MUSINGS OF A CHRISTIAN PHYSICIAN ON THE PHYSICAL AND SPIRITUAL HEALING OF MAN

A Treatise in Daily Devotional Form

JOSEPH DeMAY MD FAAP

WESTBOW
PRESS®
A DIVISION OF THOMAS NELSON
& ZONDERVAN

WestBow Press books may be ordered through booksellers or by contacting:

WestBow Press
A Division of Thomas Nelson & Zondervan
1663 Liberty Drive
Bloomington, IN 47403
www.westbowpress.com
1 (866) 928-1240

Cover photo courtesy of Bellavie Photography LLC

ISBN: 978-1-9736-9109-9 (sc)
ISBN: 978-1-9736-9110-5 (hc)
ISBN: 978-1-9736-9108-2 (e)

Library of Congress Control Number: 2020907927

Print information available on the last page.

WestBow Press rev. date: 05/21/2020

May 2019

Su	Mo	Tu	We	Th	Fr	Sa
			1	2	3	4
5	6	7	8	9	10	11
12	13	14	15	16	17	18
19	20	21	22	23	24	25
26	27	28	29	30	31	

June 2019

Su	Mo	Tu	We	Th	Fr	Sa
						1
2	3	4	5	6	7	8
9	10	11	12	13	14	15
16	17	18	19	20	21	22
23	24	25	26	27	28	29
30						

July 2019

Su	Mo	Tu	We	Th	Fr	Sa
	1	2	3	4	5	6
7	8	9	10	11	12	13
14	15	16	17	18	19	20
21	22	23	24	25	26	27
28	29	30	31			

August 2019

Su	Mo	Tu	We	Th	Fr	Sa
				1	2	3
4	5	6	7	8	9	10
11	12	13	14	15	16	17
18	19	20	21	22	23	24
25	26	27	28	29	30	31

September 2019

Su	Mo	Tu	We	Th	Fr	Sa
1	2	3	4	5	6	7
8	9	10	11	12	13	14
15	16	17	18	19	20	21
22	23	24	25	26	27	28
29	30					

October 2019

Su	Mo	Tu	We	Th	Fr	Sa
		1	2	3	4	5
6	7	8	9	10	11	12
13	14	15	16	17	18	19
20	21	22	23	24	25	26
27	28	29	30	31		

November 2019

Su	Mo	Tu	We	Th	Fr	Sa
					1	2
3	4	5	6	7	8	9
10	11	12	13	14	15	16
17	18	19	20	21	22	23
24	25	26	27	28	29	30

December 2019

Su	Mo	Tu	We	Th	Fr	Sa
1	2	3	4	5	6	7
8	9	10	11	12	13	14
15	16	17	18	19	20	21
22	23	24	25	26	27	28
29	30	31				

January 2020

Su	Mo	Tu	We	Th	Fr	Sa
			1	2	3	4
5	6	7	8	9	10	11
12	13	14	15	16	17	18
19	20	21	22	23	24	25
26	27	28	29	30	31	

February 2020

Su	Mo	Tu	We	Th	Fr	Sa
						1
2	3	4	5	6	7	8
9	10	11	12	13	14	15
16	17	18	19	20	21	22
23	24	25	26	27	28	29

March 2020

Su	Mo	Tu	We	Th	Fr	Sa
1	2	3	4	5	6	7
8	9	10	11	12	13	14
15	16	17	18	19	20	21
22	23	24	25	26	27	28
29	30	31				

April 2020

Su	Mo	Tu	We	Th	Fr	Sa
			1	2	3	4
5	6	7	8	9	10	11
12	13	14	15	16	17	18
19	20	21	22	23	24	25
26	27	28	29	30		

May 2020

Su	Mo	Tu	We	Th	Fr	Sa
					1	2
3	4	5	6	7	8	9
10	11	12	13	14	15	16
17	18	19	20	21	22	23
24	25	26	27	28	29	30
31						

The purpose of these writings is to share what I've been shown pertaining to the beautiful truths of healing available to us as believers, which took me *forever* to see. I graduated thirty-five years ago from medical school, a devoted Christian seeking to be a part of the healing ministry of Jesus Christ, but it has really just been recently that I've seen clearly just what that entails—and now it is the time to put these thoughts into writing.

This has been accomplished in the form of weekday morning emails that I started in May of 2019 in an attempt to build a "sure foundation," step by step, day by day, for the truths of what the atonement of Jesus Christ on the cross means for us as believers regarding physical, emotional, and spiritual healing. I think of these short writings as daily inoculations, like immunizations, which will eventually ensure full immunity against the deceptions and half-truths of the enemy.

Here's what we'll attempt to cover:

1. Healing is in the atonement for all believers. It's already been accomplished! This truth is *huge*, and establishing it will take the majority of our time.
2. *All* healing comes from God—I like to say that healing is not in Satan's skill set—and He has enabled the development of modern medical interventions (like vaccines) to benefit nonbelievers and believers alike. It's not wrong for Christians to seek medical care. Just realize the Source.
3. As followers of Jesus Christ, we have the authority to let the Holy Spirit work through us to effect the healing of others, of nonbelievers. Ultimately the purpose of such is to bring them to a saving knowledge of Jesus Christ, because that is of paramount importance.

Everything I say will be based on Scripture, and there will be a lot of that. The first part of our journey is going to establish why that is so important to the understanding of everything else as Holy Scripture exists in the spiritual realm and is higher than anything in our earthly realm. As we read in Zechariah 4:6, "Not by might, not by power, but by My Spirit, says the Lord."

Before we start with the daily short devotionals, I want to give a rather detailed summary of the amazing healing of a baby patient of mine that served as the impetus for this project and has forever changed my life.

I'd always believed in the healing power of Jesus Christ and viewed my life as one of service to Him via the practice of medicine, but I do realize now, looking back, that I had a deeper trust in modern medicine and its power than I did of Jesus Christ and His fully accomplished work at the cross. I went to a highly regarded medical school (Vanderbilt), graduating at the top of my class, and then went to the most prestigious navy pediatric residency program (Naval Hospital San Diego), where I was chosen chief resident my last year. I loved utilizing all the tools available to me as a pediatrician to help children get and stay well, and I enjoyed the admiration of the parents. It was pretty much still all about me.

Then *he* was born—and everything changed.

A perfectly healthy and exceptionally beautiful (honestly, most babies are ugly, right?) baby boy was born by elective caesarean section on the fifteenth of December 2017 at Williamsport Hospital in Williamsport, Pennsylvania. I had met these first-time parents for a prenatal visit and all had gone well with the pregnancy. The baby followed a perfectly normal newborn course in the hospital: breastfeeding well, voiding, and stooling with normal physical exams, etc. But there was one quirky thing: the transcutaneous meter we use to assess jaundice kept reading very low, actually zero. Now we are concerned when the babies get too jaundiced, so we like low readings, but I had never seen a zero before, and that left me just a tad unsettled.

The day came for discharge home, and the reading was still zero. I sensed that very soft, never overbearing, never loud "still, small voice" that the prophet Elijah heard in 1 Kings 19, and I told the nurse, "Let's get a bilirubin level," which is a test for jaundice. I'm no Elijah, and just getting that test would not have diagnosed this child's underlying problem. As

I was physically leaving the nursery, actually a step or two out the door, I turned around and yelled to the nurse (whom I'd worked with for twenty-five years), "And get a CBC [complete blood count] too!" She was surprised by that order, and she questioned it because she knows I don't get superfluous labs and there seemed to be no reason for that one. "Why?" she asked.

"I don't know," I said. "Just get it."

Thank God the Holy Spirit can work through even a thick-skulled person like me, because just an hour or so later, I got the frantic call from the lab that the baby's blood was full of cancer cells. He was immediately transferred to our regional tertiary-care hospital and started on chemotherapy. I got a call from the oncologist there the next day that, had the baby gone home, although seemingly perfectly healthy clinically, he would have certainly died within twenty-four hours as his kidneys would have been overwhelmed. It was then that the verse came to my remembrance that would be my rock through all that would happen subsequently, Psalm 118:17: "I will not *die*, but *live*, and proclaim the glorious works of the Lord" (emphasis added). I knew this baby was not going to succumb to the evil plans of Satan (and just how evil is that, to try to snuff out the life of an innocent baby?) but that he would be different and serve as a witness of the saving and healing power of Jesus Christ. This would mark the first of three distinct episodes in which otherwise certain death was averted miraculously.

The baby was found to have the most fulminant and deadly form of congenital acute lymphoblastic leukemia with published mortality rates of 83 percent to 100 percent (can you believe that?). He was placed in an approved children's oncology group (COG) protocol for chemotherapy, but he failed the protocol when it was found that the cancer had spread to his spinal fluid. He was placed pretty much on experimental protocols since then. The plan was to try to get his cancer down to a manageable level (measured by what's called the MRD, or minimal residual disease) and then proceed with bone marrow transplant (BMT), in and of itself a very risky undertaking for this age group. No one was very optimistic he'd even get to that point, but not only did the MRD get low enough, but also it went to zero! No appreciable disease!

So he was admitted to Children's Hospital of Philadelphia (CHoP), the world's premier children's hospital, late summer of last year for the bone marrow transplant with the father as the donor. I wasn't terribly excited about that because I believed the child was already set free and healed, and I knew the BMT would be very hard on him and would be thought of as what actually healed him if it was successful, but I trusted that the Lord would protect him and preserve the child and still receive the glory that is due only to Him.

The procedure was performed the first week of September 2018, and despite the best medical care available in the world, there were significant complications. Within two weeks, the baby was fighting for his life, in liver failure, intubated, and heavily sedated in the PICU at CHoP, and his blood work showed the return of his cancer! Can you imagine a worse scenario? This was the eighteenth of September in 2018, a day I'll never forget. The CHoP oncologist had called to let me know they had reached the end of the road, and they were going to have to withdraw support (compassionate extubation) and let the child die the following day, the nineteenth of September. Can you imagine what his parents were going through? They were being told the day of their son's death!

By the grace of God, I was not in the office when the CHoP oncologist called that evening; I saw the handwritten note from my nurse on my desk when I got back some two hours later. The oncologist had left his callback number.

Now honestly my first reaction was disbelief, followed by despair, but only very briefly because I knew *exactly* what the Word of God had said (Psalm 118:17), along with a great many other verses pertaining to this boy's healing. I looked them all up and claimed them out loud. It was my "David at Ziklag" moment (1 Samuel 30). I "strengthened myself in the Lord." I vowed to call that oncologist and plead with him not to withdraw support because this baby was not to die—not now, and not from this cancer.

So I called, and I didn't need to say a word of my rehearsed speech! The very kind oncologist forgave me for getting back to him so late, and he was actually happy that it had worked out that way because "shockingly" (his word), everything had changed since he called. Upon further review, it was discovered that the "cancer" cells were not cancer cells, and the baby was showing signs of improvement. They were not going to need to withdraw support! That oncologist said that the chances of winning the lottery were better than what happened with that baby that day. I was able to my share my faith with him by phone. I was so overwhelmed by the love of God that evening, and I will never forget that experience. That was the second, and most dramatic, rescue from imminent death I had witnessed.

Then just one week later, when the baby was still in the PICU, another miraculous event occurred (don't let anyone ever tell you that serving the Lord is boring!). It was very early in the morning, and I was having my quiet time at my office desk reading scripture. It "happened" to be the story recorded in Mark 9:25–34 of the healing of the woman who'd had an "issue of blood" for twelve years. My desktop computer was on, and I saw a new email come across, which was odd because it was 4:30 a.m. It was the baby's mom, and she was frantic. The baby was "bleeding out" into his GI tract and lungs and even his brain. He was having an adverse reaction to a blood thinner. It was feared he was not going to survive this either.

Wow, what a God we serve! Keep in mind, I'm not making any of this up. I emailed the mother what I was led to read at that time, and that was a sign that our Lord would be true to His Word and that her baby would stop bleeding and live. He did. That was the third miraculous delivery from expected death.

From that point on, the baby improved dramatically. He was finally discharged from CHoP to home in time for his first birthday. He was now cancer-free and making good progress from a growth and development standpoint, but his story wasn't over.

The first week of March of 2019, he was seen at CHoP for a routine outpatient appointment, and blood counts were obtained. Guess what?

Yep, the cancer was back, and this time they were his cancer cells. The oncologist texted me per the parents' request, asking me to call. I did, and she was very distressed. Everyone who had cared for this little guy had absolutely fallen in love with him. She laid out the last-hope plan, which was to get him into an experimental protocol for a relatively new intervention called CAR-T. As soon as possible, medical professionals would harvest a certain type of natural killer lymphocytes, T cells, from him (his cancer cells are B cells), genetically alter them by adding a receptor for the cancerous B cells (a process that takes weeks), and then infuse them back to the patient, where they would attack and kill the cancer cells. Amazingly, this would be an ongoing function of these cells for the rest of his life! The problem, though, the oncologist pointed out, was that the baby very likely would "blast out," that is, develop an overwhelming load of cancer cells before the doctors could accomplish all this. And even if he did hold out until the infusion of the killer cells, he might suffer life-threatening inflammation from the breaking down of all the cancer cells. This procedure had rarely been tried on someone this young, and it was not FDA approved. However, there were no other options.

At the end of the doctor's presentation, I said, "Okay, that all sounds good; you guys are the best, and it's a good plan. By the way, do I sound worried?"

"No," she said. "But I didn't think you would. I'd heard about you." We had a great discussion about faith and healing, and I was even able to send her some of the stuff I had written about all of this. She said at one point that everyone involved considered this particular patient to be different and had learned much from him. They called him "Professor."

So the boy didn't blast out. He went home after the harvesting of the cells, on minimal chemotherapy, and you guessed it: subsequent bone marrow and CSF (cerebrospinal fluid) studies showed absolutely no cancer! That was unexpected. Remember, this was *before* the infusion of the killer cells. The infusion took place subsequently, and the child tolerated that potentially problematic procedure beautifully without the development of the usual inflammatory reactions, which I believe was a sign that there were no remaining cells to react to! As of the time of this writing, my little patient is a thriving, cancer-free two and one half year old.

Praise God! What all of this shows - and it's all been well-documented by the wonderful doctors and staff at CHoP, both the thrilling successes and devastating setbacks - is that this little life was miraculously healed, certainly accomplished in conjunction with the best of medical science, but there was also something *more*, something *above*. His healing declares the "glorious works of the Lord" as promised right from the start.

This journey has given me such insight into the superiority of the Word of God over the things of this world, and the subtle interplay of faith and belief (they are not the same thing), and the complete defeat of Satan and his friends at the cross, and the goodness of God in enabling the development of all these tools we have in modern medicine, and the ultimate goal of witnessing to others of the grace of God through Jesus Christ our Lord. We'll start unraveling, slowly, all these things on Monday. God bless.

WEEK 1

MONDAY

First of all, let me state that I don't have any specific qualifications to opine on the Bible and what it means, except that I am a disciple of Jesus Christ and I take John 8:31–32 literally: "Jesus said to those Jews who believed in Him, 'If you abide in My Word, you are my disciples indeed. And you shall know the truth, and the truth shall make you free" (NKJV). I've come to see that the *only* perfect source of truth is Scripture because it is, as we'll prove subsequently, alive and eternal and spiritual. It edifies, informs, and perfects every other aspect of our lives. I did not go to Bible school (instead I went to medical school), I was not a religion major in college (instead majoring in biology and minoring in English), and I have never read any books about the Bible, not even Bible commentaries (I simply don't have the time—I do lots of reading to keep up with my profession). But I have always had a passion for reading and thinking about Scripture.

I believe the Holy Spirit is our best resource as believers to understanding Scripture as stated by Jesus in John 16:13–14, which says, "When He, the Spirit of truth, has come, He will guide you into all truth. ... He will glorify Me, for He will take of what is Mine, and declare it to you." Holy Scripture, the Word, is Jesus Christ (John 1:1), and it is the role of the Holy Spirit to facilitate our knowledge of Jesus Christ and His Father by giving us understanding of Scripture (the "what is Mine" in John 16:14) and allowing us to more fully see Jesus in all of Scripture. This is how we become more like Him. And in seeing Jesus, we also see the Father—"He who has seen Me has seen the Father" (John 14:9). This is what the renewing of the Christian's mind is all about, and it is the only way we can "prove what is the good and acceptable and perfect will of God" (Romans 12:2).

Please realize I'm just a layperson, but I have sought the Lord for understanding—particularly in this area of healing since I'm in the profession that deals with it. I believe He has opened my eyes to some truths that may be helpful to the church body. They certainly have been helpful to me. I have a lot to say, and it will take time, but we'll do it in rather tiny aliquots as the Lord gives me time and inspiration. I'm really looking forward to it.

And, you know, not being a minister may be an advantage. Remember that the apostle Paul, who was the first human to be given the full understanding of the Gospel, was actually taken up to heaven to learn the mysteries inherent in the Gospel (2 Corinthians 12:1–6). The man who wrote much of the New Testament (under the inspiration of the Holy Spirit) was actually, by occupation, a tentmaker (Acts 18:3). He accomplished all this other stuff in his spare time. So God can use anyone who allows Him to, but the believer needs to be equipped. There's a great verse that is for all of us, not just full-time ministers. It says, "All Scripture is given by the inspiration of God, and is profitable for doctrine, for reproof, for correction, for instruction in righteousness, that the man [or woman] of God may be complete and thoroughly equipped for every good work" (2 Timothy 3:16–17).

We'll start our journey in the understanding of the scriptural foundation for healing and how this Christian doctor applies his faith to the practice of medicine. Next time, we'll start where everything started for us as humans—in the garden.

TUESDAY

I had to completely change my way of thinking to understand and benefit from the truths about healing and living an abundant, fruitful life as a Christian. Here's what I had to get my mind around and come to accept fully: that Holy Scripture is absolute truth and eternal. Our senses, intellect, and emotions are deceiving and temporal.

Counterintuitive, isn't it? That's not what we're raised to think. We are all naturally like doubting Thomas, who would not believe that Jesus had risen from the dead until he *saw* the nail prints in His hands and *felt* the hole in His side (John 20:25). We function in the natural realm of reason by what we can see, touch, smell, taste, and hear. Makes sense, right?

But that's not how we were created to function. We were created to exist on a much higher level. To see that, we must go back to Creation, to the very start of the human race, to the garden. Before the Fall, Adam and Eve functioned in a spiritual realm and were able to communicate directly with God and God's Spirit (John 4:24). They had minds and emotions and physical bodies with all the senses, but they didn't rely solely on those aspects of their being. Those things were not needed since Adam and Eve were in perfect union with their Creator. For instance, they were naked and perfectly okay with that—they were not ashamed and saw no need to wear clothes (Genesis 2:25). All of this would change dramatically when they sinned, and every human born since would suffer the consequences.

You see, we were created as triune beings, just as God is. Whatever "made in the image of God" means, it doesn't mean that we were created to look like God physically as He has no body. But we have bodies. We were created with a body (which allows us to see, hear, touch, taste, and smell), a soul (which is eternal and composed of our intellect, emotions, and will), and a spirit (which is actually the real us, also eternal, and our way to commune with God). Adam and Eve probably had a conscience, and if they did, it was rudimentary because it was not needed. When God told Adam and Eve that they would die, and die that same day, if they ate of the one forbidden tree in the midst of the garden, it was their spirit that He was referring to. Their sin resulted from the separation of their spirits from God's. The spirit within them became dormant, and they now had to rely on the other two aspects of their being, namely, the soul (mind) and body (senses). It was indeed a fall from something much superior, and that is the way we are born—spiritually dead and separate from God. The one foolproof and perfect aspect of us as humans is not at our disposal, not unless we are born again, which results in the rebirth of our spirit. But we are getting ahead of ourselves.

Here's what I want to get across for today: spiritual things from our Creator God are always absolutely true and eternal, whereas carnal things, which have to do with our senses and emotions and intellect, are not always true—they can be deceiving (we all have experienced that) and temporary. What do we all have access to that is spiritual? Holy Scripture! Listen to Jesus in John 6:63, which says, "It is the Spirit who gives life; the flesh profits nothing. The *words* that I speak to you are *spirit*, and they are *life*" (emphasis added).

Wow. More next time.

WEDNESDAY

So we've been establishing the superiority of the spiritual over the carnal—and how the former illuminated and informed the latter but died and became dormant at the Fall—and the fact that humans were created with both natures. Every human born subsequent to the Fall is spiritually dead and doomed to rely on the carnal (mind and body) until their spirit nature is restored and they become a new creation through faith in Jesus Christ (2 Corinthians 5:17).

Now I'm using the word *carnal* to refer to all human aspects that are not spiritual; it is not meant to be a pejorative term. It encompasses our needs and activities and thoughts and emotions as humans—some of which indeed have a negative connotation, such as lust, jealousy, and lying. It encompasses the more noble aspects of our being too, like loyalty, self-sacrifice, and gratitude. We aren't all bad. But remember that even our "most righteous acts are like filthy rags" in God's eyes (Isaiah 64:6). We can only be acceptable to Him when our spirit nature is awakened and filled with the perfect Holy Spirit through our acceptance of Jesus Christ and His free gift of righteousness obtained at the cross. "For He made Him who knew no sin to become sin for us, that we might become the righteousness of God in Him" (2 Corinthians 5:21).

I believe that it is this spiritual aspect of humans that differentiates us from every other created thing, and this is what is meant by, "So God created man in His own image; in the image of God He created Him" (Genesis 1:27). Everything else was spoken into existence by God, but Adam (with Eve inside him) was formed from the "dust of the ground" by God, who then "*breathed* into his nostrils the breath of life, and man became a living being" (Genesis 2:7; emphasis added). That's when we were given His Spirit!

Just now as I'm writing this, I am reminded of the beautiful encounter between the risen Jesus Christ and His bewildered disciples recorded in John 20:19–22. This is awesome. "Jesus said to them again, 'Peace to you! As the Father has sent Me, I also send you.' And when He had said this, He *breathed* on them, and said to them, 'Receive the Holy Spirit'" (emphasis added).

Is that amazing or what? God breathed into the first Adam His precious Holy Spirit, and that Adam killed that essential aspect of our being by giving into the seduction of Satan and sinning against God. But the new Adam would come, 100 percent man and 100 percent God and full of the Holy Spirit. He would restore our rightful place before our God and breathe the Holy Spirit back into us once and for all, never to be taken away again. Praise God!

Next time we'll discuss how Satan was ever even able to pull off the Fall of Man. It has everything to do with this dichotomy of spiritual versus carnal.

THURSDAY

You might be wondering what all this theological background has to do with the healing power of faith in Jesus Christ, but please be patient. I promise you it is closely related. It is quite easy to quote Isaiah 53 and claim healing because it states, "By His stripes we are healed." Although that is indeed the case, you're just going through an exercise in positive thinking, and your soul knows it, unless you have discovered for yourself the very firm foundation your belief is set upon, such that there is absolutely no wavering, no hint of disbelief, because you know the Scriptures to be *more* true, trustworthy, and unfailing than anything you have ever experienced before and that what you believe is *superior* to what you experience in this world. In other words, things of the Spirit trump things of the world, and that's where our progenitors (Adam and Eve) erred, by believing more in the things of the world. It is this turning away from the Spirit and relying on the carnal (also referred to in the Bible as the "things of the flesh" and the "things of the world") that we will look at next.

So we left Adam and Eve in the garden, created in the image of God, filled with His Spirit, yet also equipped with an amazing intellect (God tasked Adam with observing all of His living creatures and naming them based on those observations; see Genesis 2:19) and a "fearfully and wonderfully made" physical body (Psalm 139:14). They were created perfectly, never meant to get sick or depressed or anxious and probably never meant to die. They were given complete dominion over the earth and could freely access all that God had created—all but one thing.

There were actually two trees of interest in the midst of the garden, the tree of life (which they could have eaten of and thereby lived forever, but which they did not get a chance to eat of) and the tree of the knowledge of good and evil (Genesis 2:9), and one of these was off-limits. You see, Adam and Eve were made in the image of God, but they weren't God. He was over them; they obeyed Him. And you know what? They were fine with that. He had proven Himself a lavishly loving Father, giving them everything they could possibly want. All was wonderful in Paradise, right?

Not quite. There was someone else sneaking around in that garden, and he was angry. He had suffered a great fall from the grace of God, and he had a big grudge. He had something to prove, and he saw the perfect opportunity to get back at God by messing with His perfect little creations, made on a higher level than he was as they were made in God's image and he was not. All the universe would be watching the drama of the ages play out on this little orb called Earth, and he would prove to them that God wasn't really that good, certainly not good all the time. He would show that God had an agenda.

His name is Satan, and we'll talk more about him next time, along with his plan to seduce Adam and Eve away from the spiritual and turn them toward the carnal. There is a key verse for next time, one of the foundational verses in the Bible: "For all that is in the world [carnal]—the *lust* of the *flesh*, the *lust* of the *eyes*, and the *boastful pride* of *life*—is *not* of the Father, but is of the world" (1 John 2:16; emphasis added).

FRIDAY

"We have become a show in the world's amphitheater, both to angels and to men" (1 Corinthians 4:9 AB).

The drama of the ages is about to play out on planet Earth, and there are three players: God, humankind, and Satan. So who is this Satan guy? Where did he come from? Why is he there or even allowed to be there? What is he after?

There are three angels named in the Bible—archangels, or ruling angels—namely, Gabriel, Michael, and Lucifer. Satan is Lucifer, and he was probably the greatest of God's creations to that point, referred to as "son of the morning" in Isaiah chapter 14. It is this chapter, and Ezekiel 28, where we find the greatest details of this created being. And here's a *big* point that we need to keep in mind: Satan was *created* by God; he is not God, nor is he equal to God—not even close. Whatever he is, we do know for certain what he is not:

- **Omnipresent.** Satan is one individual entity. He can only be at one place at one time, but he does have a lot of "friends" that do his evil bidding. Revelation 12:4 alludes to the possibility that a full third of the angels went with him in his revolt. I would point out, though, that even if that is true, they're outnumbered two to one!
- **Omniscient.** Satan's knowledge is limited, and I would argue less than that of a redeemed human, as "the fear of the Lord is the beginning of knowledge" (Proverbs 1:7). Specifically, he cannot read your mind or know your thoughts. He can hear you, though, and that's why it's so important to *speak* out your faith when appropriate. There's a very popular saying attributed to Saint Francis of Assisi: "Preach the Gospel at all times. ... When

necessary, use words." But that's not in the Bible, and the Gospel is primarily shared by words as Romans 10:14 says: "And how shall they believe in Him of whom they have not *heard*?" (emphasis added). And it was Jesus's words that amazed the Jews, as much as His miracles. In John chapter 8, the chief priest sent his guards to arrest Jesus (v. 32), but they came back empty-handed, so the chief priest asked them, "Why have you not brought Him?" The officers answered, "No man ever spoke like this Man!" (vv. 45–46). My favorite verse regarding this has Jesus talking to a tree—out loud! It's recorded in Mark chapter 11. Jesus was hungry, and He came to a fig tree to eat the buds of the spring season, but the tree was fruitless. "In response, Jesus *said* to it, 'Let no one eat fruit from you ever again.' And His disciples *heard* it" (v. 14; emphasis added). The point is, there is power in our words as believers when we are directed by the Spirit, but we must make sure what we say is in accordance with the Word of God as "death and life are in the power of the tongue" (Proverbs 18:21).

So we kind of diverged there. We'll do that a lot. There's no firm script here. It's all good to my way of thinking. In the end we're setting the foundation for the superiority of Scripture and why it's so hard for us to see that it is superior.

There is one more quality that God has that Satan does not, and that's omnipotence, or all-powerfulness. We'll deal with that next time.

2

WEEK

MONDAY

So we're in the garden. Humankind is God's perfect, innocent, Spirit-filled but free-willed creation, and they (and by "they" I mean Adam *and* Eve because they were considered as one entity by God. Remember, Eve was taken out of Adam) were both created at the same time on the sixth day of creation. Likewise, when a Christian man marries a Christian woman, the two become in God's eyes actually *one*. It is not a figure of speech: "Therefore a man shall ... be joined to his wife, and they shall become one flesh" (Genesis 2:24). There is no gender discrimination with God—never has been. They are thriving, enjoying their role as gardeners and communing perfectly with their Creator. Had things continued on in this fashion, they would have eventually, no doubt, eaten of the tree of life and been allowed to live forever in their "fearfully and wonderfully made" bodies, and their offspring would have spread out to inhabit the entire earth and rightly rule over it. Humankind was given that kind of authority over this earth (Genesis 1:28).

I am thankful that this seemingly idyllic scenario didn't play out because then the Mystery of the Ages would not have been solved. I have to skip a bit ahead in the story here because, at the rate at which I'm digressing and following rabbit trails (as above), it will take forever to get to where I intend to go. The universe at that time was questioning the very nature of God, which is love as stated in 1 John 4:8, and the "foundation of His throne," which is righteousness and justice (Psalm 89:14). The lie had been spread (by the father of lies; John 8:45) that God really wasn't who He portrayed Himself to be, that He was holding something back, and that He was keeping everyone else from being like Him, and if God had protected His little perfect humans from all temptation, that lie would be furthered. "See," it could be said, "God isn't really *that* good; He can't even trust His free-willed children to serve Him. He has a hedge around them, and that's not *fair!*"

So God had to leave His precious little ones in that idyllic garden unattended, to function on their own with what they'd been given, which included the Holy Spirit, but it also included a soul (which is comprised of the mind and emotions) and a physical body. And they would have to face temptation. We know who that involves: Satan. We started talking about him last time, and we were describing what he is *not*, namely, omnipresent and omniscient. Now we'll see that he's also *not* omnipotent. But because these are meant to be short and frequent postings, and given that I do have a busy day job, we'll do that next time.

TUESDAY

So Satan is not omnipotent; only God is all-powerful. But he is powerful, and that is evident in the Bible, where he is referred to as "the prince of the power of the air" (Ephesians 2:2). In Job, we see him able to appear before God Himself, presumably as the authority over this earth, and present his plans to harm Job (Job 1:6). Now it should be noted that he was thrown out from the presence of the Lord some time earlier (Isaiah 14:12; Ezekiel 28:16), and it was humankind who was to have the authority on this earth. We're getting to how that got all messed up and how Satan took over our position of authority and our standing before God.

And in Daniel chapter 10, we see Satan (referred to as the prince of Persia) fighting with Michael, one of the powerful archangels of God, and delaying the answer to Daniel's prayer. He was apparently a formidable enemy. After all, he did convince a third of God's angels to side with him.

But, you say, that was all before the cross; Jesus hadn't defeated him yet. That's very true, but Paul certainly recognized Satan's power in Ephesians 6:12: "For we do not wrestle against flesh and blood, but against *principalities* and *powers*, against the rulers of the darkness of this age, against spiritual hosts of wickedness in the heavenly places" (emphasis added). Sounds scary, doesn't it?

Nope, Paul is just stating who the enemy is, the one against whom we "wrestle," not the one to whom we lose. Look what else he says, which puts it all in perspective: "Having *disarmed* principalities and powers [the same words used in Ephesians], he made a *public spectacle* of them, *triumphing over* them in it" (Colossians 2:15; emphasis added). And don't forget this awesome verse, a good one to memorize: "For I am persuaded that neither death nor life, nor *angels* nor principalities nor powers, nor things present nor things to come, nor height nor depth, nor any other *created thing* [i.e., Satan], shall be able to separate us from the love of God, which is in Christ Jesus our Lord" (Romans 8:38–39; emphasis added).

When Jesus said with a loud voice on the cross, *"It is finished!"* (John 19:30), He meant it, and Satan was defeated once and for all.

But that hasn't happened yet in our story. We're still in the garden. Satan is very smart, crafty, and cunning (Genesis 3:1), and he has hatched a plan to get back at God and dethrone Him, a very well thought out, intelligent, and seemingly *perfect* plan to knock out the foundations of His rule and prove that He is not all love, not all the time. Next time, we'll unravel that.

WEDNESDAY

So we have set the stage for one of the two most consequential days in human history, the Fall of Man, which necessitated the second most important day to occur four thousand years later. *That* day would actually be *the* most significant day in the history of the universe, the day of the crucifixion of Jesus Christ. And although we know the exact time of the salvation of humankind (3:00 p.m., the time of the evening sacrifice), we don't know the exact time of the Fall, but knowing our Lord, I suspect it was three in the afternoon when this happened also.

We go to Genesis chapter 3 for the story. We'll take it slowly because understanding what went on here is crucial to understanding the roles of faith and belief in healing and their relation to modern medicine, which is the purpose of this series. We'll unravel this in little snippets because that's the format I was given and it works for my schedule. And I think it's a wonderful way to digest truth and knowledge anyway, in little recurrent pieces that build one on another. It's the way God intended us to learn from Him. "Let My teaching drop as the rain, My speech distill as the dew, as raindrops on the tender herb, and as showers on the grass" (Deuteronomy 32:2). What if all the water in the atmosphere fell at once, in one big splat?! Then what was meant to be good would be disastrous. We wouldn't be able to handle it all at once. Likewise, the glory and knowledge of the Lord is too much for us, too wondrous, to absorb it all at once. The gentle rain is what we need. So these messages are short and sweet, usually taking up no more than a single page.

There will be lots of Scripture because I don't want you to just take my word for what we'll be discussing. God's Word is our lifeline: "Man shall not live by bread alone, but man lives by every word that proceeds from the mouth of the Lord" (Deuteronomy 8:3). In fact, as we'll see in due time, not realizing this is what precipitated our fall. It would be best through all these postings to have your Bible at hand because seeing the verses in your own Bible helps you to remember them. At least it does for me.

Next time we will look at Satan's crafty plan to ensnare the first Adam, which worked so well that he would try using it once again—many, many years later, on the second Adam.

THURSDAY

"Now the snake was the most clever of all the wild animals the Lord God had made. One day, the snake said to the woman, 'Did God really say that you must not eat of any tree in the Garden?'" (Genesis 3:1 NCV).

And so starts the temptation of humankind. Satan has taken the form of a created animal, the snake (or serpent), which had already been known to Adam and Eve as a crafty, cunning, subtle animal that apparently could converse with them since they didn't seem to be startled by this wild animal talking to them. And Satan starts out true to form, by *questioning* the authority of God's Word—postulating that Adam and Eve didn't hear God correctly, and *lying*, which is a consistent characteristic of Satan—and twisting God's Word to imply that He forbade eating of any tree. In truth, God had told Adam and Eve that they could eat of *every* tree in the garden, and eat *freely*, except for one (Genesis 2:16–17).

This particular character trait of Satan—lying—was emphasized by Jesus, who considered it his basic nature. Look at John 8:44: "When he [Satan] lies, he speaks his native language, for he is a liar, and the father of lies" (NIV). Wow, that's pretty strong language, but Jesus knew that spreading lies about the goodness of God was the modus operandi of Satan and was part of how he planned to overthrow God.

This is born out in that amazing chapter about Satan, Ezekiel 28, but it's implied rather than clearly stated. For next time, see if you can find what I'm alluding to in that portion of Scripture. Of course, even though Satan is a defeated enemy, and has no power over us (as believers) except what we give him, he is still in the business of spreading lies about, and misrepresenting, God. Some things never change.

FRIDAY

So Satan is up to no good in the garden. He is out to seduce the human race (composed of just two people at that time, but representative of all of us to come), and his attack is two-pronged: (1) Lie about God's Word so that its authenticity and power will be questioned, then (2) go after humankind's carnal nature—their emotions, intellect, and physical senses. It's a formidable plan and if he pulls it off, it will put God in a quandary because—remember this—Satan's ultimate goal is to bring God down by proving that He is not all about love and that He is not really just and righteous. Profound stuff here.

We were discussing the first attack. Look at these verses in Ezekiel 28:

"By your great skill in *trading* you have increased your wealth, and because of your wealth your heart has grown proud" (v. 5; emphasis added).

"By your many sins and *dishonest trade*, you have desecrated your sanctuaries" (v. 18; emphasis added).

This chapter starts out as a prophecy against an actual human man, the king of Tyre, with Tyre being a great ancient city of trade and commerce. The first ten verses are about him, including verse 5, above. So he was a wise and skillful trader. But starting with verse 11, there is a dramatic change as the subsequent verses through verse 29 are obviously not talking about a man. Look at these verses:

- "You were the model of perfection, full of wisdom and perfect in beauty" (v. 12).
- "You were in Eden, the garden of God" (v. 13).
- "You were anointed as a guardian cherub" (v. 14).
- "You were blameless in your ways from the day you were created" (v. 15).

This was no man; this was Satan. But there was a similarity with the ancient king of Tyre: they were both involved in *trade* (the Old English word used in the King James Version is *traffick*). And just what was that trade in? What was he trafficking? We'll uncover that next time.

3
WEEK

MONDAY

Let me be probably the first to wish you a happy Memorial Day, since I do these really early in the morning. I thought of taking today off from writing, but this stuff is just too good! Remember that fundamental verse (at least to this series), namely, John 6:63, in which Jesus says, "The words that I speak to you are spirit, and they are life." What a great way to start our day, right? I find it hard not to write about the things of the Lord. I love Jeremiah's take on this passion, in chapter 20, verse 9: "His word is in my heart like a burning fire, a fire shut up in my bones. I am weary of holding it in ... indeed, I cannot" (NIV).

So we are looking at the fall of Satan before we turn to the the Fall of Man because they are intimately related. In Ezekiel 28, Satan is described as a "trafficker" or "trader," and it says that whatever he was trading in would lead to his downfall. "Through your [Satan's] widespread trade, you were filled with violence, and you sinned" (Ezekiel 28:16).

And what was he spreading (trading) throughout the universe? *Lies!* He was murmuring and whispering untruths about the goodness of God and His righteousness, causing God's creation to question His very nature, namely, love.

Actually, to my thinking, Satan was the first created being to do this, that is, to lie. God simply can't lie. Did you know there are things God can't do? This is one of them, and it's scriptural: "It is *impossible* for God to lie" (Hebrews 6:18) and "God, who *cannot* lie" (Titus 1:2). But Satan? Remember what Jesus said? "He [Satan] was a murderer from *the beginning*, and does not stand in the truth, because there is no truth in him. When he speaks a lie, he speaks his native language, for he is a liar, and the *father of lies*" (John 8:44; emphasis added). That's pretty clear, isn't it? It is Satan's nature to lie, and it would result in his banishment from the presence of God, but not his destruction—not yet. In our story, he's still very much alive and doing what he does best, lying about God's Word and causing God's newest and most cherished creation, humankind, to question Him and get their focus out of the spiritual realm and into the carnal realm in the garden.

Sorry. This one was a bit longer than usual, but I had the time. Have a great holiday.

TUESDAY

So here's a good question: Why is Satan even in the garden? Why is he still around at all? We've seen that he had started a "whispering campaign" of lies about the goodness and justice and righteousness of God and that God had expelled him from His presence, casting him out of heaven along with his converts. "So I drove you in disgrace from the mount of God, and I expelled you, O guardian cherub, from among the fiery stones … so I threw you to the Earth" (Ezekiel 28:16, 17).

Couldn't God have completely destroyed Satan and his "friends" right then and there? Shouldn't He have?

The answers are yes and no. Yes, He certainly had the power and authority to obliterate His created but fallen angels, but no, it wasn't the wise thing to do, and He knew that. What does an evil, authoritarian dictator do to his opposition? He squelches all his enemies, scorches them. If God had done that in the face of all those questions Satan had been promulgating, there would have been even more questions, more division. Was God hiding stuff from the rest of the universe? Was Satan onto something?

No. That would not be the way to prove once and for all that God is love, that He's good all the time. There had to be another way. And here I'm going to state a quote of mine. It's not absolute truth, but I believe it was given to me to concisely summarize the core of our Christian faith, which is at the foundation of all healing and everything else that comes from belief in Jesus Christ. Here it is:

The cross is the sign of the ransom paid by the love of God to satisfy the justice of God and preserve the righteousness of God.

It will take us weeks, maybe months, to fully explain that one sentence, but for now in our story, Satan is alive and well and has already created a chink in the armor of humankind by causing them to question the Word of God, allowing access to humankind's carnal nature, which is what Satan is going after next in the garden.

WEDNESDAY

"So when the woman saw that the tree was *good for food*, that it was *pleasant to the eyes*, and a desirable tree to *make one wise*, she took of its fruit and ate it" (Genesis 3:6; emphasis added).

"For all that is in the world—the *lust of the flesh*, the *lust of the eyes*, and the *pride of life*—is not of the Father, but is of the world" (1 John 2:16; emphasis added).

These are two very related scriptures, are they not? And they have to do with the carnal (intrinsic to humans) nature of humankind. Satan is targeting Adam and Eve's senses (taste and vision) and emotions / psychological makeup as Satan had said to Eve, "For God knows that in the day you eat of it [the fruit] your eyes will be opened, and you will be like God, knowing good and evil [making you wise]" (Genesis 3:5).

Now I want to remind you again, because it's essential, that Satan had to first knock humankind down from the spiritual realm in which they so beautifully functioned, in perfect communion with their Father, who is Spirit, to get them to think and act on a carnal level. Adam and Eve were the only two humans he had to accomplish this for; all subsequent humans have been born spiritually dead as God had warned: "For in the day that you eat of it you shall surely die" (Genesis 2:17). As Bob Dylan proclaims in the song "Saved," "I was blinded by the devil, born already ruined, stone-cold dead as I stepped out of the womb."

And this is huge. We are born entirely carnal; that is our default. It's what we're comfortable with. The things of the world are natural to us; the things of the spirit are not. We weren't created that way—quite the opposite. It was a very significant and consequential day in the garden.

THURSDAY

So we're discussing how we humans died to all things spiritual in the garden and how we are born to function at the lower, carnal level, relying on our senses, intellect, and emotions, all of which are imperfect and potentially deceiving and temporary, that is, not eternal.

But when we are saved, that is, when we accept the free gift of salvation offered by Jesus Christ and His finished work on the cross, that scenario is completely changed. Our spirit person is awakened, and we are once more able to commune with our Father. We are "new creations," and "all things have become new" (2 Corinthians 5:17). We are now able to function on a much higher level, having access to things that are eternal and true. That presents a problem for Satan because he can't compete with the absolute eternal truths of God's Word, and he knows it.

So what does he try to do to us Christians? And by the way, he spends a lot of time on us. He doesn't have to worry about the lost; they are already his. They are born his. Just think about that. The amazing thing to my thinking is that anyone is ever saved at all as we are born already in the clutches of Satan, spiritually dead, and therefore with no natural desire for the higher things of God. Paul says that it should be clear to all people that there *is* a God from the intricacies and awesomeness of Creation (Romans 1:20), but it's sure not clear to fallen humanity how to get right with Him.

Wow, so many questions and so little space to examine them, but I promised to keep these things short and sweet, right? So next time we'll look at how any human can even have a chance at salvation and how Satan tries to dumb down those of us who are saved.

FRIDAY

We start this morning with this profound verse from "Amazing Grace," written by John Newton in 1779, "'Twas grace that taught my heart to fear, and grace my fears relieved."

It isn't just the melody that makes that old hymn the greatest of all time (and I guarantee you, we'll be singing it in heaven); it's the lyrics. And the foregoing verse basically sums up the whole Gospel.

We were wondering how we, as fallen humans, can bring ourselves to a saving knowledge of Jesus Christ since that involves some measure of spiritual discernment, but we are born spiritually dead. The answer is that we can't. That's how utterly hopeless we are. But remember, "While we were yet sinners, Christ died for us" (Romans 5:8).

It is the Holy Spirit who draws us in, who gives us even the desire to seek the Lord, as Paul points out in 1 Corinthians 12:3: "No one can say that Jesus is Lord except by the Holy Spirit." And that is entirely because of the goodness of God, which we are endeavoring to prove, because it is "the goodness of God that leads you to repentance" (Romans 2:4).

What then is our role? Our role is to accept that grace, to put our faith in Jesus Christ and what He did for us. That's all we can do as our human efforts to please God could never be enough.

Wow, I wasn't planning to go that far off topic, but it's all good. Surely somebody needed to hear that. But here's the big picture that we are trying to paint: there is a dichotomy between the spiritual and the carnal that was never meant to be, and it explains how we as humans ever got sick to start with and why we as believers don't have to stay that way. We'll get there eventually. Patience!

4
WEEK

MONDAY

So we've been teasing out the differences between things spiritual and things carnal. The bottom line is that we are born fully carnal ("in the flesh" as the Bible puts it), subject to imperfect thinking and senses and emotions and sickness and depression and anxiety, etc. *But* as believers we have access to something much superior, the spiritual realm. Here's a great verse: "For to be carnally minded is *death*, but to be spiritually minded is *life* and *peace*" (Romans 8:6; emphasis added).

I want to focus on two words this morning, *instantaneous* and *gradual*, and contrast the Fall of Man with the salvation of fallen humanity. When we are saved, that is, respond to the Holy Spirit's beckoning, our spirit person, that part of us dormant at birth, is *instantaneously* revived and made perfect. We are flawless in God's eyes. This is seemingly too good to be true, but it is true, and it makes sense to God. "'Come now, and let us reason together,' says the Lord, 'Though your sins are like scarlet, they shall be white as snow'" (Isaiah 1:18).

However, the other two components of our being, the soul (mind/intellect/emotions) and the physical body, are not changed immediately. The transformation of these carnal aspects is *gradual* and occurs as we allow more and more of the perfect spiritual aspect of our lives to permeate the carnal aspects. It's a gradual dying to ourselves and a becoming more like Jesus. This is called sanctification. It's a process, and it won't be complete until we get to heaven.

Boy, I'd love to digress here and explain how to go about doing this sanctification thing, because we tend to make it too hard and focus on our efforts, and this has everything to do with the healing of our bodies and minds as believers, but I need to finish this contrast first.

At the Fall, when Adam and Eve sinned against God, their spirits *instantaneously* died as God had warned, but their souls and minds were initially unchanged. However, their spiritual death triggered a *gradual* process of deterioration of their bodies, minds, and emotions such that they experienced sickness, despair, want, and eventually death. It was never supposed to be that way for humankind. O the consequences of original sin!

Today's message is too long, but we won't end on a negative note. Here's the good part: "But, you [believers] are *not* in the flesh, but in the Spirit, if indeed the Spirit of God dwells in you" (Romans 8:9; emphasis added). Praise God!

TUESDAY

We have seen how humans became infected with disease, emotional dysfunction, cognitive dysfunction, aging, and even death due to the sin of the "first Adam," which nullified the overriding spiritual influence on their carnal natures. We have seen how putting our faith in Jesus Christ revives that spiritual element and fully restores it so that we are *justified* before God for all eternity as if we have never sinned. We are righteous in His eyes as seen in 2 Corinthians 5:21: "For God made Him, who knew no sin to be sin for us, that we might become the righteousness of God in Him." This is *justification*, and although it is ridiculously good news, most Christians don't have a hard time conceptualizing this and accepting it.

But where does that leave our still present carnal aspects? How do they get progressively transformed so that we have the mind of Christ and are healthy? And is it even scriptural to assume this could even happen, that this *sanctification* (becoming more like Jesus in our daily walk with Him) is even possible?

Well, it is. Here are some supportive scriptures:

- "But we have the *mind* of Christ" (1 Corinthians 2:16; emphasis added).

- "Beloved, I pray that you may prosper and be in *good health*, just as your soul prospers" (3 John 1:2; emphasis added).
- "Because as He [Jesus] is, so are we *in this world*" (1 John 4:17; emphasis added).

My wife and I had the privilege a few years ago to visit the Accademia Gallery in Florence, Italy, where Michelangelo's *David* is housed. By the way, I believe that particular artist was divinely inspired. Just viewing the *David* sculpture is awe-inspiring. I think Michelangelo captured perfectly both the complete confidence young David had in the Lord and his utter disdain for this non-God-fearing heathen who had the audacity to make fun of David's covenant God. I think David viewed the encounter as a mismatch—in his favor!

But what I was especially drawn to was the hallway exhibiting the unfinished sculptures, also known as the *Prisoners*. Michelangelo worked without the benefit of a rough model. He claimed he could "see" the forms inside the blocks of granite, and his job was to set them free. But these works were never completed; there were bodies at various degrees in the process of "escaping" from the formless rock. It struck me that this is a beautiful analogy of our sanctification process. We are to be continually emerging more into the light of the Gospel, into the spiritual realm, and leaving farther and farther behind our carnal natures as they are progressively transformed (Romans 12:2), aiming for the perfect will of God.

And just how is that accomplished? Today we went way over; it will have to wait until tomorrow.

WEDNESDAY

"Now there were certain Greeks ... who came to Philip [one of the disciples], and asked him, saying, 'Sirs, we wish to see Jesus'" (John 12:21, 22).

So here's the question we've been building up to, and it's super important: How do we accomplish this "transformation" that Romans 12:2 alludes to?

How do we become more like Christ and allow His perfect Spirit, which is already in us, to invade and permeate our minds, emotions, and physical bodies? We have heard lots of ways of doing this—at least I have during my Christian walk—but they don't seem to work. We were told we had to pray more and harder, and fast, and give of our time and money to the poor, and tithe, and try our very best to obey, and volunteer in the church. These are all *really* good things that we ought to be doing, but none of these things truly transforms us.

No, I've come to see there is really only one thing, what Jesus referred to as "that good part, which will not be taken away" in Luke 10:42. It's in the opening verse: *We must see Jesus!*

And not physically, because even while He was physically here on this earth, both before and after the cross, He emphasized that it was better that He not be physically with us for us to best experience Him. Want scriptural proof?

"Nevertheless, I tell you the truth. It is to your advantage that I go away" (John 16:7).

This beautiful and profound truth is dramatically played out on the road to Emmaus, found in one of my favorite portions of scripture, Luke 24, verses 13–32. Read them for next time, then read them again. For me it's a reset of the garden, where a newly resurrected Jesus Christ, in bodily form, "walks" with two of His disciples (two of the seventy), namely, Cleopas and his wife, and communes with them as Creator God did every day in the cool of the evening with His beloved Adam and Eve in the garden.

THURSDAY

We'll spend some time on this road to Emmaus. For one thing, it's seven miles long and we're walking. But the truths found on this road are potentially life-transforming; I know because they have been for me.

It's Resurrection Sunday, the first day of the week, and Jesus Christ has just defeated sin and death, and is risen. It's early in the morning, but He has already presented Himself to Mary Magdalene and other women who were followers of his (Luke 24:10)—all women. I find that, in and of itself, to be awesome given the lower status afforded to women at that time, not just by the Jews (who should have known better) but also by every culture of the day.

But then Jesus does something very peculiar. He turns onto the road to the small town of Emmaus, instead of continuing on into Jerusalem to meet the Eleven. He does this, we'll see, for only one express purpose: to talk with—commune with—two other followers of his, not part of the original Eleven but no doubt part of the seventy (Luke 10:1).

Why? I think because those two disciples were a couple—husband and wife. That's my conjecture. Scripture doesn't clearly state this, but only one of them is identified by name, Cleopas, in verse 18 of Luke 24, so this idea makes the most sense to me given the already stated lower class status of women and the fact that these two individuals are so intimately identified everywhere else in scripture as the "two of them" (Mark 16:12). It seems reasonable to me that the other is Cleopas's wife.

So we have the Lord walking and communing with a married man and woman, the first couple He appears to after He defeated Satan. Where have we seen a similar scenario? Here's a hint: It was just after the Fall, and it was in the garden. We'll see an amazing comparison next time, on the road to Emmaus.

FRIDAY

"And they heard the sound of the Lord God walking in the Garden in the cool of the day, and Adam and his wife hid themselves from the presence of the Lord God among the trees of the Garden. Then the Lord called to Adam and said to him, 'Where are you?'" (Genesis 3:8–9).

So we're contrasting God, and His interactions with the first couple in the garden after their fall from grace, and Jesus Christ, after demonstrating God's grace in redeeming fallen humankind and His interactions with the first couple He encountered subsequently. It is this latter encounter that will reveal to us how we are to "see Jesus" in our lives on this earth, unlocking the abundant, prosperous, healthy, productive lives we are to have in Him. Exciting stuff, right?

But first a neat diversion, and I really like this one. God's question to Adam and Eve "Where are you?" is the first true recorded *question* in the Old Testament. I told you before to check out everything I'm saying with Scripture and make sure it lines up. Please check out Genesis 3:1, which indeed does come before Genesis 3:9. There's a question mark there. But if you read closely, you see it's not a true question. Instead Satan is twisting around God's Word, misquoting Him. It's his attempt to change an absolute statement, which ended originally in a period, into a lie that ends in a question mark. And you know what, that's a pretty good characterization of the two: God deals in absolute truth, which always ends with "Amen!" and "Yes!" and is rock solid, whereas Satan deals in questions and the blurring of truth and shaky ground. He's unsettled.

Even if you don't buy the first question argument, you certainly have to admit it's the first question God has for humankind: "Where are you?"

Now here's the neat thing. Look at the first question recorded in the New Testament. Of course we start at Matthew 1:1, and we keep reading. We get to chapter 2, the second verse: "Where is He who has been born King of the Jews?"

Wow, do you see what the Holy Spirit did there? The first question recorded in Holy Scripture, a question God asks of humankind, occurs when God is looking for His lost, wayward, sinful children, and the first question recorded in the new covenant is asked by these same lost, wayward, sinful children as they are looking for their Savior, who was prophesied at the same time of the Fall, in Genesis 3:15!

If the awesomeness, complexity, and beauty of Holy Scripture doesn't just floor you, then you're just plain dead! This stuff is unbelievable, and we're just getting started on the road to Emmaus.

5

WEEK

MONDAY

So we've just started our journey to Emmaus, and we're drawing some parallels to the Garden of Eden, because I think the encounter between the Lord Jesus Christ, who had just defeated Satan, and Cleopas and his wife offers a "reset" back to the *way* that we were originally created to function, which Adam and Eve had forfeited. Both involved a human couple (husband and wife) and their Lord. In the garden, Adam and Eve had just sinned against God, turning over their loyalties to Satan, and they were scared and trying to *hide* from the Lord. They "hid themselves from the presence of the Lord God" (Genesis 3:8).

It is a very different situation on the road, where the two disciples are heading out of Jerusalem, sadly discussing the events surrounding the Crucifixion. "So it was, while they conversed and reasoned, that Jesus Himself drew near and went with them. But their *eyes were restrained*, so that they did not know him" (Luke 24:15–16 NKJV; emphasis added).

This encounter is mentioned one other place, briefly, in the Bible, in Mark 16:12: "After that, He appeared *in another form* to two of them as they walked and went into the country" (emphasis added). I like the New King James Version best of all translations, and that's what I will be primarily using, but I like to compare to others also. Here's the *New Testament for Everyone* translation: "After this, He appeared in a different guise to two of them as they were walking into the countryside."

So Jesus was actually *hiding* His identity from the two disciples. Adam and Eve didn't want God to see them, and Jesus didn't want Cleopas and his wife to see Him! Wow, this is neat stuff. And there's a very beautiful reason for this contrast, but (and don't you just hate when I do this?) that will have to wait until next time.

TUESDAY

We're in Luke 24, with Jesus and Cleopas and his wife walking toward Emmaus, and the disciples think that a stranger has joined them; Jesus's true identity is hidden from them. They don't recognize Him physically, nor do they recognize His voice. They are distraught because their Master has been killed, and they fully thought He was going to be their Messiah and deliver them from the rule of Rome (Luke 24:19–21). Now all hope is gone; their Deliverer has failed, and they are on their own.

On their own. That takes me back to the garden, and sinful Adam and Eve, who had severed their spiritual ties with their Creator Father and were hiding from Him. They must have felt very alone. God, who is, remember, just and righteous, had to punish humankind for their sin; He had to keep His promise that they would die if they were to eat of the tree. He couldn't just "look the other way" and forgive them, because the foundations on which His throne are built, namely, righteousness and justice (Psalm 89:14), would be destroyed. But how could He just throw them away and desert them if His very nature is love? You can see why Satan had thought he had outsmarted God Himself in the garden: game, set, match!

Little did Satan know—because, remember, he is not omniscient—that God had a *plan*, formulated before the very creation of the world (Ephesians 1:4), to make everything that had gone so wrong right again. That plan would culminate in the cross. The haunting prophecy of such was given in that very same garden: "And I will put enmity between you [Satan] and the woman, and between your seed and her Seed; He shall bruise your head, and you shall bruise His heel" (Genesis 3:15).

And now we're there. The cross had been accomplished; victory over sin, disease, and even death was won, and Jesus had created an opportunity to tell His followers *how* to appropriate that victory into their lives, and grow in Him, and live the abundant, healthy, productive life that is inherent in the Atonement. I promised last time to reveal that this morning, but I had to set the stage first and get things into perspective. We'll pick it up next time, on the road to Emmaus.

WEDNESDAY

"And Jesus said to them, 'What kind of conversation is this that you have with one another as you walk and are sad?' Then the one whose name was Cleopas answered and said to Him, 'Are You the only stranger in Jerusalem, and have You not known the things which happened there in these days?'" (Luke 24:17–18).

Then the two disciples, who, like all the others, never did quite get it regarding Jesus's teachings concerning His mission during this First Coming—that is, that He came to save humans from sin and all its consequences, and He wasn't interested in overthrowing Rome, and He knew that He must die and be raised the third day—began to reveal their thoughts about Jesus in verses 19–24. They thought of Him as a prophet and were hoping that He would redeem Israel from Roman oppression, but then the religious leaders forced the Roman rulers to condemn Him to death and crucify Him. That was three days prior, and now there were rumors that His tomb was found empty that very morning, but "Him they did not see" (v. 24).

So they were confused and discouraged and anxious—just a mess! And Jesus was *right there* next to them! Wouldn't it be just awesome if Jesus had revealed who He was and let them physically see Him, touch Him, and embrace Him and be encouraged by Him, so that they felt better about everything? Wouldn't it?

That's not quite what happened. "Then He said to them, '*O foolish ones*, and slow of heart to believe in all that the prophets have spoken! Ought not the Christ to have suffered these things, and to enter into His glory?' *And beginning at Moses and all the prophets, He expounded to them in all the Scriptures the things concerning Himself*" (vv. 25–27; emphasis added).

Wow, there are so many life-transforming truths packed into those verses. We'll start unpacking next time, on the road to Emmaus.

THURSDAY

I've been working toward today's post for a while now. It's kind of a little epiphany, so *pay attention*! (Just a little humor this early morning.)

We left Jesus Christ actually scolding His beloved disciples, Cleopas, and Cleopas's wife for not knowing the Word of God and therefore not understanding who He was and what He had just accomplished at the cross, but He is staying hidden from their eyes. They do not recognize Him. Not yet.

And what Scripture should they have been familiar with? Did they have the Bible?

Yep, they had the first part of it—the Old Testament. Did you know the entire Old Testament was written and readily available to the Jews of Jesus's time? It had already been translated into Greek (the Septuagint). These Holy Scriptures are actually all about Jesus Christ, when properly interpreted. We'll get into that fully later. But for now, I want to point out the supreme importance Jesus is placing on knowing Scripture and seeing Him in it.

So I've been given some statements that have been very helpful to me in conceptualizing the truths of this great Christian faith of ours. I already gave one of them, about how the cross was necessary to prove the love of God without compromising the justice and righteousness of God. Remember that? Well, this next one has been even more beneficial to me because it gives a profound insight into the role of healing in the life of believers. Here it is:

Knowing Scripture, and seeing the face of Jesus in all of it, is what allows our perfectly revived spirit nature to permeate and *renew* our minds, emotions, and physical bodies (our carnal nature) such that we can fully participate in the *healing* of our minds and emotions and bodies, which has been already provided for us in the Atonement of Jesus Christ at the cross.

There is lots there, and it will take us weeks and plenty of Scripture to make this come alive. For now I am just very thankful for that conversation Jesus had with us on…the road to Emmaus.

FRIDAY

Last time we dropped a spiritual bombshell: It is by properly discerning and interpreting Holy Scripture, and by seeing that ultimately all of Scripture is about Jesus Christ and His finished work on the cross, that we can unlock all the blessings and gifts available to us, ("Blessed be the God and Father of our Lord Jesus Christ, who has blessed us with *every* spiritual blessing in the heavenly places in Christ" [Ephesians 1:3; emphasis added]), which includes our healing. And it is better to see Jesus in Scripture than even to see Him physically, as weird as that seems, because He wants us to see Him with spiritual eyes, that perfect part of us (once we're saved), rather than with our physical, carnal eyes, which are not perfect. John 20:29 reads, "Jesus said to him, 'Thomas, because you have seen Me [physically], you have believed. Blessed are those who have not seen and yet have believed [spiritually].'"

Wow, there is so much truth tightly wound up in the foregoing paragraph, and we need to slowly unravel it and digest it little by little because then it will seep deep into our souls. I wish I had an outline for you going forward. I wish I had an outline for *me* going forward! I've asked for such, but I was given this verse instead: "The wind blows where it wishes, and you hear the sound of it, but cannot tell where it comes from and where it goes. So is everyone who is born of the Spirit" (John 3:8).

We're going to let the Holy Spirit lead. That's always best, albeit a little unnerving, because I'm a planner by nature, and His way is to have us rely on His perfect timing and guidance, rather than on our own predictable and set plans—kind of like blowing in the wind.

That leading is taking us next to a discussion of the age-old duel between belief and works. Notice that in the opening paragraph, about the way to receive the healing we are after, there is no mention of what we have to *do* but plenty about what we have to *believe*. The one leads almost effortlessly to the other. Yet so many of us have it completely backward, and that leads to frustration and stagnation, which is exactly what Satan wants as he knows he can't rob us of our salvation, but he sure can try to rob us of our joy and peace and our rest in the Lord.

We'll start that next time, blowing in the wind.

6
WEEK

MONDAY

So I've tried to establish that getting to know (see) our Lord and Savior through Scripture and drawing nearer to Him is what activates the promises (including healing) that are legally ours because of the exchange of our sin (which resulted in disease and death) for His righteousness that occurred at the cross. "For He [God] made Him who knew no sin to be sin for us, that we might become the righteousness of God in Him" (2 Corinthians 5:21). What an awesome verse!

But we have to *believe* the Word of God if we are to benefit from it because, as we'll come to see, it is that faith/belief in Holy Scripture that allows us to *rest* in the finished work of Jesus Christ and not try to accomplish our healing through our own *works*.

First, though, I want to explain how I have come to see these super important terms *faith* and *belief*. Are they the same thing? I haven't heard what I'm about to present preached anywhere, and you may not agree with it, but I've found this way of thinking very helpful to me—and it is in accordance with Scripture—and it has helped me deal with the question we've all had as believers at one time or another, namely, "Do I have enough faith for this?"

First, faith and belief are *not* the same. Here's my definition of faith: the *confident expectation*, based on scripture, that what you are praying for will come to pass.

Paul described faith as "the substance of things *hoped* for" (Hebrews 11:1; emphasis added). You can't be saved without faith, so every Christian has faith. Here's the thing that I think will be a bit hard to swallow: every

— 32 —

Christian has the *same* amount of faith! Look at Romans 12:3, again the words of Paul: "For by the grace given me I say to every one of you: Do not think of yourself more highly than you ought, but rather think of yourself with sober judgment, in accordance with *the* measure of faith God has given you" (NIV; emphasis added). It should be noted the King James Version also says *the* measure, but the New King James Version, which I've said before is my favorite, gets this verse wrong and says *a* measure of faith.

Look at Jesus's own words in Matthew 17:20: "If you have faith as a mustard seed [which is apparently the smallest seed ever], you will say to this mountain, 'Move from here to there,' and it will move; nothing will be impossible for you." Wow! We'll come back to this chapter next time, when we define *belief,* but know this: you don't ever have to question whether you have *enough* faith. That's not the question. You do have enough faith. The question is *in what* have you placed your faith. And if the answer is Jesus Christ and His cross, then you're just fine.

I knew this one would be lengthy; it's a big subject. We'll continue next time.

TUESDAY

So we were defining *faith*, that *confident expectation*, and *hope* that we place in Christ Jesus, our "hope of glory" (Colossians 1:27), without which we cannot please God: "No one can please God without faith, for whoever comes to God must have faith that God exists, and rewards those that seek Him" (Hebrews 11:6 GNT).

We postulated that we all as believers (and we couldn't be believers without faith, because "we are saved by Grace through Faith" (Ephesians 2:8), have a "full measure" of faith and have enough for any challenge that comes our way as long as our faith is properly placed in Jesus and His finished work on the cross. Don't ever question that.

But there is a deeper thing, I think, and that's *belief.* Here again is how I picture faith:

Faith is the *confident expectation* that what you are praying for *will come to pass*.

Here's how I picture belief:

Belief is the *unwavering conviction* that what you are praying for *has already come to pass*.

Wow, do you see the subtle but profound difference? The verse that lit this up for me is one of the most important verses in the Bible for me, Mark 11:24. Listen to the words of Jesus: "Therefore I say to you, whatever things you ask for, when you pray, *believe* that you *receive* them, and *you will have them*" (emphasis added).

This is how I see the difference between faith and belief: Faith is an *instantaneous* gift from God, perfectly complete and at our disposal when we accept Jesus as our Savior, but belief is a gradual manifestation of our growing closer to Jesus and becoming more like Him by "seeing" Him in Scripture such that we get to the point that we can absolutely *know* that what He *says* (His Word) is true, no matter what the *circumstances* that we *see* and *experience* in this carnal world.

That's a lot to digest, isn't it? It will all become clearer when we return to an amazing story of the importance of belief in Matthew 17, next time.

WEDNESDAY

So this morning we'll set the stage with scripture. Meditate on it, and ask yourself the question, "Why were the disciples unable to do what they were tasked to do, and not only tasked to do, but also given the authority and power to do?" The answer will have practical applications for us. Here's a teaser: Their failure was not due to what we've been told.

> Then He [Jesus] called His twelve disciples together and gave them power and authority over all demons and to cure diseases. He sent them to preach the kingdom of God and to heal the sick. (Luke 9:1–2)

After these things the Lord appointed seventy others also, and sent them two by two before His face into every city and place where He Himself was about to go. … Then the seventy returned with joy, saying, "Lord, even the demons are subject to us in Your name." (Luke 10:1, 17)

And when they had come to the multitude, a man came to Him, kneeling down to Him and saying, "Lord have mercy on my son, for he is an epileptic and suffers severely; for he often falls into the fire and into the water. So, I brought him to Your disciples, but they *could not* cure him." Then Jesus answered and said, "O faithless and perverse generation, how long shall I be with you? How long shall I bear with you? Bring him here to Me." And Jesus rebuked the demon, and it came out of him; and the child was cured that very hour. Then the disciples came to Jesus privately and said, "*Why could we not cast it out?*" So Jesus said to them, "Because of your *unbelief*; for assuredly I say to you, if you have faith as a mustard seed, you will say to this mountain, 'Move from here to there,' and it will move; and nothing will be impossible for you. However, *this kind* does not go out except by prayer and fasting." (Matthew 17:14–21; emphasis added)

As a pediatrician, I find the visual imagery here to be striking. Even to me seizures are scary and intimidating, and they certainly were for the disciples. But Jesus wasn't fazed, and He went on to do the will of His Father. We'll see how next time.

THURSDAY

So the disciples were explicitly given the authority and power to cast out demons and cure diseases by Jesus. Wow, just think about that. And it appears as though, for the most part, they did exactly that.

But there was something different about this boy, something that resulted in their failure to heal him. You know what it was? Look at these descriptions of what they were witnessing, from the perspectives of Matthew, Mark, and Dr. Luke, respectively:

- "He is an epileptic and *suffers severely*; for he often *falls into the fire* and often *into the water*" (Matthew 17:15; emphasis added).
- "Wherever it seizes him, it *throws him down; he foams at the mouth, gnashes his teeth*, and *becomes rigid*" (Mark 9:18; emphasis added).
- "He *suddenly cries out, it convulses him* so that he *foams at the mouth*; and it departs from him *with great difficulty, bruising him*" (Luke 9:39; emphasis added).

These very dramatic behaviors scared the disciples to death, and they let what they physically saw overwhelm what they knew the Words of Jesus to be. They no longer *believed* they had the power to do what Jesus had told them to do. They fell from the spiritual to the carnal. It's called *unbelief*. And Jesus made that clear to them. When they asked why they couldn't cast out the evil spirits, Jesus answered, "Because of your *unbelief*" (Matthew 17:20; emphasis added).

Now notice that it wasn't because they didn't have faith that they *could* do what Jesus had already given them the power to do, as they had been consistently doing His will and casting out demons and healing diseases. But when confronted with an overwhelming assault on their *senses*, they didn't hold on to that *unwavering conviction* that God's Word is true, and they gave into the carnal.

Next time we'll look at another example of this lack of belief, namely, the story of the only mortal man who ever walked on water, albeit briefly.

FRIDAY

So let's reset the big picture. We simply have to do this on occasion. Although it seems that we get off topic at times, we really don't. We're headed along a trajectory that will end in a fuller understanding of our physical healing as believers, and the roles of faith and belief, and how, or if, modern medical science fits in. It's just that we'll take a few side roads as the Spirit leads. I guess I should point out that everything we've discussed up to this point pertains only to believers. If you're not one—if you've never accepted Jesus Christ as your Savior—then you might as well get saved so that all of this amazing stuff will apply to you during your time on this earth. And you'll get an eternity of bliss, beauty, and joy to boot. The alternative is really bad, and once you die, there's no recourse. "How shall we escape if we neglect so great a salvation?" (Hebrews 2:3). This gift of salvation is free, but you do need to qualify and there's only one qualification: you have to be a sinner. You have to be lost.

I have thus far endeavored to show that we as believers have a revived and perfect spirit nature and are flawless in God's eyes. This was made possible by the sacrifice of Jesus Christ on the cross, where He took the just penalty for all our sins and made us righteous. That defeat of sin took care of all the consequences of sin, including disease, anxiety, depression, and poverty, all of which were conquered on the cross. Our "work" now is to approximate that renewing of our carnal minds and bodies by allowing our perfect spiritual realm to permeate and transform the rest of us. That is accomplished by seeing Jesus in His Word and meditating on His Word because His Word is Spirit, and that's the realm of our being that we are to *primarily* function in since we were created that way. The spiritual aspect will inform, enhance, and improve everything else we are and everything else we do.

Integral to all of this, we must have faith and belief. The faith part is a given for believers since it is a manifestation of the hope we had in the first place to accept the promptings of the Holy Spirit. We are saved by grace through this faith (Ephesians 2:8). But belief in the Word of God as absolute truth, no matter what the situation—that unwavering conviction that is rock solid—is a more gradual process and is something that grows stronger as we see Jesus more fully and clearly. The main impediment to being well and having an abundant Christian life is *unbelief*, not lack of *faith*, as seen in John 13:58: "Now He did *not* do many mighty works there *because of their unbelief*." That's where we left off last time.

Sorry, I had to get this summary of the last month of posts in, and in one message. I just had to. We'll look at another example of unbelief next time.

MONDAY

"Now in the fourth watch of the night, Jesus went to them, walking on the sea … and Peter … said, 'Lord, if it is You, command me to come to You on the water.' So He said, 'Come.' And when Peter had come out of the boat, he walked on the water to come to Jesus. *But,* when he *saw* that the wind was boisterous, he was afraid; and *beginning to sink*, he cried out, saying, 'Lord, save me!'" (Matthew 14:25–30; emphasis added).

This fascinating story is told only in the Gospel of Matthew. I find that interesting, in that Mark was thought to write his Gospel primarily based on Peter's testimony, and no mention of this legendary event featuring Peter is found in Mark. Perhaps Peter wasn't especially proud of this "failure" on his part, but it should be pointed out that, as far as I know, Peter was the only mortal man to ever successfully walk on water for any length of time.

Now you might be thinking that Peter had unusually strong faith that empowered him to get up out of that boat amid a raging storm and even start walking on the sea. But remember this is Peter we're talking about, who would completely turn on Jesus and deny Him not just once, but three times at His trial, and who was constantly having to reaffirm his faith by saying that he was the one disciple who would do anything for Jesus, and follow Him anywhere, and love Him more than the other disciples did. No, Peter was no pillar of faith. Remember that point I was trying to make before? We all as believers have enough faith to do our Lord's bidding. That's reassuring, but why then did Peter fail?

He had enough faith; he just didn't have enough belief. He started out with his focus on the face of Jesus, not aware of any physical thing around him, just the face of Jesus. And he was doing what no mere person had ever done before or has done since. *But* (and that can be a really bad word) when he *saw* the wind and noticed immediately thereafter he was actually *sinking*, he didn't overcome those physical stimuli with a rock-solid *belief* based on the Word of God, which had clearly told him, "Come." The proper response on Peter's part would have been to say, "So the wind is pretty violent, and the waves are rough, and I'm a man with a body who is supposed to, based on physics, sink, *but* [it can be a good word also] Jesus said that I should come to Him, and that is what I can fully trust. He will provide a way for me to get to Him no matter what I'm sensing, and I will go to Him!"

Wow! I'm getting inspired by all this. As good an example of the importance of belief that this story is, there's a better one, found in the Old Testament, a phenomenal story. We'll look at it next time.

TUESDAY

We are examining the importance of belief, and we have cited a couple of examples of unbelief. Let's now look at, to my way of thinking, the most amazing example of belief in the Bible. It's found in Genesis 22. I've heard that this portion of Scripture is revered more than any other by the Jews, and that's fascinating since, although the story is ostensibly about Father Abraham and his son Isaac, it's *actually* about Father God and His *only* Son, Jesus. The Jewish people don't see it that way now, but they will someday (Zechariah 12:10–11).

Note that we are so focused on this belief thing because it is through this that we can see Jesus in Scripture and become more like Him, and it is belief that allows us to perform good works pleasing to the Lord and according to His will. We're taking on this age-old battle between belief and works, which is another reason I want to look at this story, because it clearly demonstrates the proper relationship between the two. Ready?

First of all, we need to see the proper order of things. This is crucial because if we put the cart before the horse, we will ultimately fail. Before Genesis

22 is Genesis 15, where the Lord God appears to Abram (that was his name before God changed it in chapter 17) in a vision and is comforting and reassuring Abram because he had no children and he was getting *very* old, as was his wife. When God initially called Abram to follow Him, back in Genesis 12, Abram was already seventy-five years old. God had promised to make him "a great nation" (v. 2)—yet he had no kids! So here Abram is reminding God of this, and the Lord gently does the following:

"Then He brought him outside and said, 'Look now toward heaven, and count the stars, if you are able to number them.' And He said to him, 'So shall your descendants be'" (Genesis 15:5).

Wow! This is the middle of a desert, absolutely no artificial light. Can you imagine how full of stars that nighttime sky would have been? The stars were innumerable for sure. Now we have some idea of how awesome stars are, and of all the different kinds and sizes and stages, and an estimate of the total number (at least one billion trillion). And here God is saying to this childless old guy who has a barren wife almost as old as he that he is going to have as many offspring as the number of stars in the sky! What would you say to that? We'll see Abram's response, and God's response to his response, next time.

WEDNESDAY

I want to start out this morning by finishing a discussion regarding the awesome stars God showed to Abram in Genesis 15—at least one billion trillion of them. One would think the scripture would devote a fair amount of time to the creation of such given the great effort it would have required, right? Here's the sum total of the account:

"He made the stars, also" (Genesis 1:16).

Wow! That's it? A billion trillion unbelievably powerful huge balls of energy were seemingly created as an *afterthought*, a *parenthetical*, a "*by the way*"?! What kind of God is this? And why, if He is our God, are we scared and anxious about the relatively petty things we struggle with? Before God took Abram outside, he told him, "Do not be afraid, Abram. I am your shield, your exceedingly great reward" (Genesis 15:1).

I think Abram realized that because he had just been told an incredibly unbelievable prophecy, that his descendants would be as innumerable as the stars. This went against all biology and science and rational thought. It went against everything his carnal intellect and emotions and senses told him. So what did he do?

"And he [Abram] *believed* in the Lord, and He *accounted it to him for righteousness*" (Genesis 15:6; emphasis added).

I know it seems like I say every verse I quote is foundational and super important, but this one really is. Trust me. We're going to get to the story of Abraham offering up Isaac as a sacrifice, and we'll rightly use that as an example of great faith and belief, but that "work" is *not* what justified Abraham before God; it was his *belief* that occurred on that starry desert night. Amen!

THURSDAY

"And the Scripture ... preached the Gospel to Abraham beforehand ... so, then, those who are of faith are blessed with Believing Abraham" (Galatians 3:8, 9).

"Now it came to pass, after these things, that God tested Abraham, and said to him, 'Abraham!' And he said, 'Here I am.' Then He said, 'Take now your son, your *only* son, Isaac, *whom you love*, and go to the land of Moriah, and offer him there as a burnt offering on one of the mountains of which I shall tell you'" (Genesis 22:1–2; emphasis added).

"For God so loved the world that He gave His *only begotten* Son, that whoever believes in Him should not perish, but have everlasting life" (John 3:16; emphasis added).

"And suddenly a voice came from heaven, saying, 'This is My *beloved* Son, in whom I am well pleased'" (Matthew 3:17; emphasis added).

So this morning we start dissecting the offering up of Isaac, found in Genesis 22. It is a true historical story but also a type of things to come. Abraham probably already had a pretty good idea of God's ultimate plan of salvation, starting when God first called him to leave his country in Genesis 12, when God told Abraham He would make of him "a great nation" (see Galatians 3:8), but this event would have given a lot more clarity since it was obviously primarily about God and His Son. Notice the emphasis on "only son" and "whom you love" in verse 2 of Genesis 22. Interesting, right? Abraham had *two* sons at that time, Ishmael and Isaac. Only God had one Son. And what about that love thing? Isn't that superfluous? Wouldn't any father love his son?

God wanted to emphasize just how much the Son was loved. He was looking two thousand years into the future, when He would have to actually turn away from the one most beloved thing in the universe to Him and let His obedient, sinless Son take the punishment for all the sins of fallen humankind, an act of love so overwhelming that the universe would never question the great love of God again. God is allowing a similar event to play out now in the land of Moriah, but it will have a very different ending as we will eventually see. But we'll take our time in this incredible land of Moriah.

FRIDAY

So we're starting in Genesis 22. I gave the first two verses yesterday. Every amazing thing that is to happen in this chapter came to pass "after these things." We ought to quickly explain what "these things" in Abraham's life were:

1. As we read in **Genesis 12**, Abram is called by God to leave everything and follow Him (kind of like Jesus calling the disciples, eh?), to go to an unspecified land, "a land that I will show you," and he would be the patriarch of a "great nation." So Abram leaves Ur and heads for Canaan.

2. As we find in **Genesis 13**, Abram is given the land of Canaan by God (not by the United Nations or some peace plan or political arrangement. Israel currently occupies just a small portion of the

original land God gave Abram; they're not going anywhere), and God more specifically promises to give Abram *lots* of kids: "I will make your descendants as the dust of the earth; so that if a man could number the dust of the earth, then your descendants also could be numbered" (v. 16).

3. In **Genesis 15**, as already mentioned, we see where God takes Abram outside into the starry desert night and tells him to count the stars. "So shall your descendants be." And for the first time it is stated that Abram "*believed* in the Lord, and He accounted it to Him for righteousness" (vv. 5–6). It is then that the Abrahamic covenant is drawn between Abram and God, an immutable covenant.

4. In **Genesis 17**, God reaffirms His covenant with the newly named Abraham and makes male circumcision the physical sign of it. I've performed literally thousands of circumcisions in my career, and I think of this covenant sign every time, but remember, it is *not* part of the new covenant as seen in Colossians 2:11: "In Him you were also circumcised with the circumcision made without hands." It is also in this important chapter that Sarah (previously known as Sarai), Abraham's wife, ninety years old (Abraham was ninety-nine!), is told that she will bear a son and that he is already named. "Sarah, your wife, shall bear a son, and you shall call his name Isaac" (v. 19).

5. **Genesis 18** tells us that shortly thereafter, the preincarnate Jesus appears to Abraham and Sarah, confirming the pregnancy with Isaac (I personally think this is when Sarah became pregnant. I'm probably the only person on earth who thinks that, but the life of Isaac would turn out to be very much a type of Christ, and Jesus said twice to Sarah that He would return to her "according to the time of life." I take that to mean nine months) (vv. 9–13).

6. We find in **Genesis 21** that the promised son, Isaac, is born (vv. 2–3)! This would have been impossible in the natural, carnal world and would have absolutely sealed Abraham's *belief* in God's Word because what He had promised did indeed come to pass.

Wow, I really went on too long this morning. This stuff may seem boring to you, but I absolutely *love* it, and I suspect you do, too. We've set the background for Abraham's journey up a mountain…in the land of Moriah.

8
WEEK

MONDAY

"God … said to him, 'Abraham!' And he said, 'Here I am'" (Genesis 22:1).

"The Lord called to him from heaven and said, "Abraham!' So, he said, 'Here I am'" (Genesis 22:11).

We're examining some examples of belief in the Bible, and we've just begun looking at the most dramatic and inspiring of examples, found in Genesis 22. We've seen how God had already mightily worked in the life of Abraham. I am struck by the way God interacts with him, almost in a word-for-word fashion, in these two verses. It's like an endearing script; there's a familiarity there with the exclamation of Abraham's name and his pat response. You know what that reminds me of?

When I want to give my wife a hard time about something, I don't call her by the usual intimate name I use, namely, Kate, but I shout out, "*Kristen!*" And she slowly, knowing I'm toying with her, says a drawn-out "Yes?" I think that's what's going on between God and Abraham here. Call me weird, but I just get that sense. And the reason my wife and I converse like this is that we are, in addition to husband and wife, the best of *friends*. One could say best friends forever (BFFs).

Here's my point: God and Abraham were BFFs! "What?" you say. Well, I can prove it. Look at 2 Chronicles 20:7: "Are you not our God, who drove out the inhabitants of this land before Your people Israel, and gave it to the descendants of Abraham, Your *friend forever*?" (emphasis added). Wow! And in Exodus 33:11, God speaks to Moses as His friend.

Try to get your mind around this. You know that unbelievably awesome God who created all the stars as an afterthought? That great God of heaven? He allows us to be His friends! We have no business having that kind of access to God. There's no way we can comprehend this, and God knows that.

"For My thoughts are not your thoughts, nor are My ways your ways, says the Lord. For as the heavens are higher than the earth, so are My ways higher than your ways, and My thoughts than your thoughts" (Isaiah 55:8–9).

Certainly a diversion this morning, but a really good one for a Monday morning, I think. Next time we start the three-day journey to the land of Moriah.

TUESDAY

Our topic is belief, and we're spending a long time on it because it is crucial to appropriating all the benefits and blessings of the cross to our earthly lives. And we're dissecting Genesis 22 slowly. We're just starting verse 2. But I'm telling you, this is the best way to really meditate on Scripture: tear off small portions first thing in the morning and chew on them all day, essentially slowly *eating* the Scripture! Look at the words of Jesus: "I am the living bread which came down from heaven. If anyone eats of this bread, he will live forever" (John 6:51). Wow.

"Take now your son … and go to the *land of Moriah*" (v. 2; emphasis added).

So just where is this special place that God chose to be the site of the most dramatic story in the Old Testament? At the time, Abraham was living in the southern portion of the land God had given him, Canaan (which basically was where Israel is today, but it encompassed a much greater area), in a place called Beersheba (Genesis 21:31–33). Moriah was an area of hills a two-to-three-day journey north of there, and it would turn out to be where Jerusalem was built, the City of God, a place very, very dear to God's heart because Solomon's temple would be built there, on Mount Moriah, as seen in 2 Chronicles 3:1, and Jesus Christ would suffer and die there, probably very close to where Abraham would offer up Isaac, foreshadowing the most important event in the history of the universe. The word *Moriah* itself means "Yahweh is awesome!" Jesus absolutely loved Jerusalem as seen in Luke 19:41–44, in fact: "Now, as He [Jesus] grew near, He saw the city [Jerusalem], and wept over it."

No little detail in the Bible is unimportant; there is great significance in this land of Moriah. When Jesus comes back the second time to earth, as conquering King, He will arrive there, in Jerusalem, on the Mount of Olives (Zechariah 14:4), and He will rule from there, and there will be a glorious "New Jerusalem" (Revelation 3:12). So it's an awesome place, that land of Moriah. Abraham is about to get up "early in the morning" and head for it with his miraculously given son—next time.

WEDNESDAY

"I will make you and the woman hate each other. Your children and her children will be enemies. Her Son will crush your head, and you will bite His heel" (Genesis 3:15 NIRV).

"Therefore David ran and stood over the Philistine [Goliath], took his sword and drew it out of its sheath and killed him and cut off his head with it. … And David took the head of Goliath and brought it to Jerusalem" (1 Samuel 17:51, 54 NKJV).

I know what you're thinking: *What do these verses have to do with Genesis 22?* The answer is: virtually nothing! It's a diversion. I love diversions, but they are always related to some degree.

We were describing the land of Moriah and the fact it was a hilly area that would become the site of Jerusalem. Abraham will shortly be heading up one of those hills to sacrifice Isaac, but the topic today is an event that occurred in this same area, probably on a hill, two thousand years later, and that place was called Golgotha, also known as the "Place of a Skull" (Matthew 27:33). Luke calls it Calvary (chapter 23:34); the Latin term *calvarium* means "skull." Why the name? And why is there just one skull involved? Remember, nothing in Holy Scripture is insignificant.

It has been suggested that there were geographic features of this hill that made it look like a skull, but I like the following possibility better. You see, Goliath, who was from the city of Gath, was a type of Satan, wholly opposed to God to the point of even mocking Him and striking fear in God's people. David was a type of Christ; in fact, one of the names used by Jesus was "Son of David." So you see a type of fulfillment of Genesis 3:15 in the story of David and Goliath. And the Bible makes the point that David cut off Goliath's head and brought it to Jerusalem. Why would he have done that? Jerusalem was not a prominent city for the Israelites at that time.

This isn't in the Bible, but Jewish tradition indicates that David buried Goliath's head in Jerusalem, building a mound, or hill, over it, and it was called—you guessed it—Golgotha (a conflation of *Goliath* and *Gath*). And it was there the ancient prophecy was fulfilled because the only true Seed of a woman (indicating an immaculate conception), Jesus Christ, crushed Satan's ugly head once and for all! Praise God.

Wasn't this diversion neat? And it was still about this land of Moriah.

THURSDAY

Happy Fourth of July! What better way to start the day than reading from the book that shows the only Way to true freedom and independence.

"So Abraham rose early in the morning and saddled his donkey, and took two of his young men with him, and Isaac his son; and he split wood for the burnt offering, and arose and went to the place of which God had told him. Then, on the third day Abraham lifted his eyes and saw the place afar off. And Abraham said to his young men, 'Stay here with the donkey; the *lad and I* will go yonder and worship, and *we* will come back to you'" (Genesis 22:3–5; emphasis added).

"By faith Abraham, when he was tested, offered up Isaac, and he who had received the promises offered up his only begotten son, of whom it was said, 'In Isaac your seed shall be called,' concluding that God was able to raise him up, *even from the dead*, from which he also received him in a figurative sense" (Hebrews 11:17–19; emphasis added).

And this next quote is from a human book by a Christian author, J. R. R. Tolkien, so it's not absolute truth, but I've always been intrigued by the question, and it is apropos to the topic at hand:

"Is everything sad going to become untrue? What's happened to the world?" This is what Sam asked of Gandalf in *Lord of the Rings: The Return of the King.*

In a sense, Abraham and Samwise Gamgee were in a similar potentially dark place; all that had been promised and that was good and uplifting and proper was being pulled away and spiraling downward. The son of promise, without whom there could be no fulfillment of the promise, was to die. That was Abraham's dilemma. With Sam, Frodo's sidekick in the final book of the *Lord of the Rings* trilogy (and probably the true unsung hero of the story), all things good in the world had been seemingly consumed by the evil of Sauron and his dark forces. All was lost. But then Sam awakened to find Gandalf, the good wizard, thought to certainly be dead, still alive, which is what prompted his unusually worded but profound and extremely Christian question, "Is everything sad going to become untrue?" Just seven words, and so strangely arranged, not "Are all things going to be made right again?" which would have made more sense to me. No, Sam is essentially asking if it is possible for all the bad and sad and evil of the past to be completely obliterated such that it would be as if it *had never even occurred*!

The answer is found in the words of the great Old Testament prophet Jeremiah. Next time. Enjoy the holiday.

FRIDAY

"But *this* is the covenant that I will make with the house of Israel after those days, says the Lord: I will put My law in their *minds*, and write it on their *hearts*; and I will be their God, and they shall be My people. No more shall every man teach his neighbor, and every man his brother, saying 'Know the Lord', for *they shall all know Me*, from the least of them to the greatest of them, says the Lord. For I will forgive their iniquity, and *their sin I will remember no more*" (Jeremiah 31:33–34; emphasis added).

Wow! Do you realize what this is saying? Not only are all the horribly bad and sad and depressing things of the past forgiven, but also they are all *forgotten* when we put our faith in Jesus Christ and accept His salvation, purchased at the cross. It is as if they never occurred! It is as if they were all untrue, and the only truth now is our life in Jesus Christ. This is the new covenant. And don't let that part about the "house of Israel" confuse you. We as Gentiles are partakers of this salvation first as Jesus was rejected by the Jews ("But through their [Israel's] fall, salvation has come to the Gentiles" [Romans 11:11]), but they will be grafted back in at the end. This covenant is for us; we, as believers, are brand new, and the old stuff is *gone*. Not just improved upon, not just cleaned up, but *gone*! Look at this:

"Therefore, if anyone is in Christ, he is a *new creation*; old things have *passed away*; behold *all things have become new*" (2 Corinthians 5:17).

So, *yes*, Samwise Gamgee, yes. Everything sad *can* become *untrue*, and it already has for believers. But what does this have to do with Father Abraham and Isaac and belief and Genesis 22? Everything! Abraham knew this truth already. I'll prove that next time in the land of Moriah.

9
_____
WEEK

MONDAY

So last week we read in Genesis 22 that Abraham was fully convinced that he would return from the mount of sacrifice with Isaac in tow (v. 5), and we read in Hebrews 11 that Abraham "concluded" that such would be the case *even* if it meant God would allow him to kill Isaac so that God could raise the boy from the dead (v. 19)!

Do you see the absolute, unwavering *belief* Abraham had in the promises God had given him regarding Isaac? It was a foregone *conclusion* to him. He didn't tell the waiting party that he "hoped" to come back with Isaac, God willing, because he *knew* the Word of God, and he *knew* God was willing. There was no set of circumstances that would cause him to waver, and that's what I mean by belief. That is where I want to live! God absolutely *loved* this attitude of Abraham. Just watch as we pick up the narrative:

"So Abraham took the wood of the burnt offering and laid it on Isaac his son; and he took the fire in his hand, and a knife, and the two of them went together. But Isaac … said, 'Look, the fire and the wood, but where is the lamb for a burnt offering?' And Abraham said, 'My son, God will provide for Himself the lamb for a burnt offering'" (Genesis 22:6–8).

So what was Abraham actually thinking here? He was fully planning to kill his son, yet he told Isaac that the sacrifice would be there. Was it a white lie, told because he was trying to calm down his son?

Hmm. Here's what I think: Abraham was so sure of the outcome that the details didn't matter; he wasn't anxious or scared. I believe Isaac picked up on that and wasn't scared himself. I think there may have been a lot less actual drama occurring up on that mount than we'd like to imagine, and truth be known, there was something else, something *alive*, up there with Isaac and Abraham. Abraham never saw it coming up on a mount in the land of Moriah.

TUESDAY

So Abraham had figured out this belief thing I'm trying to explain, and he was headed up a mount in Moriah to offer up his son of promise as a sacrifice, knowing that one way or another he would return with his son intact. He absolutely believed the Word of God, which had promised many, many descendants to Abraham, and therefore Isaac was to have at least one child. At present he was just a "lad" and had no progeny yet. It was obvious to Abraham that Isaac would either be spared, or, more likely, sacrificed and then brought back to life. This is what he *knew*. This was *belief*, and God acknowledged that, and respected that, and *rewarded* that (Hebrews 11:6).

Here's why I say that, and this is how I view this subtle interplay of faith (which we all have equally) and belief, which is an acquired thing and strengthens as we grow in the Lord. You see, in addition to what he knew, Abraham had a *hope*, a *confident expectation* also, namely that God would provide the sacrifice and spare the death of Isaac as we saw last time (Genesis 22:8). God didn't specifically say that at all; He told Abraham to kill Isaac! This expectation was a sign of Abraham's faith, but it was a well-founded *hope*, not an absolute certainty to him. His belief was manifest in his statement in verse 5 that Isaac would return down that mount with him because that was in accordance with God's Word.

And here's the thing: Abraham's *belief* is what allowed his *faith* to be *fully realized*! Look at what actually happened up on that mount:

> And Abraham stretched out his hand and took the knife
> to slay his son. But the Angel of the Lord called to him
> from Heaven and said, "Abraham, Abraham!" So he said,
> "Here I am." And He said, "Do not lay your hand on the
> lad, or do anything to him; for now I know that you fear

God, since you have not withheld your son, your only son, from Me." Then Abraham lifted his eyes and looked, and there behind him was a ram, caught in the thicket by its thorns. So Abraham went and took the ram and offered it up for a burnt offering, instead of his son. (Genesis 22:10–13)

Wow! Abraham's belief was unwavering, and because of that his hope was realized and his faith was sufficient. We're going to spend more time on this mount in the land of Moriah, but next time we'll take a side trip to ancient Babylon, where a few of the descendants of Abraham and Isaac will demonstrate for us another example of exactly what I'm talking about here. It will be awesome.

WEDNESDAY

God loves us recklessly, absolutely recklessly. What kind of God gives His most treasured and beloved Son away to become a human and then suffer and die and become sin, just so we, who had turned our backs on Him, could once again be reunited with Him? What kind of God "leaves the ninety-nine" to go after the lone lost one (Luke 15:4–7)? What kind of God gives us both the desire and the ability to do His will and then rewards us for doing it (Philippians 2:13; Hebrews 11:6)? It is a reckless love.

And we must *believe* recklessly! We need to have that unwavering, go-for-broke, no-plan-B attitude regarding believing in the absolute truth of the Word of God *no matter what*! As we just saw, Abraham knew that. Young David knew that when he rejected King Saul's armor and sword and took five stones (one for Goliath and one for each of his brothers) and his slingshot to kill the giant who had defiled his God (1 Samuel 17). The prophet Elijah knew that when he called down fire from heaven at Mount Carmel upon the false prophets of Baal—just him against four hundred fifty of them (1 Kings 18). And young, innocent Mary knew that when the archangel Gabriel told her an astonishingly unbelievable thing, namely that she, a virgin, would give birth to the Son of God and He would reign over His people forever. What did she say? "Let it be to me according to your word" (Luke 1:26–38).

That's what I call *belief*. And now we'll look at the equally inspiring story of three young captive Jewish boys who were all in for their God, who knew that "everything sad *could* become untrue," and who showed that unwavering conviction in the truth of God's Word, even in a far-off, foreign land and even as slaves. It is found in the book of Daniel, chapter 8. We all know the story well, that story of Shadrach, Meshach, and Abed-Nego and the fiery furnace. Read it for next time; it's always awesome. But I want to focus not on their deliverance, which we love to reflect on, but on their unwavering conviction (belief) that made the outcome a rather moot point. Next time, in Babylon.

THURSDAY

A quick summary of Daniel chapter 3: King Nebuchadnezzar, the most powerful man on earth, erects a huge golden image (I suspect of himself) and decrees that all his subjects must fall down (not just bow down) and worship this image upon the signal of special music that would be played. Anyone refusing this command would be thrown into a burning, fiery furnace and be consumed.

The three young Jewish captives Shadrach, Meshach, and Abed-Nego (their Babylonian names) had already made it clear that they would only serve and worship the one true God, the God of Abraham, Isaac, and Jacob. Therefore, they did not fall down and worship on cue, and this enraged the king. He gave the order to his soldiers to bring these rebels to him, and he gave the boys an ultimatum: "Now if you fall down and worship the image which I have made, good! But if you do not worship, you shall be cast immediately into the midst of a burning, fiery furnace. And who is the god who will deliver you from my hands?" (Daniel 3:15).

And don't we just *love* the answer these three kids gave to mighty Nebuchadnezzar? "O king, we have no need to answer you in this matter. If that is the case, our God whom we serve is *able* to deliver us from the burning, fiery furnace, and He *will* deliver us from your hand, O king. *But if not*, let it be known to you, O king that we do not serve your gods, nor will we worship the gold image which you have set up" (Daniel 3:16–18; emphasis added).

Wow! What a statement of belief, right? It's that unwavering, absolute *knowing* that God would come through no matter what—no fear—that caused the fiery furnace to have no power over them. Victory was theirs—case closed.

Or was it? Is something missing here? Why that "but if not" phrase? Were they really that certain of the outcome? Did it even matter?

Rats! We're out of time. I can't wait for tomorrow, because what I'm going to share was a revelation to me, and I think it's really true. It should bless your socks off! Next time.

FRIDAY

So there's a fairly recent popular Christian song by MercyMe that, I'm sure, was written based on this story of Shadrach, Meshach, and Abed-Nego and the fiery furnace. It's called "Even If," and it goes like this (emphasis added):

> I know You're *able*, and I know You *can*
> Save through the fire by Your mighty hand.
> But even if you don't …
> My *hope* is You alone.

It's a really good song, and I like it, and it does perfectly reflect the position of these three young men when confronted with a seemingly impossible challenge, but I'm telling you, neither Daniel 3 nor this song *fully* reflects the situation and position of *us* as believers. Here's why:

Shadrach, Meshach, and Abed-Nego were Old Testament believers. Everything they could do to please God was done on *credit*. Jesus Christ, our Savior, hadn't yet come to live with us, and suffer, and die. Satan and sin and death and sickness had not been defeated yet. The Holy Spirit, who empowers us, had not been given yet; that would occur when "Pentecost had fully come" in the second chapter of Acts. These boys had to look forward to the cross. Their *hope* had not yet been *realized*!

But that's *not* the case with us, not anymore. Jesus has come, and almost exactly two thousand years ago, at a specific time and place, He absolutely annihilated Satan and all his ugly friends. And now "behold, all things have become *new*" (2 Corinthians 5:17; emphasis added). Everything sad has become untrue. As Bob Dylan says in the song "Pressing On," "What's been lost has been found … what's to come has already been." In short, our *hope* has been *realized*.

And here's my attempt to convey all this in short, compact statements:

Faith is the *hope*.

Belief is the *reality*.

And it's a new reality, just for believers, and actually much more real than the carnal reality of the world. I would rewrite that MercyMe song to say this: "I know You're *able*, and I know You *can*, and better yet, *I know You already have!*"

Wow! And it's all entirely, absolutely because of Jesus Christ and His atoning work on the cross. Amen!

I told you this would be a good one! Have a great weekend in the Lord.

MONDAY

Happy Monday! I mentioned last time the song "Even If" by MercyMe and modified it some, but it's basically a doctrinally sound song. However, there are occasional Christian songs out there that are not, and it's important to recognize this because music has a way of getting deep into your soul without your permission, and you don't want to be deceived. Following are some examples of doctrinally unsound songs that come to mind, starting with the rather strangely titled "Blessings," by Laura Story. Here's the refrain:

> What if Your blessings come through raindrops?
> What if healing comes through tears?
> What if a thousand sleepless nights are what it takes to know You're near?
> What if the trials of this life are Your mercies in disguise?

Wow, this is such a common and destructive misconception, that God puts us believers through trials and suffering and stress to make us better Christians. *No, no, no!* We will face trials—Jesus promised that (John 16:33)—but they are *not* from God; He is *good*, and He is *good all the time*. We pointed out previously that the main lie of Satan is exactly that God isn't *really* that good; He is hiding something. But that question was settled once and for all at the cross, for all the universe to see. Look at these verses:

"Every *good* gift and every *perfect* gift is from above, and comes down from the Father of lights, with whom there is no variation or shadow of turning" (James 1:17; emphasis added).

"Do you despise the riches of His *goodness* … not knowing that the *goodness* of God leads you to repentance?" (Romans 2:4; emphasis added).

If causing pain, suffering, and anxiety is God's way of showing His "mercies in disguise," then wouldn't His Son Jesus, who said Himself that He only does what the Father does (John 5:19), have demonstrated this during His three-and-a-half-year ministry on this earth? All He did was go around healing and saving everyone He encountered; there is not one record of Him making someone sick or poor or troubled. He *calmed* the storms; He didn't cause them!

So here's the deal: We need to stop blaming God for our problems! Let's grow up, take our thumbs out of our mouths, and just *thank* Him for sending His Son to sacrifice for us, such that we are "blessed with every spiritual blessing in the heavenly places with Christ" (Ephesians 1:3). Here's a great verse for us, mentioned earlier, John 16:33 (emphasis added): "In this world, *you will have trouble*; but be of *good cheer*! I have *overcome* the world!" We really need to stop whining!

You know, my wife says I'm too critical. I don't think so. Do you think I'm too critical? I just get worked up when this amazingly awesome God of ours is blamed for anything. I was planning to just spend one morning on this topic of popular songs with errant doctrine, but I've got more… tomorrow.

TUESDAY

Okay, yesterday's writing was possibly a bit overly critical, and I apologize. As far as "whining" is concerned, I should be pointing nine fingers at myself if I'm pointing one at the songwriter. I come by it honestly, though, being a man. We whine *way* more than women, and that goes all the way back to the garden. Eve was the first to sin, but at least she owned up to it. Look at Adam's response when God asked him if he had eaten of the forbidden fruit: "The *woman* whom *you* gave to me … *she* gave me of the tree" (Genesis 3:12). What a whiner!

But I do want to press on, in a constructive manner, and examine another currently quite popular song, namely, "Confidence," by Sanctus Real. Here's the refrain:

> So give me faith like Daniel in the lion's den.
> Give me a hope like Moses in the wilderness.
> Give me a heart like David; Lord, be my defense
> So I can face my giants with confidence.

Sounds okay, right? Lots of good words like *faith*, *hope*, and *heart*. But I'm telling you, any one of those great Old Testament saints would have given anything to have what we have as New Testament saints to face our giants, namely, the "abundance of grace, and the gift of righteousness" (Romans 5:17). They were sinful men, not yet having been reconciled to God, not righteous in His eyes. All three lived under the Law and had not received the Gospel, for "the Law was given through Moses, but grace and truth came through Jesus Christ" (John 1:17). We are now the "righteousness of God in Christ" (2 Corinthians 5:21) and have the Holy Spirit living *in* us (which they did not have), who reveals the very mind of Christ to us and teaches us the things of God (2 Corinthians 2:12–13).

So I don't covet the faith, or hope, or heart of these carnal men, but I long for the mind of Christ, which we already have as believers (1 Corinthians 2:16). It is way, way better.

Just one more example, and this one is shockingly inaccurate. The song is "Prodigal," by Sidewalk Prophets. Here's the refrain (emphasis added):

> Wherever you are, whatever you did,
> It's a page in your book, but it isn't the end.
> Your Father will meet you with arms open wide,
> *Come running like a prodigal.*
> *Come running like a prodigal.*

Yeah, apparently they never read the story. It's found in Luke 15, which we'll discuss tomorrow.

WEDNESDAY

"And he arose and came to his father. But when he was still a *great way off*, his father *saw* him and had compassion, and *ran* and fell on his neck, and kissed him" (Luke 15:20; emphasis added).

We all know the story of the prodigal son. It's not about the son; he acted foolishly the entire time. It's all about the father, who represents God and His relentless, overwhelming love for us, who are represented by the prodigal. It is that reckless love that leaves the ninety-nine to go after the one lost sheep (as told just a bit earlier in chapter 15) and *rejoices* when the lost is found ("There will be more joy in heaven over one sinner who repents" [v. 7]). It is the embodiment of Romans 5:8: "But God demonstrates His own love toward us, in that while we were yet sinners, Christ died for us." The only thing the son did was *allow* the father to find him. That's all any of us can do. We can't save ourselves. The message of that song is all wrong in that the emphasis is on the action of the prodigal, which didn't even occur (he didn't run back home; the father ran to him), and not on the incomprehensible love and forgiveness of the father.

Just one more song. This one begs the question, "Is anyone editing these lyrics?" It's "In the Eye of the Storm", by Ryan Stevenson and Brian Christopher Fowler, and here's the refrain:

> In the eye of the storm, You remain in control.
> In the middle of the war, You guard my soul.
> You alone are the anchor when the sails are torn.
> Your love surrounds me, in the eye of the storm.

This is a great message of God's protection, *but* isn't the *eye* of the storm really peaceful, calm, serene, and quiet? Isn't it? We need God's protection *in the midst of storm*, not in the peaceful eye of the storm. I know I'm splitting hairs here, for the overall message is right on.

We end on a positive note: the Hillsong groups (United, Worship) are awesome. Not only is their music beautifully anointed, but also the lyrics are spot-on. I suspect Hillsong's pastoral staff approves of all the lyrics to ensure they are scripturally correct. Great idea! A moving example of their music is "So Will I (100 Billion ×)." Listen to it. I cry every time.

So this side trip is officially over. Tomorrow we attend to some unfinished business on our way up a mount in the land of Moriah.

THURSDAY

So our subtopic is belief vs. works, probably more commonly referred to historically as faith vs. works, but I think belief is the more appropriate concept as I've explained previously. We're examining the offering up of Isaac, found in Genesis 22. This is cited as a great example of an amazing work performed by Abraham that *justified* him before God, triggering all the blessings that God had already promised. We'll get to those verses (15–18) shortly.

But what I'm endeavoring to show, based on Scripture, and vital to our Christian walk and enjoyment of all the blessings promised us, including healing, is that the *justification* of Abraham occurred previously, in Genesis 15, when Abraham "believed in the Lord, and He accounted it to him for righteousness" (v. 6). The act of obedience Abraham carried out in chapter 22 was a direct consequence of that belief, and it *did* justify Abraham, but not before God. I'm going to skip ahead now because we'll have to set more foundation to support what I'm about to say, but the offering up of Isaac served two primary purposes: (1) to foreshadow the future offering up of Jesus by His Father, which was the most awesome act of *love* and *obedience* ever seen in the history of the universe, and (2) to justify Abraham before us humans. For us it is a concrete example of belief becoming reality no matter the circumstances.

Wow, that's pretty profound stuff, and enough to ponder for this morning. We'll get to all this, but as the Spirit directs. First we will look at the *provision* of God for us, demonstrated up on Mount Moriah:

"Then Abraham lifted his eyes and looked, and there behind him was a ram caught in a thicket by its horns. So Abraham went and took the ram, and offered it up for a burnt offering *instead* of his son. And Abraham called the name of the place, The-Lord-Will-Provide; as it is said to this day, 'In the Mount of the Lord *it shall be provided*'" Genesis 22:13–14; emphasis added).

That's our topic next time—in the land of Moriah.

FRIDAY

We've seen that Abraham headed up Mount Moriah with Isaac, fully convinced that he would return *with* the boy intact (his belief), one way or another, but most likely after killing him and having God raise him from the dead. Abraham was also hopeful that God would *provide* the sacrifice to take the place of Isaac (thereby demonstrating his faith). We've examined the Scriptures supporting these statements already.

Now we see that the sacrifice, the ram, is right up there on that mount with them. As I put it before, the reality of Abraham's belief fulfilled the hope of his faith. I keep repeating this stuff because it's pretty deep. It is not intuitively obvious but true and life-changing.

But where did that answer to prayer, that sacrifice, come from? It wasn't seen along the way up the mount. God didn't just make it spontaneously materialize at that second (He could have done that, but God is not capricious, as Albert Einstein famously said. He works within His creation).

So just two possibilities: the ram was coming up the mount *behind* Abraham and Isaac, or the ram was coming up the mountain *on the other side*! I love the second scenario; what a beautiful mental image for us as Christians. We believe for the answer to our prayer, for the provision for our need, and we see no sign of it coming to fruition, but we hold fast and push on, *knowing* that the answer, the sacrifice, is on the way. We just can't *see* it, or *sense* it with our carnal nature. It's heading up *the other side*, and it will be right where we need it at just the right time, at the very hour of our need. That is *belief*. That is what this story, and indeed this entire series we've embarked on, is all about. We rely on our renewed spiritual nature, not our carnal nature, and as we do that more and more and see our belief rewarded more and more, we become more confident and grow stronger in the Lord; we emerge further from the dark granite into the light and beauty of our Lord.

Wow, this is good stuff. And we're not done learning from this story that takes place on a mount in the land of Moriah.

11
WEEK

MONDAY

We're working through Genesis 22. Isaac has been offered up and spared. But there's more to this story. Actually, to my way of thinking, the most important (certainly not the most dramatic, but the most important) part is yet to come.

"Then the Angel of the Lord called to Abraham a second time out of heaven, and said: 'By Myself I have sworn, says the Lord, because *you have done* this thing, and have not withheld your son, your only son—blessing I will bless you, and multiplying I will multiply your descendants as the stars of the heaven and the sand which is on the seashore. ... In your seed all the nations of the earth shall be blessed, *because you have obeyed My voice*'" (Genesis 22:15–18; emphasis added).

So our current topic is belief vs. works, and my premise is that absolute belief in the Word of God will lead to appropriate works that are in accordance with God's will and pleasing to Him. Our works are a fruit of our belief and do not in and of themselves make us righteous. So what's going on here? It appears as though the Lord is going to bless Abraham *because* of what he *did*. It was this act of obedience that justified him before God. That's what this passage seems to indicate, right?

I think not. Here's what I think is going on here, and it is consistent with "the whole counsel of God" and the Gospel: the act that Abraham carried out on Mount Moriah *demonstrated for us* his belief. It wasn't for God's benefit but for ours. It didn't justify Abraham before God but instead justified him before us, and this was necessary because of our carnal nature, that is, the way we perceive truth via our senses and emotions. I want to go to a New Testament passage, Matthew 9:1–8, to support this concept. Read it for next time; it is a beautiful healing story, one that will give us insight pertaining not just to Abraham but also to us and the amazing relationship between forgiveness of sin, which can't be seen, and physical healing, which can be seen. Next time.

TUESDAY

The act of obedience carried out by Abraham on Mount Moriah was a *physical manifestation* of the underlying, unwavering belief he had in the Word of God. We are now going to see an example of healing as a *physical manifestation* of the forgiveness of sin. In both cases, that which is *not seen* results in that which is. This particular story is so important that it is told in all three synoptic Gospels, and—here's the interesting part—almost exactly word for word. The Holy Spirit wanted us not to miss this great truth.

And here's the truth: Jesus Christ viewed remission of sin and healing as synonymous! I'm serious. We'll soon prove that Scripturally. So what does that mean for the believer? Here's another compact statement of mine that I'll just throw out there for now and then later take the appropriate amount of time to support:

If you are saved, then you are healed!

That same solid conviction (belief) that you and I both have regarding our salvation must needs be applied also to the truth of our healing. This revelation is so important, yet so hard for us to grasp because of our carnal nature, that our Lord instituted one of our only two sacraments as believers, Holy Communion, to remind us of it, and remind us of it often. We'll go deeply into this later, but for now know that there are *two* elements in Communion, and only one of them signifies remission of sin. What's the other one for? This sacrament of Communion is so important that all four Gospels mention it, *and* the resurrected Jesus Christ Himself revealed it separately to the apostle Paul to share with the church in 1 Corinthians 11. I can't wait to get into this more, but first things first. Here's the portion of scripture in question, also found in Mark chapter 2 and Luke chapter 5:

> Then behold, they brought to Him a paralytic lying on a
> bed. When Jesus saw their faith, He said to the paralytic,
> "Son, be of good cheer; *your sins are forgiven you*." And
> at once some of the scribes said within themselves, "This
> Man blasphemes!" But Jesus, knowing their thoughts,
> said, "Why do you think evil in your hearts? For which is
> easier to say, 'Your sins are forgiven you,' or to say, 'Arise
> and walk'? But that you may know that the Son of Man
> has power on earth to forgive sins." ... Then He said to
> the paralytic, *"Arise, take your bed*, and go to your house."
> And he arose and departed to his house. (Matthew 9:2–7;
> emphasis added)

Sorry this one is so long. I couldn't see how to make it any shorter. Next time.

WEDNESDAY

So we're making the transition now to a new theme, one I will call "Seeing the Unseen," which will examine how unwavering belief in the Word of God unlocks the physical healing provided for believers at the atonement. It's going to be awesome. We'll start with that story of the paralytic, but first one more point before we leave Genesis 22 and the land of Moriah.

"So Abraham returned to his young men" (v. 19).

Do you notice something odd in this concluding verse of the story of the offering up of Isaac? The sacrifice-to-be who was spared, namely, Isaac, isn't mentioned! Wow, you would think the fact that Isaac *did* return down that mount, just as Abraham promised, would be newsworthy, but he's not mentioned at all.

You know why, don't you? As we said earlier, this story wasn't really about Isaac and his father, Abraham, but about Jesus Christ and His Father, and in that latter event the sacrifice did not come down Mount Calvary. He did die, after absorbing the righteous punishment for all the sins of all the world. What an awesome thought!

But we know what happened three days later, and because of the victory of Jesus Christ over sin and death, we as believers are forgiven—our spirit nature is revived—and we are made new creations, free to allow the renewing of our carnal nature (mind / intellect / emotions / physical body) by becoming more like Jesus via seeing Him in scripture as the Word of God is all about Him and His Spirit. Then our spirit person will ever more permeate our minds and bodies, making us whole, for "as He is, so are we in this world" (1 John 4:17). That definitely includes our physical healing as Jesus is not sick. But to accomplish that you have to believe in things you can't see (that is what true belief is all about) so as to give birth to things you can see. This is what we will deal with now as we leave the land of Moriah and move into the realm of seeing the unseen, as stated beautifully by Paul in 2 Corinthians 4:18: "We do not look at the things that are seen, but at the things that are not seen. For the things that are seen are temporary, but the things which are not seen are eternal." Amen.

THURSDAY

Depending on the translation, the story we're about to examine from Matthew 9, Mark 2, and Luke 5 is titled "A Paralytic Is Healed" or, less commonly, "A Paralytic Is Forgiven," but I've not seen it called anywhere what it truly represents: "A Paralytic Is Forgiven *and* Healed." I gave the Matthew account earlier this week, but the wording as to Jesus's noting the faith of the paralytic's friends, and the forgiving and subsequent healing of the man, is virtually word for word in all three versions although recounted by three different authors. That's the importance the Holy Spirit is putting on what took place here.

The Mark and Luke accounts, however, also include the part of the story we probably remember the most: "Then behold, men brought on a bed a man who was paralyzed, whom they sought to bring in and lay before Him. And when they could not find how they might bring him in, because of the crowd, they went up on the housetop and let him down with his bed through the tiling into the midst before Jesus" (Luke 5:18–19).

And Jesus noticed. All three versions have the exact same next line: "When He saw their faith" (v. 20).

The main recollection I have of this story, growing up in Sunday school, is of the absolute importance of the faith of these men and how it was *because* of that faith that the paralytic was healed. Isn't that what you remember?

But then I actually read it for myself, over and over, and realized that probably *everybody* who was sick in that crowd received healing that day. Look at Luke 5:17: "And the power of the Lord was present for Him to heal the sick" (NIV). Plus we know that Jesus was prone to heal all who needed it: "And He cast out the spirits with a word, and healed *all* who were sick" (Matthew 8:16; emphasis added). Remember how we defined faith, namely as a "confident expectation" that God's Word is true and that our prayers will be answered? I would venture to say that just about every sick person there had faith that they would be healed, or else they wouldn't have even been there! Just like we believers are all given the same measure of faith or else we couldn't be saved.

No, Jesus wasn't noticing some exceptional degree of faith that compelled Him to do good. He was after something else here, something much greater, something unseen. Next time.

FRIDAY

We pick up the story of the paralytic:

"He said to him, 'Man, your sins are forgiven you'" (Luke 5:20).

Hmm, unusual response, isn't it? This paralyzed man is brought before Jesus to be healed. His faith and the faith of his friends was for his healing. He wasn't asking for his sins to be forgiven; there were animal sacrifices he could bring to the temple for that, under the Old Testament sacrificial system. He just wanted to be healed.

But Jesus's words, although shocking to the scribes and Pharisees in attendance there, were not out of line as every Jew knew that all diseases and infirmities were the result of sin. Just look at the famous story of the blind man: "Now, as Jesus passed by, He saw a man who was blind from birth. And His disciples asked Him, saying, 'Rabbi, who *sinned*, this man or his parents, that he was born blind?'" (John 9:1–2; emphasis added).

Of course their limited, superficial view that all disease was the result of the individual sins of the person or the parents was wrong, and Jesus refuted them, but the deeper truth is this: All disease/sickness/infirmity/depression/anxiety in humans is a consequence of original sin, of the Fall of Man. Disease is intimately related to sin, and the *only* way to deal with the *disease* problem is to *first* deal with the *sin* problem. They all kind of intuitively knew this, but they were more focused on the miraculous, dramatic healings Jesus was performing (this was very early on in His ministry), on what they were *seeing*, rather than on the implications of such, that is, that these miracles *couldn't* occur unless humankind was somehow dealing with their sins. But that they couldn't *see*.

So Jesus decided to press the point, and thereby get the religious folk there very upset, because He was going to make them acknowledge the unseen, which is eternal and trumps the seen, which is temporal. We'll see what happened next week.

12
WEEK

MONDAY

We left the paralyzed man (obviously in need of healing) lying on his bed right in front of Jesus, who was most likely healing people right and left. This very needy man had just gone to great lengths to get to Jesus; he and his friends were confidently expecting (i.e., having faith) that he would be healed. And so were the watching scribes and Pharisees. No-brainer, right? Jesus would, of course, heal him straightaway.

But Jesus wasn't one to do the expected; He was constantly turning everyone's world upside down. He simply said, joyfully, to the paralytic, "Son, be of good cheer; your sins are forgiven you" (Matthew 9:2).

Wow, what a loaded statement. Jesus fully well knew that the experts in the Law were all there, and they well knew that *only* God could forgive sin. Look at the Old Testament prophet Isaiah: "I, even I, am He who blots out your transgressions for My own sake; and I will not remember your sins" (Isaiah 43:25). They weren't going to let that statement go.

"And the scribes and the Pharisees began to reason, saying, 'Who is this who speaks blasphemies? Who can forgive sins but God alone?'" (Luke 5:21).

They were right; they just didn't realize Jesus was God. They hadn't "reasoned" deeply enough to see that these healings could not have occurred unless there was remission of sin, so Jesus must be God. Jesus, planning to help them see this, said the following:

"Why are you reasoning in your hearts? Which is easier to say, 'Your sins are forgiven you,' or to say, 'Rise up and walk'?" (Luke 5:22–23).

Now Jesus apparently didn't give them time to answer this amazing question, but we have the time, and it's a really good question in that it has everything to do with the seen being a manifestation of the unseen. We just don't have time today; we will tomorrow.

TUESDAY

Profound question from Jesus (would we expect anything less?): Which is the easier work, to *say* "Your sins are forgiven" or to *say* "Arise and walk"?

Here's the key difference: The former command requires no physical proof of success; you can't *see* that sins are forgiven. The latter command is all about physical proof. Success can be quantified; you can *see* it.

Jesus's point to the scribes and Pharisees is exactly that: they thought he was *claiming* to do something no person could do, only God. They knew the act of forgiveness of sin would be an impossibly hard task, and Jesus had no right saying He could do it, since in their view He couldn't, so physical healing would be the more difficult task. But they were seemingly ignorant of the fact that disease was a direct consequence of sin and that there could be no healing if there was still sin, so Jesus beautifully and powerfully said:

"'But that *you may know* that the Son of Man has power on earth to forgive sins'—then He said to the paralytic, 'Arise, take up your bed, and go to your house'" (Matthew 9:6; emphasis added).

Wow! That should have made it obvious, but it didn't. You see, the Jews were, in a sense, blinded to the revelation that Jesus Christ was their Messiah, even though, as we'll see later, no one *ever* healed humans of their diseases before, since no one before had the authority to do so. They didn't get it. Look at their responses to all of this:

- "Now, when the multitudes saw it, they marveled and glorified God, who had given such power to men" (Matthew 9:8).

- "All were amazed and glorified God, saying, 'We never saw anything like this!'" (Mark 2:12).
- "And they were all amazed, and they glorified God and were filled with fear, saying, 'We have seen strange things today!'" (Luke 5:26).

You might think that all sounds great, but what's missing? They did not acknowledge the Healer as God, as the Messiah, but simply as an empowered man. They lacked spiritual discernment.

So what is the answer to Jesus's question? To *claim* to be able to forgive sin was easy; to *accomplish* the forgiveness of all our sins was a whole different matter, the most difficult task in the history of the universe, full of suffering and shame. And Jesus knew it was coming, and soon, and that it would be accomplished. We'll see next time just what that means for *your* healing, which can be *seen* and experienced on this earth because of your belief in the *unseen*.

WEDNESDAY

It's the last day of July! We've been in this series for two and a half months. Can you believe it? We started out in the garden, then traveled down the road to Emmaus, and then spent a good amount of time in the land of Moriah. Now we're exploring how to see the unseen.

We've covered a lot: how we were created to function primarily in the spiritual realm, in perfect communion and harmony with Creator God, which Adam and Eve did for a time in the garden. But that part of us died via original sin, and we fell to function entirely in the carnal realm of mind/emotions/conscience and physical body / senses. That's how all humans start out at birth, "born already ruined." But that spirit person who was dead is revived at salvation, and that part of us is *perfect* in God's eyes; we are *justified* before Him. However, our souls and bodies are not immediately transformed; they need to be gradually renewed (Romans 12:2) in a process called *sanctification*. We've seen on the road to Emmaus how Jesus instructed us to do that, to *see* Him in all of scripture, and to meditate on that and become more like Him (have the "mind of Christ"

(1 Corinthians 2:16) as we emerge from the darkness of our carnal nature to the beautiful light of our Lord. We saw the importance of *faith*, that confident expectation of hope in our Lord, and *belief*, that unwavering conviction that everything promised to us in Holy Scripture is absolutely true, no matter what, and has already come to pass for us as demonstrated so well by Abraham in the land of Moriah.

Now we're *seeing*, because of that *belief*, that the Atonement of Jesus on the cross not only provided the forgiveness of our sins but also accomplished the physical healing of our earthly bodies as stated by Jesus Himself in the healing and forgiving of the paralytic. That means the following, and don't you ever forget it:

If you are saved, you are healed!

And here's the really neat part: Everything I've said has been supported by Scripture; it is all true. You can wholly believe it. Or not. It's entirely up to you as our God is a "perfect gentleman" and never overbearing.

You know, I wasn't planning this summary today. But reading over it, I see it's pretty good. Save it; it will be a good reference going forward.

What I was planning was to show *how* our healing became part of the Atonement. Here's a teaser: there was *no* atonement for healing in the old covenant. Try to prove me wrong. For next time.

THURSDAY

So our subtopic is "Seeing the Unseen," and we've thus far established that the highly visible healing of our minds and bodies, as believers, is a result, and direct consequence, of the forgiveness of our sins. The seen is manifest *because* of our belief in the unseen. All this was made possible by the atonement for our sins and healing, which Jesus Christ accomplished at the cross. Now I want to set the foundation as to how all this came to be so that it becomes more real than anything you're experiencing carnally, as it is all based on the absolute truth of the Word of God and is superior to everything carnal.

Let's start with the term itself, *atonement*. What does it mean? Remember that *Lord of the Rings* question we answered previously, of whether everything sad could me made untrue? *That* is atonement. It means to make amends for, or *right*, a previous *wrong*. And the wrong we're referring to here is, of course, *sin*. Our focus now will be on the atonement for sin because that must come first, before the atonement for healing.

The atonement for sin is a very big deal in the Old Testament; lots of time is spent on this topic. However—and this is very interesting to me as a physician—although there is much emphasis on forgiveness of sin in the old covenant, there is no provision for the atonement for healing. Certainly healing is talked about, but primarily in the form of prophecy; cases of actual physical healing are as rare as hen's teeth (which is a rare thing, but it does occur; there are actually strains of chickens with teeth) in the Old Testament. We'll get into the fascinating reason why later, but first we'll deal with the atonement for sin. It all starts where we've always begun before: in the garden.

"Unto Adam also and to his wife did the Lord God make coats of skins and clothed them" (Genesis 3:21 KJV).

This was right after the Fall—I mean right after it. God was all about temporarily atoning (covering over) the sins of His precious humans, and that was what this verse is all about. Here's the haunting question for tomorrow: Where did God get those skins?

FRIDAY

"This is because the life of the body is in the blood, and I have given you rules for pouring the blood on the altar to *remove your sins*, so you will belong to the Lord. It is the *blood* that *removes the sins*, because it is *life*" (Leviticus 17:11 NCV; emphasis added).

"And according to the Law, almost all things are purified with blood, and without shedding of blood there is no remission (of sin)" (Hebrews 9:22).

So, back in the garden, the first man and woman sinned and became immediately cut off from God, dead spiritually. There could be no communion with the Father without the remission (cancellation/removing) of sin. God chose to make the *shedding of innocent blood* the vehicle to accomplish that as seen in these verses.

I do not find in Holy Scripture a definitive reason why this had to be the case; it was the decree of a holy God. In truth, Christianity is a very "bloody" religion, which can be an initial turn-off for some, but to us who are washed in the blood of Jesus Christ, it is truly a beautiful thing. For all eternity, the glorious Jesus Christ, who is worthy of all praise, will be seen as "a Lamb, as though it had been slain" (Revelation 5:6).

But we're getting ahead of ourselves. The Messiah had been prophesied already, but He was not to come for four thousand years. God was to institute an effective, but temporary, solution for the sin problem, and it would involve the shedding of *innocent* blood. No human would be innocent again at birth, so humans would not suffice.

But animals are innocent; they aren't capable of sinning. So God Himself offered the first sacrifices for our human sin by killing two innocent animals and fashioning the skins (I bet leather, and really nice leather) into coats, or "coverings" for Adam and Eve. Such is the love of our God and the goodness of His heart. The precedent had been set, and it would serve as an inferior, temporary solution for sin. It could not be perfect because, although animals are *innocent*, there is a problem: they are not *human*. We'll pick up on this point next week.

WEEK

MONDAY

It's a new week the Lord has given us. Let's reset. Our goal since the beginning has been to show what is available to us as New Testament believers regarding physical healing, and we've set the Scriptural foundation for justly claiming that healing is in the Atonement accomplished by Jesus Christ at the cross, in addition to the remission of sin. It is this obliteration of the sin debt that leads to the manifestation of our healing. We're now looking further into this whole concept of atonement, and how and why the cross came to be, and how the problems of sin and disease were handled in the Old Testament as there were, of course, believers then also. We're going to focus now on the old sacrificial system God put in place to temporarily deal with sin, and after that we'll see why there was not a similar propitiation for disease available to Old Testament believers.

It won't be boring. This topic is chock-full of types of Jesus Christ and the cross and is an excellent example of what our Lord asked us to do on the road to Emmaus, that is, see Him in Old Testament scripture. "And beginning at Moses and all the Prophets, He expounded to them in all the Scriptures the things concerning Himself" (Luke 24:27).

As important as this shedding of innocent animal blood to cover the sins of humans was, it was imperfect because only an innocent, sinless human could serve as an adequate sacrifice, and until Jesus Christ, that was not possible. And Jesus would not come to live with us for four thousand years! That's an awful lot of animals that had to bleed and die innocently.

So one has to wonder (and God loves for us to ponder His ways and inquire of Him; "'Come now, and let us reason together,' says the Lord" [Isaiah 1:18]). Why the wait? Why would God wait four thousand years to send the Savior, when the plan for such was formulated by the Godhead from the start? "All who dwell on the earth will worship Him, whose names have not been written in the Book of Life of the Lamb, *slain from the foundation of the world*?" (Revelation 13:8; emphasis added). Why not send Him for Cain and Abel?

I don't have a Scriptural answer for that question, but I have my thoughts, for what they're worth—next time.

TUESDAY

"The Lord is not slack concerning His promise, as some count slackness, but is longsuffering toward us, not willing that *any* should perish, but that *all* should come to repentance" (2 Peter 3:9).

I think this verse explains why Jesus Christ, our Messiah, our Deliverer, was not sent to us to become one of us, to dwell with us, and to suffer and die for us until the time He did come. In short, the timing of all the divine interventions in the course of human history has been for the express purpose of *maximizing* the number of people to be *saved* and *minimizing* the number to be *lost*. And I believe that process is ongoing; it's still fluid—which is why Jesus Himself said of the timing of His Second Coming, "But of the day and hour *no one knows*, not even the angels of heaven, but My Father *only*" (Matthew 24:36; emphasis added).

It was therefore beneficial to that ultimate outcome to have humankind prove that left to their own devices after the Fall, they would completely *fail*. "Then the Lord saw that the wickedness of man was great in the earth, and that every intent of the thoughts of his heart was *only evil continually*" (Genesis 6:5; emphasis added).

This led to the wiping out of the perverted human race in the Flood with only Noah, who was still 100 percent human, and his family being saved. That was a major reset there, but it was necessary to allow the human race to have any chance at salvation. And by the way, a chilling thought comes to mind here. Go back to Matthew 24, which we just referenced, verses 37–39. The times just before the Second Coming of our Lord will be very similar to the days of Noah in that every thought will be only of evil continually. Wow!

Man, I wish we had more time. I often start writing these thinking I don't have much to say, but I always end up with way too many things to say—and that's not because of me. The Lord has *a lot* to say to us, and this is how we *grow* in Him. Next time we'll pick up right where we're leaving off.

WEDNESDAY

We're musing about God's plan of salvation and why it took four thousand years of human existence for the Savior to come. We've just seen that after the Fall, the human race (and by the way, every scientist agrees now that there is just *one* human race, no matter what the skin color. I think this is very supportive of creationism and detrimental to evolution) became perverted (by intermingling with the fallen angels) and had to be wiped out except for Noah's family. Humans got a fresh start in a sense, but not really, as they were still born with the sin nature intact and the spirit person dead, and they again had no desire to commune with God or to have any spiritual aspect to their lives, so they became very strong and innovative and arrogant since they all spoke the same language and were of the same anti-God mind-set. (Does any of this sound familiar?) And they were *not* going to let God destroy them ever again; they would build a "tower whose top is in the heavens" (Genesis 11:4). So again, to ensure a future great harvest of human souls who would become the sons and daughters of God and commune with Him eternally, the triune God said, "'Come let Us go down and there confuse their language, that they may not understand one another's speech.' So, the Lord scattered them abroad from there over the face of all the earth" (Genesis 11:7–8).

So *that's* how different people groups and different languages and people living in just about every locale on earth came to be! That is so much more logical than what I was taught in school, that groups of people would "migrate" from the larger group to different locales that suited them better and then settle there. Since everyone is pretty sure (yes, scientifically speaking) that human life did originate in the Middle East (the Fertile Crescent), I always wondered, as an impressionable young student, why in the world anyone in their right mind would migrate from the beautiful weather and agriculture of that area to northern Alaska! It never made sense. The truth is, a loving God "moved" them supernaturally and *equipped* them to like their new environments and thrive there. But this move accomplished something else: it made human beings a little less arrogant and less self-sufficient. It made them possibly more attuned to the things of God—to spiritual things.

We're not getting way off track here, trust me. We're showing why there needed to be an atonement for human sin before Jesus Christ came and why it took so long for Him to come. I'm trying to compactly cover four thousand years of human history in a few paragraphs; have patience. We'll pick up from right here tomorrow, but I do want to say one more thing this morning that might shock you. Although humankind was sinning like crazy during this time of human history, and although there were surely negative consequences of that sin, God wasn't holding the people responsible for their sins. Does that seem odd? I'll prove it next time.

THURSDAY

"For until the Law, sin was in the world, but sin is not imputed when there is no Law" (Romans 5:13).

Isn't *that* interesting? If we're to believe this astonishing verse, written by the apostle Paul, then we must confess that all humans from Adam and Eve (who, by the way, *did* have their sin imputed to them, obviously) to the giving of the Ten Commandments on Mount Sinai twenty-six hundred years later were not being held responsible for their many sins. *Impute* is an accounting term meaning "to charge to one's account." Now there were natural consequences for their sins, but God wasn't going to use those sins against them. They had not been given any rules, so how could they be responsible for breaking the rules? Conversely, Adam and Eve had *one* rule, and they broke it.

This plays into the whole plan of salvation that God put in place. Humankind was lost to Him. There was the prophecy of the Savior to come, someone who would "crush Satan's head" (Genesis 3:15 NCV), but humankind had to be in a position to understand that they *needed* a Savior. Not only that, but also, remember, this earth and the human experiment "were like a show for the whole world to see—angels and people" (1 Corinthians 4:9 NCV), because God was kind of on trial here to see if He was truly just and righteous and whether His very nature was love. At this point, it was becoming clear that humankind could not save themselves; they were ensnared by sin and usually did wrong rather than right, causing a guilty conscience, and they were getting sick and dying, and life was onerous and hard. Yet God couldn't easily communicate with His lost and separated children, because they functioned pretty much exclusively on a carnal basis, and He is Spirit. I think this verse conveys the heart of God trying to reach us before the Savior. "The eyes of the Lord run to and fro throughout the whole earth, to show Himself strong on behalf of those whose heart is loyal to Him" (2 Chronicles 16:9).

That's how He found Abraham, from the land of Ur (now part of Iraq), which was a game changer because this man was going to do something unique among humans at that time. He was going to *believe* what God told him without being able to physically see the result of that belief. He was going to "see the unseen" and be the example for us as to how to please the Lord. This was six hundred years before the Law.

We're making progress explaining this awesome plan of salvation and why it took four thousand years for Jesus to show up. Patience. More tomorrow.

FRIDAY

We're halfway through the journey to Jesus, two thousand years, and Abraham is on the scene. Humankind has been struggling mightily, but now there is hope because God has said He will use Abraham and his descendants to start shining the light of the Gospel to His lost children, and it would be based on belief, not works, as we so carefully examined in the story of the offering up of Isaac in Genesis 22. And the covenant between God and Abraham (and remember, believers, *we* are also children of Abraham) would be *forever*!

"And I will establish My covenant between Me and you and your descendants after you in their generations, for an *everlasting* covenant, to be God to you and your descendants after you" (Genesis 17:7; emphasis added).

Abraham would miraculously have Isaac, whose name is a true reflection of the heart of God, meaning "he will laugh; he will rejoice," and Isaac would have Jacob, whose name would be changed to Israel, and he would have twelve sons, which would be the tribes of Israel. This nation would be collectively known as the "children of Israel," and they would serve as the beacon of God's light in the world and of hope. And the promised Messiah would come from them, specifically from the tribe of Judah, and specifically from a virgin girl from that tribe (Isaiah 7:14).

But that would take another two thousand years. Something very significant and, in a way, very tragic would have to come about first. And I mean that it *had* to come about because, remember, the whole universe was watching this human drama play out on planet Earth and trying to decide if God was really good and just and righteous, and whether or not He was this way all the time, even with His fallen little free-willed humans who'd been made in His image. How was He going to deal with their sin problem? God had human beings on a sort of probation up to this point; they were sinning, for sure, but *not against Him*, as He had not given them laws and rules since the one given in the garden. Things were in limbo. The universe was still unsettled, and things were about to get even worse. That's where we'll pick up next week. There's another mountain looming on the horizon, and it's not Mount Moriah; it's Mount Sinai. Wow!

14

WEEK

MONDAY

"Then the children of Israel groaned because of the bondage, and they cried out, and their cry came up to God because of the bondage. So God *heard* their groaning, and God *remembered* His covenant with Abraham, with Isaac and with Jacob. And God *looked* upon the children of Israel, and God *acknowledged* them" (Exodus 2:23–25; emphasis added).

We left off last week with the children of Israel living under the Abrahamic covenant of blessings, based on Father Abraham's unwavering conviction (belief) in the Word of God, but they were struggling with this concept of believing in the unseen and of relying wholly and completely on the grace and mercy of God, which is counterintuitive to our carnal nature. These "stiff-necked," that is, rebellious, people kept frustrating the grace of God, and they ended up in bondage as slaves in Egypt.

But God, demonstrating His great love for all of us and His faithfulness to His covenant with Abraham, His friend, did not forget them as seen in the foregoing verse. This was all part of the plan. The universe was watching, and they were seeing that human belief in God was weak and unsustainable. Human beings didn't have *within themselves* the *power* to *rest* in the *goodness* of God. They wanted to be in control because that was more natural and comforting to them, and they ended up literally and figuratively in bondage.

Now relax. That is *not* the case for New Testament believers. We are empowered to continue on in belief and rest in the Lord, for He has come and set us free on the cross *and* (this is essential) has sent the Holy Spirit to live within us. And you know what He does: "But you shall receive *power* when the Holy Spirit has come upon you" (Acts 1:8; emphasis added).

Wow! There is so much really good stuff to cover here. I mentioned Mount Sinai last time, and what will happen there will usher in a hugely important component of God's plan of salvation for all humankind. It will also show *why* there had to be an Old Testament atonement for sin, but we can't go there yet. We first need to see how these lost children get out of bondage, both literally and figuratively. We'll look at the Exodus and the Passover next time.

TUESDAY

Let's look now at the verses given yesterday, Exodus 2:23–25. The children of Israel are not living freely in the land of promise, Canaan, but are slaves in Egypt under Pharaoh Amenhotep II, and they've been there for four hundred years! They've pretty much forgotten their God and His covenant with them. In verse 23 they are seen groaning and crying out because of their bondage, but *not to God*! They are desperate for deliverance, but they don't remember *whom* to turn to. Remember, they didn't want to be completely dependent on God previously, and they got their wish, and now they are completely broken. And you know what? That's where we need to be also to experience the fullness of God's love for us.

And what did God do? He *heard*, and *remembered*, and *looked* upon them, and *acknowledged* them, without their even asking Him to, because they were already in an immutable covenant with Him. Isn't that awesome? He hadn't changed; He just needed to wait until they would see their *need* for Him.

That word *acknowledged* is interesting to me. It's the Hebrew word *yada*, and it means "to make oneself known in an intimate way"—and I mean an *intimate* way. Look at Genesis 4:1: "Now Adam *knew* Eve his wife, and she *conceived*" (emphasis added). That word *knew* is the same word *yada*. Wow! The Lord showed that to me for the first time today. God was going to reveal Himself, His true nature, to them in an intimate and powerful way.

I'm going to say something here that isn't logical, but I know it's true because it fits with the "whole counsel of God" (Acts 20:27) and is consistent with what I know of the heart of God. This revelation of the true heart of God, of His *love*, is not going to be seen through the amazing, miraculous ten plagues on Egypt that will subsequently unfold in the next several chapters of Exodus but in what occurs at a simple dinner the children of Israel hold on the evening of the tenth plague, known appropriately as the Passover. It's a moving, beautiful representation of what is going to come *after* what is coming at Mount Sinai in just a couple of months, and it's all about *innocence*, and *blood*, and *atonement for sin*. We'll examine it closely because this special dinner would be reenacted every year by the Jews. Jesus honored it and gave it new meaning. We also partake of it frequently as believers. It all started in Exodus 12, which we'll get into next time.

WEDNESDAY

> Now the Lord spoke to Moses and Aaron in the land of Egypt, saying, "This month shall be your beginning of months; it shall be the first month of the year to you. Speak to all the congregation of Israel, saying, 'On the *tenth* of this month every man shall take for himself a lamb ... for a household.' ... Your lamb shall be without blemish, a male of the *first year*. You may take it from the sheep or from the goats. Now you shall keep it until the *fourteenth* of the same month. Then the whole assembly of the congregation of Israel shall *kill* it *at twilight*." (Exodus 12:1–6; emphasis added)

There are two chapters in the Old Testament that are worth remembering and reading often because they provide the most clear foreshadowing of Jesus Christ and the cross. One we've already looked at: Genesis 22. The other is this one, Exodus 12. We will, in due time, examine many other types of Christ in the Old Testament, and also the numerous direct prophecies regarding Him, because that is what He instructed us to do on the road to Emmaus: to *see* Him more clearly and become more like Him by meditating on Him in Scripture. And by the way, I've come to realize that there is no end to this process, as Scripture is inexhaustible and eternal, and the more I comprehend, the more I see just how little I know. This sanctification thing will continue until I go to Him or He comes for me.

This chapter is awesome, bursting with revelation and drama; no Hollywood script could compare. Yet the main symbol for me in this fantastic story of protection, and death, and blood, and treasure, and supernatural health, and haste is a mild, innocent, absolutely adorable one-year-old lamb or kid. I'm sure we've all experienced these little animals in person, and there is nothing alive on this earth that is more innocent, harmless, and lovable.

God is about to set His people free; Pharaoh was not moved by the nine previous plagues, but this one he could not deny as all the firstborn of every Egyptian *and* their animals were to die at midnight, including Pharaoh's. The Israelites, however, would be spared. Chapter 12 gives all the details of this ceremony of divine protection, which would become known as the Feast of Unleavened Bread, or Passover. This is what Jesus celebrated at the Last Supper and what we celebrate as Holy Communion. It's that important.

It all starts with a lamb. Note in the foregoing scripture that the lamb is to live with the family for five days, from the tenth to the fourteenth day of the month, and then be sacrificed "at twilight" on the fourteenth.

As we've said before, nothing is insignificant in Scripture, and the five days of living with and examining the sacrifice are important. Obviously the lamb represents Jesus Christ, the Lamb of God (John 1:29). What did the five-day period have to do with Him? We'll see tomorrow morning.

THURSDAY

"Then, *six* days before the Passover, Jesus came to Bethany" (John 12:1; emphasis added).

"The *next day* a great multitude that had come to the Feast, when they heard that Jesus was coming to Jerusalem, took branches of palm trees and went out to meet Him" (John 12:12–13; emphasis added).

It's the first Palm Sunday, the Sunday before Easter. The chronology laid out in John shows that the Feast of Passover would be in five days as seen in the foregoing. Jesus had dinner with His friends, Mary and Martha and their brother, Lazarus, who was raised from the dead by Jesus in Bethany, a small town just outside of Jerusalem, on Saturday night, six days before Passover. The next day was His triumphal entry into Jerusalem, riding on a young donkey (v. 14). Look at this awesome prophecy about the coming Messiah, written five hundred years before He came:

"Rejoice greatly, O daughters of Zion! Shout, O daughter of Jerusalem! Behold, your King is coming to you; He is just and having salvation, lowly and *riding on a donkey*" (Zechariah 9:9; emphasis added).

Wow! So now the "Passover Lamb" has arrived in His "household," and He will present Himself to them in Jerusalem and let them question Him and examine Him on Monday the tenth, on Tuesday the eleventh, on Wednesday the twelfth, and on Thursday the thirteenth, which would be the night of the Passover feast. And then on Friday the fourteenth, Passover Day, He would be crucified!

At what time was the initial one-year-old Passover lamb to be killed? Do you remember? *Twilight.* We'll look at an awesome similarity with that next time, tomorrow, which just happens to be a Friday!

FRIDAY

"Then the whole assembly of the congregation of Israel shall kill it at *twilight*" (Exodus 12:6; emphasis added).

"Now it was the *third hour*, and they crucified Him" (Mark 15:25; emphasis added).

"Now it was about the *sixth hour*, and there was darkness over all the earth until the *ninth hour*. Then the sun was darkened, and the veil of the temple was torn in two. And when Jesus had cried out with a loud voice,

He said, 'Father, into Your hands I commit my Spirit.' Having said this, He breathed His last" (Luke 23:44–46; emphasis added).

The Word of God is amazingly specific. The adorable, innocent sacrificial lamb was to be killed "at twilight" on the fourteenth of the month. What does that mean? When exactly is that? Interestingly, the Jewish day started at sunset, that is, in the evening. The term *twilight* means "the time of the going down of the sun" and can mean anytime from when the sun starts to decline in the sky until sunset, or "at the going down of the sun" as stated in Deuteronomy 16:6. Traditionally, the actual time of the sacrifice of the lamb was 3:00 p.m. Got it?

Now we jump ahead to the actual event that this first Passover was foreshadowing—the Crucifixion of Jesus Christ, to occur some fourteen hundred years later. The Jews started the hours of daylight at 6:00 a.m.—that was hour 0. So the third hour was 9:00 a.m., and that was the time the recently tried and convicted and scourged/beaten Jesus Christ arrived at Golgotha to be nailed to the cross. Now here's something neat. We are eventually going to get to Mount Sinai and the Law and the formal institution of the sacrificial system set up by God for a temporary atonement for sin. There will be *lots* of sacrifices, and many on a daily basis, but just look at this particular one:

"Now this is what you shall offer on the altar: *two* lambs of the first year, *day* by *day continually*. One lamb you shall offer *in the morning*, and the other lamb you shall offer *at twilight*" (Exodus 29:38–39; emphasis added).

Wow! Jesus was put up on the cross right at the time of the "morning sacrifice," but He wasn't dead yet. No, He was very different from any previous sacrifice because He *couldn't* be killed; He would have to *give up* His life, and that He would not do until the time of the evening sacrifice, twilight. Man, I really wish we could go on with this right now, but we're over our usual limit. Next week will be great. Have a wonderful weekend.

15
WEEK

MONDAY

Our current topic is the Passover, a beautiful *preview* of the perfect, ultimate plan of salvation that the Godhead had designed from time immemorial to save humankind from their sin and reunite them with Father God, foreshadowing the perfect sacrifice of Jesus Christ on the cross, which would not occur for fourteen hundred years. Last week, we left Jesus on the cross in a sense since we had to wait out the weekend, but keep in mind, and this is important, that Jesus Christ did not stay on that cross! As believers, we remember and revere the cross image, that "emblem of suffering and shame," but we are not to picture Jesus as *still* on the cross, which is shown on a crucifix. I think that's an important distinction. Satan would have just loved for Jesus to stay nailed to that cross because then He would not have been able to defeat him and conquer sin, disease, and death. But our Lord did rise on the third day, and He is *alive* and well, seated at the right hand of the Father! Amen.

"Now from the sixth hour until the ninth hour there was darkness over all the land" (Matthew 27:45).

"Now there were in the same country shepherds living out in the fields, keeping watch over their flocks by night. And behold, an angel of the Lord stood before them, and the *glory* of the Lord *shone* around them" (Luke 2:8–9; emphasis added).

Neat distinction here. The Light of the world, Jesus Christ, came to dwell with us as one of us in the middle of the night, in darkness, but the sky was illuminated like never before or since. The dark became light.

From 12:00 noon until 3:00 p.m. on Good Friday, the day of the Crucifixion, the brightest time of day, there was total darkness over the entire earth. This was no natural eclipse. The Lamb of God was drawing all the righteous judgment for our sins, and all our infirmities and sickness, upon Himself such that He would "be made to be sin" (2 Corinthians 5:21). The agony and suffering He went through those three hours would not be viewed by humans. God turned the lights off, not just to humans but also to the universe, all of whom were watching intently, and even to Himself. Even He had to turn away.

I want to expand on this tomorrow because, as you may have gathered already, the main focus of this series on healing has been and will continue to be the Healer, not the healing, as that is the proper order of things. We'll examine two portions of Scripture, Mark 15:34 and John 12:31–33, next time.

TUESDAY

"Now when the sixth hour had come, there was darkness over the whole land until the ninth hour. And at the ninth hour Jesus cried out with a loud voice, saying, 'Eloi, Eloi, lama sabachthani?' which is translated, 'My God, My God, why have You forsaken Me?'" Mark 15:33–34).

Haunting, isn't it? The perfect, sinless Son of God, the pride and joy of the universe, had just absorbed, in His decimated body, all the sin of humankind. He was made to *be* sin. Now please note that Jesus never *sinned*—He was perfect in all His ways—and He never succumbed to sin, but He drew into Himself all the bad and sad, all the judgment. Here's a very important verse that proves that but is often misunderstood:

"'Now is the *judgement* of this world; now the ruler of this world will be cast out. And I, if I be lifted up from the earth, will draw all *peoples* to Myself.' This He said, signifying by what death He would die" (John 12:31–33).

I was taught as a young child that this awesome verse was proof that if one simply professed Jesus as Lord appropriately and preached about Him correctly, that is, if Jesus was "lifted up," then all humankind would accept Him as their Savior. But that is not true. For one thing, we all know that many people will reject Jesus, even when the true Gospel is presented to them, but also look at verse 33. Jesus Himself said this portion of Scripture was about the manner of His death, and that would be crucifixion. The wooden cross Jesus was nailed to had to be "lifted up" into the air, suspended between heaven and earth, before it was slammed down into the hole dug for it to keep it upright. That's what He meant by "lifted up." And what was He drawing to Himself?

This is where the confusion comes in. Note that the word *peoples* in verse 32 is italicized in your Bible; the KJV and NIV use the word *men* instead, but both are wrong because the original Greek does not have any word there. Those words were added by the translators (that's what the italics signify) since they thought it would make more sense that way, but it completely changes the intended meaning. It should read, "Will draw all to Myself." And what is that "all"?

Hmm, we're out of time for this morning. Meditate on this for tomorrow.

WEDNESDAY

"And if I, if I be lifted up from the earth, will draw all things to Myself" (John 12:32 DRA).

This particular translation of Holy Scripture was the first from Latin to English, and it dates from the sixteenth century, but it gets this foundational verse as close to accurate as any translation I could find. What Jesus is saying He will draw unto Himself on the cross is the "thing" stated in the prior verse:

"Now is the *judgement* of this world" (John 12:31; emphasis added).

That's it. And that He did, absorbing all the righteous penalty that should have been meted out to us for all our sin and disobedience, for *billions* of humans—all who have ever lived or will live—as He would "draw *all* things" (v. 32). He was the Passover Lamb of God who would "take away the sins of the world!" (John 1:29).

But there was such a crucial difference between the innocent one-year-old little lamb of the first Passover and the Son of God, who would come fourteen hundred years later: the lamb was sacrificed quickly and humanely; there was no suffering. The Jews would go to great lengths subsequently, with all the sacrificial animals to come, to treat them well, because they had to be "without blemish" to serve as a sacrifice, and to kill them according to strict laws so that there would be no stress or suffering for the innocent animal.

Such was not the case with Jesus Christ as He was made to *suffer* and bleed and die, not just bleed and die. And, man, did He suffer, to a degree no person had ever before or has ever since. Look at Isaiah 42:14: "His appearance was so disfigured that He did not look like a man, and His form did not resemble a human being" (HCSB).

The animal sacrifices had to bleed because in such was the remission of sin, as we have shown previously, but Jesus's bleeding was intimately intertwined with great suffering all along the way. From the sweating of blood arising from His anxiety in the garden of Gethsemane, to the bleeding from His forehead because of the crown of thorns, to the bleeding from His face (this is hard for me to write) thanks to the plucking of His beard, to the bleeding from His raw back after the relentless scourging, such that there was no flesh left on His back, to the bleeding from His hands and feet from the three cruel nails pounded into His body at the cross, to the spilling of blood from His precious side because of the spear plunged into Him … Wow! Why? Why? He didn't need to suffer at all to forgive our sins—and forgive them for eternity—and give us everlasting lives. Why? Why all the unimaginable physical suffering? I so wish I could get out this morning all that's bursting within me, but this is more than enough to chew on today. God bless.

THURSDAY

You know, I've heard it preached before that the physical suffering of Jesus Christ was not what He dreaded so much; it was the separation from the communion with His Father. And He was indeed distanced from His

Father, as that had to be in order to satisfy the righteous judgment of God and prove once and for all that God is love. That was so vividly shown in Mark 15:34, when Jesus exclaimed from the cross, "My God, My God, why have You *forsaken* Me?" (emphasis added). Jesus had never before referred to His Father as "God" (in the Greek, *theos*, a generic term for any god, even pagan gods); He always called Him His Father. On the cross, the Son realized the Father had turned away, had forsaken Him. There's a verse about all this in Isaiah 53, that famous messianic chapter, written seven hundred years before Jesus, that is difficult to comprehend:

"But it was the Lord who decided to crush Him and make Him suffer. The Lord made His life a penalty offering" (Isaiah 53:10 NCV).

I know I simply can't get my mind around that; it is a level of love for us that is beyond all reason and understanding, and which proved to the universe two thousand years ago that God is *good*, and God is *love*, and Satan is a liar.

But the physical suffering was truly overwhelmingly agonizing for Jesus. In the garden, He actually prayed for the "cup" to be taken away from Him (Luke 22:42). The word *cup* here signifies the wrath of God (Psalm 75:8). But He did submit to the will of His Father, and "then an angel appeared to Him from heaven, strengthening Him" (Luke 22:43). But this would be the last time He received any supernatural assistance during His passion; He would absorb all this physical suffering as 100 percent *man*! That is hugely significant because He did this for you and me. No matter what physical or emotional affliction we're dealing with, He already bore it all on Himself, and it took a great toll. In fact, Jesus was almost beaten to death *before* He got to the cross. It would have been disastrous had He died before getting to the cross, because He *had* to die *on the cross* to redeem us from the curse of sin. "Christ has redeemed us from the curse of the law, having become a curse for us (for it is written, 'Cursed is everyone who hangs on a tree')" (Galatians 3:13). Even He could not "bear His cross," and a black man, Simon the Cyrene, was pulled from the crowd to carry His cross to Golgotha. We are *never* to forget just how much He suffered. I'm going to share a very personal story about this tomorrow.

FRIDAY

"For all those who have eyes, and all those who have ears / It is only He who can reduce me to tears." This comes from "When He Returns" by Bob Dylan.

As men, we try to keep our composure and play tough—we're not to cry like babies—but this Jesus of ours … well, here goes:

An event happened to me many years ago, and a visual image was deeply etched into my mind that would come to the surface often. It would always disturb me on a deep level and invariably bring tears and a rush of emotion. I never knew why until just recently.

I was driving during daylight from home to my office, in town, going probably just 35 mph (honestly), when a little rabbit ran out in front of my car. I guess I was daydreaming a bit because I didn't notice until it was too late. I ran the bunny over. I felt the bump as the big SUV tires crushed that little body, which was sickening for me because I really try to avoid these little critters as much as is safely possible. And if I had been paying attention, I would have been able to safely brake and swerve and miss this one. I instinctively looked in the rearview mirror as I drove on, and it's what I saw then that riveted itself to my very soul.

The little rabbit's body was crushed, but not his head. I saw him try as hard as he could to lift his head and scamper away with his body, but to no avail. He was *suffering*; he was *dying*, but he wasn't dead. He was in pure anguish, his body *crushed*, in terrible pain, and *all alone*, no one to rescue him and make everything all right. After a few more tries, he couldn't muster the strength to even raise his head, so he laid it down for good.

Yeah, I was crying, and crying good, because it was *my* actions that had caused all that suffering and pain and anguish; the bunny was *innocent*. How I wished I had just run over his head initially; at least he wouldn't have suffered. That mental image, always as clear as the day it happened, of an innocent animal suffering and dying because of me, all alone, forsaken (I wanted so badly to turn around and rescue him—make everything sad to be untrue), has been with me ever since, deep inside. It would come to the surface all too often. And I would cry every time. For years and years.

So I eventually asked the Lord to take that memory from me so it wouldn't haunt me anymore. And then He showed me what I should have seen all along. This wasn't about some rabbit; it was about Jesus! It was to be a reminder to me of the awful price paid for my salvation *and* my healing as that is the only reason the precious Lamb of God was made to suffer, for my healing on this earth, and the price Father God had to pay to turn away and forsake His beloved Son. O how He would have wanted to save His only Son from all of that. And I was *never, ever* to forget it. None of us are. That's why Jesus would initiate the sacrament of Holy Communion, to be celebrated "often." We'll eventually get to that.

Yep, I'm crying. But you know what I think? When God sees me getting all choked up over Jesus and the cross and His love for His Son, I think He sees me as the strongest I will ever be. I have a hunch that's the case.

I'm not even going to apologize for the length of this one. Have a wonderful weekend. How can you not after all this?

16
WEEK

MONDAY

Happy Monday! Let's get out the map of our journey from the glove compartment and see where we're at and recount where we've been. It's good to stop and take stock once in a while.

The focus from Day 1, three and a half months ago, has been on laying the foundation to prove that healing is in the Atonement for believers, culminating in the statement a couple of weeks ago "If you are *saved*, then you are *healed*." We've worked toward that astonishing statement slowly and meticulously, piece by piece, as a lawyer would present a case (it is difficult for me to make that comparison since MDs and JDs are not often complimentary of each other. Remember that analogy between a lawyer and a catfish? One is a horrible, scum-sucking, bottom-dwelling scavenger, and the other is a fish). John describes Jesus as our "Advocate" (the Greek word *parakletos*, which means "lawyer/counselor") before the Father in heaven, pleading our case (1 John 2:1). Now we're pondering why it had to take four thousand years from the first sin before Jesus would come to save us.

We've come a long way already, starting in the garden, going through the Great Flood, getting dispersed all over the earth at the Tower of Babel, and landing in Ur of the Chaldeans (modern-day Iraq), where we met believing Abraham, whose covenant with God, based on belief and not works (Genesis 15:6), is still in effect for us. Abraham had Isaac, who had Jacob, who had twelve sons, and these chosen people would become known as the children (or nation) of Israel. They were to be totally dependent on the goodness and grace of God via belief as a model for the world to see, but they couldn't fulfill that plan. They were weak and ended up in captivity in Egypt for four hundred years!

Now they're getting ready to blast out of that place of bondage. The next major event on the road toward Jesus is about to take place, and it will change everything. Please remember, up to this point human beings were sinning like crazy and suffering terribly from the consequences of that sin, but they weren't sinning against God as He had not given them rules to keep since that first one in the garden. And remember, the whole universe was intently observing our beautiful blue orb to see what God was going to do with His little sinful humans created in His image. Would He forgive them entirely, give them a "free pass"? If He were to do that, His justice and righteousness would be compromised because there had to be a punishment for their sin. Would He destroy them completely? Then how could He claim that His very nature was love? Things were still unsettled; the universe was on edge. God's children were still lost and suffering.

And then something really awesome happened. That's where we are now: at the Passover. It is a simply beautiful, amazing *preview* of the ultimate answer to all these questions, not to occur for fourteen hundred years. We're going to examine it more, a lot more, starting tomorrow.

This one had to be really long because it's a summary of twenty-six hundred years of human history from a theological perspective. Sorry!

TUESDAY

"Then they are to take some of the blood and put it on the sides and tops of the doorframes of the houses where they eat the lambs" (Exodus 12:7 NIV).

"Take a bunch of hyssop, dip it into the blood in the basin and put some of the blood on the top and on both sides of the doorframe. When the Lord goes through the land to strike down the Egyptians, He will see the blood on the top and sides of the doorframe and will pass over that doorway, and He will not permit the destroyer to enter your houses and strike you down" (Exodus 12:22–23 NIV).

"I see the world in grace. I see the world in Gospel" (from the song "Wonder" by Hillsong United).

We're deep into the Passover. The innocent little sacrificial lambs were allowed to live with their host families for five days, bonding and becoming an intimate part of the family, and then humanely, without suffering, killed at twilight (3:00 p.m.) on the fourteenth day of the month. The blood of the lamb was to be displayed as described in the foregoing verses. That's the topic this morning.

Why the Hillsong quote? Remember the road to Emmaus? My position is that we are to strive to "see" Jesus Christ and His cross in "all of Scripture" (Luke 24:27), and this is an example of such. There are two basic movements in our physical world that have huge spiritual implications, and they are (1) *horizontal*, that is, a back-and-forth movement, and (2) *vertical*, an up-and-down movement. Got it? Horizontal (back and forth) and vertical (up and down).

So take your finger and make an imaginary horizontal line in the air, using a back-and-forth movement, in front of you. Then go to the center of that imaginary line and make a vertical, up-and-down line with the down more than the up. What sign have you made? Yep, the sign of the cross. That's exactly what the Lord saw in the foregoing verses from Exodus 12, as the blood of the lamb was smeared *horizontally* on the top of the doorframe and *vertically* on the sides. He saw the cross and knew that everything hidden within that cross was *safe* and *protected* from the destroyer, as this was all about Jesus Christ and His once-and-for-all sacrifice on His cross, to occur fourteen hundred years later.

Wow! I love it. This is what we really are to do: appreciate Jesus in all of Scripture so that we get to know Him better and become more like Him, renewing our minds to conform more with the mind of Christ. We'll look at another example of the sign of the cross in the Old Testament tomorrow.

WEDNESDAY

So it's hump day for the world, but for us believers, "every day with Jesus is sweeter than the day before." We'll start this day with some really inspiring

Scripture from the Old Testament that, most likely, you've never thought of as inspiring before, but bear with me.

> He who offers the sacrifice of his peace offering to the Lord shall bring his offering to the Lord ... the fat with the breast he shall bring, that the breast may be *waved* as a *wave offering* before the Lord. Also, the right thigh you shall give to the priest as a *heave offering* from the sacrifices of your peace offerings. For the breast of the *wave offering* and the thigh of the *heave offering*, I [God], have taken from the children of Israel, from the sacrifices of their peace offerings. (Leviticus 7:29–34; emphasis added).

So we're jumping ahead again (it's kind of hard to tell a long story when you, and everyone reading, already know the ending) from the Passover to just several weeks down the road of God's salvation plan for humans. The seminal occurrence on Mount Sinai has ushered in the sacrificial system for the nation of Israel, and the foregoing is an example of one of the numerous offerings to be observed, specifically, a peace offering for the priests. The animal to be sacrificed could be a goat, sheep, or ox. The meat of the breast and thigh is for the priests to eat; the offering is for them. This ceremony is first described in Exodus 29.

But note what is done before the part is put on the altar to be burnt. The smaller breast part is held up and *waved* horizontally, back and forth, before the Lord. The much larger and heavier right thigh is *heaved*, a vertical, upward motion, to throw the part up onto the altar.

Wow! What does the Lord see? Horizontal, back and forth, and vertical, up and down—the cross! *That*, the future cross of Christ, is what allowed these temporary sacrifices to work at all, praise God!

You've got to admit, this stuff is good. Seeing Jesus in new and fresh ways is truly life-changing. One more really neat example of the cross in the Old Testament next time.

THURSDAY

So our broader topic is God's plan of salvation, and why it took four thousand years for Jesus to come, and how God was dealing, or not dealing, with sin prior to Jesus, and we're sojourning now on the first Passover. We've got more to cover, but we're first seeing Jesus, and specifically His cross, in this ceremony and other instances in the Old Testament.

This next example will take the rest of this week and possibly into the next to discuss in full because it's subtle and takes some explaining. I first noticed this by looking at a graphic in my old MacArthur Study Bible, and I saw something that should have been obvious, but no mention of its significance was made, nor could I find a reference to what I was seeing in any of my numerous other Bibles, but I think it's really neat.

We're again jumping ahead to after Mount Sinai, two years after the Exodus. The children of Israel are wandering through the wilderness; they are mobile. They've constructed the tabernacle according to plan, which they carry with them and which is at the center of their encampments when they are not on the move. We pick up the story in Numbers 1 and 2. We are told how the thirteen tribes of Israel were to position themselves around the tabernacle, and how many men over the age of twenty, and fit for war, were in each camp (tribe). Now, as you recall, there were only twelve sons of Jacob, but the Levites (the tribe of Moses and Aaron) were the priests, and they camped right around and near the tabernacle. They were not to be counted as they did not go to war. The children of Joseph were split into two tribes, Ephraim and Manasseh, and that's how we have twelve tribes still to be placed around the tabernacle. The twelve tribes would position themselves in groups of three tribes each, heading out in columns north, south, east, and west from the tabernacle, with the tabernacle in the center. Can you picture that?

The people were to be numbered, and those numbers are very telling because, remember, nothing in Holy Scripture is insignificant and it is *all* about Jesus and His cross.

"Every one of the children of Israel shall camp by his own standard, beside the emblems (flags) of his father's house; they shall camp some distance from the tabernacle of meeting" (Numbers 2:2).

Tomorrow we'll go through the numbers specifically. If you could, please have a blank sheet of paper, a pencil, and some sort of ruler handy; no need for a protractor, or compass, or slide rule! (Yep, I lived in the era of those, and they were so much better for our little developing brains than electronic tablets. Just saying.) Have a great Thursday.

FRIDAY

"On the east side, toward the rising of the sun … Judah shall camp. And his army was numbered at 74,600. Those who camp next to him shall be the tribe of Issachar, and his army was numbered at 54,400. Then comes the tribe of Zebulun. … And his army was numbered at 57,400. … On the south side" (Numbers 2:3–10).

And so the narrative goes, on and on, numbering the fighting men of each tribe and their positioning. When all is told, there were approximately two hundred thousand men to the east of the tabernacle, one hundred thousand to the west of the tabernacle, and one hundred fifty thousand to the north and south, respectively, arranged in straight columns. (Remember, these were just the fighting men; the total Israeli population was over two million!)

Do you have your paper, pencil, and ruler? Make a central dot on the paper, then draw a straight line downward two inches and label that "east." In the same fashion, extend a line one inch long above the dot (west), and then one-and-a-half-inch lines extending both to the right (north) and the left (south). What have you drawn? Can you believe this?! When God looked down on His chosen children in the wilderness, for the time absolutely still lost to Him, He saw the cross, and not just any cross, but the Roman cross with the longer downward post, which, by the way, wasn't even in fashion at that time. He saw the cross that Jesus Christ would suffer and die on. And God would remember what was to come, and show favor to His people, and protect them and provide for them. Wow!

This is a great way to end this week, I think. Next week we'll start out by explaining why Judah was mentioned first and why that tribe was on the east, "toward the rising of the sun." A hint: Who's called the Lion of the tribe of Judah?

Have a great weekend.

17
WEEK

MONDAY

Happy Labor Day! You know, labor has a very different look in the spiritual world than in the carnal world. There's only one thing we are to "labor" for in the kingdom of God. Look at this amazing scripture:

"There remaineth therefore a *rest* to the people of God. For he that is entered into His rest, he also hath ceased from his own works, as God did from His. Let us *labour* therefore to *enter* into that *rest*" (Hebrews 4:9–11 KJV; emphasis added).

Wow! Now I know Philippians 2:12 says to "work out your own salvation," but that doesn't mean to work *for* your salvation; that is a gift. The Greek word used here for "work out" means to knead out, or pound out, or unwrap—that sort of thing. We do have to utilize this "gift of righteousness" (Romans 5:17).

The following verse, Philippians 2:13, one of my all-time favorites, says, "For it is God who works in you, both *to will* and *to do* for His good pleasure" (emphasis added). Where, I ask, does that leave room for our self-righteous efforts?

I hadn't planned any of that, but it's all good.

We just saw the crucifixion cross in the way the children of Israel camped around the tabernacle. Judah was the largest tribe, and the first mentioned, and was camped to the east of the tabernacle. We'll end today with two portions of scripture and a much less important, but nonetheless intriguing, *Lord of the Rings* quote, which we'll start examining tomorrow. Enjoy the holiday.

Now when they drew near Jerusalem ... at the Mount of Olives, then Jesus sent two disciples, saying to them, "Go into the village opposite you, and immediately you will find a donkey tied, and a colt with her. Loose them and bring them to me." ... They brought the donkey and the colt, laid their clothes on them, and set Him on them. And a very great multitude spread their clothes on the road; others cut down branches from the trees and spread them on the road. Then the multitudes ... cried out, saying, "Hosanna to the Son of David! Blessed is He who comes in the name of the Lord! Hosanna in the highest!" (Matthew 21:1–9)

"Behold, the Day of the Lord is coming ... and in that day His feet will stand on the Mount of Olives, which faces Jerusalem on the east" (Zechariah 14:1, 4).

"Look to my coming on the first light of the fifth day. At dawn, look to the east." (Gandalf said this to Aragorn in *The Two Towers* from the *Lord of the Rings* series.)

TUESDAY

There are two "triumphal entries" of Jesus Christ into Jerusalem recorded in Scripture. The first is known as Palm Sunday, which already occurred some two thousand years ago and is well-documented. The second has not occurred yet, "but of that day and hour no one knows, not even the angels of heaven" (Matthew 24:36). This will be at the Second Coming of Jesus Christ. In both instances, He comes in from the east! The Scriptural proof of that was given yesterday morning. The Mount of Olives is a ridge just east of Jerusalem. Hence the importance of the tribe of Judah, from which Jesus descended, and the largest of the tribes, being positioned to the east of the holy tabernacle. Again, nothing in scripture is insignificant, and it all ultimately has to do with Jesus and His finished work on the cross. If you find me saying that a lot and making a big deal of it again and again, *good*! And get used to it because we will *forever* be proclaiming, "Worthy is the Lamb who was slain to receive power and riches and wisdom, and strength and honor and glory and blessing!" (Revelation 5:12).

The Palm Sunday entry is recorded in all four synoptic Gospels. There should be a movie just of it because it was so beautiful and dramatic. I like Matthew's account best. The people were sincerely enthralled to see Jesus, including all the children. "And the children crying out in the temple and saying, 'Hosanna to the Son of David!'" (Matthew 21:15). "All the city was moved, saying, 'Who is this?' So the multitudes said, 'This is Jesus, the prophet from Nazareth of Galilee.' ... Then the blind and the lame came to Him in the temple, and He healed them" (vv. 10, 11, 14).

But not everyone was happy. Check out what the "religious folk" said: "But when the chief priests and scribes saw the wonderful things that He did ... they were *indignant*, and said to Him, 'Do you hear what these are saying?' And Jesus said to them, 'Yes. Have you never read, *"Out of the mouth of babes and nursing infants you have perfected praise"*?'" (vv. 15–16; emphasis added).

And here's the take-home message for this morning: Jesus was quoting Psalm 8:2, but He tweaked it a bit (which He, by the way, being the Word, has the right to do). This is what David said in Psalm 8:2: "*Out of the mouth of babes and nursing infants you have ordained strength*" (emphasis added).

Wow! I'm telling you, I know this is true. There is strength in praising the Lord! As Nehemiah 8:10 says, "The joy of the Lord is my strength."

I thought that was neat. We'll take up the second triumphal entry tomorrow.

WEDNESDAY

Zechariah was one of the last Old Testament prophets, and he prophesied a lot about Jesus. We're discussing the two triumphal entries of Jesus into Jerusalem, and Zechariah goes into detail about both. The Palm Sunday entry is as follows:

"Rejoice, greatly, O daughter of Zion! Shout, O daughter of Jerusalem! Behold, your King is coming to you; He is just and having salvation, lowly and riding on a donkey" (Zechariah 9:9).

Wow! That was written five hundred years before the fact—with pinpoint accuracy. Notice it was daylight when this arrival occurred. The Second Coming is then addressed by this faithful prophet in chapters 12–14, and it's a completely different scenario: "Thus the Lord my God will come, and all the saints with You. It shall come to pass in that day that there will *be no light; the lights will diminish*. It shall be one day which is known to the Lord—neither day nor night, *but at evening time it shall happen, that it will be light*" (Zechariah 14:6–7; emphasis added). This turning of *night* into *day* was to take place just to the *east* of Jerusalem on the Mount of Olives. The desperate children of Israel, surrounded in Jerusalem, were to "at dawn, look to the East." Then they will finally see their Messiah, whom they rejected the first time, and "they will mourn for Him as one mourns for His only son, and grieve for Him as one grieves for a firstborn" (Zechariah 12:10).

Awesome stuff. You know, I'm the ultimate lark, arising *very* early each morning, and I can tell you from great experience that the time of night just before the dawn is special. It is indeed the darkest time of the night, and there is a palpable expectancy in the air as if all of creation is holding its breath, hoping that the dawn will come, that the sun will rise. I liken that to our fallen state, both as humans and with regard to creation itself, all "looking for the *blessed hope* and *glorious appearing* of our great *God* and *Savior Jesus Christ*" (Titus 2:13; emphasis added). Amen!

Okay, we are done with this mini diversion about the significance of the east. Now we'll get back to seeing the sign of the cross in the Old Testament, then it's back to the Passover, and then we'll get back on the road of God's salvation plan for humankind, culminating in the cross of Jesus Christ. It's all good.

THURSDAY

"Then the Lord instructed Moses, 'Make a poisonous serpent out of bronze and fasten it to a pole. Anyone who has been bitten and who looks at it will live.' So, Moses made a bronze serpent and fastened it to a pole. If a person who had been bitten by a poisonous serpent looked to the serpent, he lived" (Numbers 21:8–9 ISV).

The children of Israel were still wandering through the wilderness, until all the unfaithful generation who did not believe they could possess the Promised Land the first time (except for Joshua and Caleb, who did believe), had died. In Numbers 21 they were again "very discouraged" and spoke against God and Moses. This God had taken meticulous care of His rebellious chosen people, even in their disobedience. He had provided water for all two million of them in the middle of a desert and fed them daily with manna from heaven. Their clothes miraculously never got old, and their shoes never wore out! For forty years! Yet this was their response: "There is no food or water, and our soul loathes this worthless bread." Can you believe it? "So the Lord sent fiery [poisonous] serpents among the people, and they bit the people; and many of the children of Israel died" (Numbers 21:5–6).

Does that seem a bit harsh? Let's look at it this way: these people were in a desert that was normally loaded with venomous snakes; that was their habitat. The fact that they hadn't been attacked by these snakes previously was a sign of divine protection, but these people were never pleased with anything, and there was a lesson to be learned here, because although they were under the Law at that time, God's heart was for grace and mercy. The people realized they had sinned against God and asked Moses to intervene for them, to pray to the Lord to "take away the serpents from us" (Numbers 21:7).

But God had a better plan. The Israelites would find salvation even in the midst of the trouble, even *after* they had been bitten. Read the introductory verses carefully. This salvation was *only* for those who had been bitten, only for those who *needed it*. You know how I see this, don't you, as I'm a grace person and I view this as saying that the *only* qualification for salvation is that you have to be "bitten" by the curse of sin. You'll probably not hear that preached anywhere, but remember, I'm a doctor, not a preacher.

Man, this is really getting good. I hate to have to stop, but we'll pick up right here and end the week with a bang tomorrow morning.

FRIDAY

"And as Moses lifted up the serpent in the wilderness, even so must the Son of Man be lifted up, that whoever believes in Him should not perish but have eternal life" (John 3:14–15).

We all know John 3:16; these are the two verses before it, and Jesus is referring to our story in Numbers 21. To save the people, Moses was instructed to make a *bronze* serpent and *fasten* it to a *pole*. Nothing is insignificant, right? Why bronze and not gold or silver, two very much more precious metals?

Bronze is associated with the *judgment* of God upon sin; all the utensils associated with the animal sacrifices performed in the court of the tabernacle, including the altar, were made of bronze. And this bronze, coiled serpent was somehow to be attached to a wooden pole. Most images you'll see of this show the snake coiled vertically around the upright pole, much like the medical symbol of a staff and a snake, but that seems impractical to me; the snake would slide down the pole. Moses's instructions were to "fasten" it to the pole, and I think, just knowing how awesome Scripture is, that the snake was fashioned around a horizontal crossbar, which was then attached to the vertical pole! Where have we seen that before? This lifted snake-carrying pole would have looked like a cross, thereby combining two of the most despised and feared emblems known to humans: the serpent and the crucifixion cross. *Just looking* at it resulted in the *healing* of the *already bitten* children of Israel. It would be as if they had never been bitten; indeed, everything sad was made untrue. The curse was reversed; all was made brand new! And why? Because the *righteous judgment* of a *just God* was drawn to that cross, and not the people. Wow!

That explains again the words of our Lord in John 12:32: "And I, if I be lifted up from the earth, will draw all _____ to Myself." That blank would be filled in with the word *judgment,* and that timeless act of obedience on the cross satisfied the *justice* of God and secured the *righteousness* of God, while saving us believers and restoring us to a personal relationship with the great God of heaven forever and ever, empowering us to live abundant, healthy, productive, and impactful lives on this earth. And this is all because of the *love* of God. Amen!

Back to the Passover next week. Have a blessed weekend.

18
WEEK

MONDAY

We return to the first Passover, recorded in Exodus 12. We left after the Passover lamb was slain and its blood smeared on the lintels and doorposts of the Israelites' homes (the sign of the cross), saving their firstborn children from death, foreshadowing the salvation provided for all humans from sin by the shedding of the blood of Jesus Christ on Calvary. But the ceremony was not over; there was a second component: dinner!

"Then they shall eat the flesh on that night; roasted in fire, with unleavened bread and with bitter herbs they shall eat it. Do not eat it raw, nor boiled at all with water, but *roasted in fire*—its head with its legs and entrails. You shall let none of it remain until morning, and what remains of it until morning you shall *burn with fire*" (Exodus 12:8–10; emphasis added).

The sacrificial lamb was to be roasted intact and eaten—*all* of it. This part of the Passover was every bit as important and consequential as the shedding of the lamb's blood. And this is what we will now concentrate on for the next several days as it will further buttress our position that healing is fully provided for believers in the atonement of Jesus Christ, because just look at the results for these enslaved, impoverished, weak children of Israel after properly observing the elements of the Passover the night before they left Egypt:

"He also brought them out with silver and gold, and there was none feeble among His tribes" (Psalm 105:37). That's unbelievable and miraculous. These were lowly *slaves*, yet their proper observing of the Passover changed everything.

I want to draw our attention to three requirements stated in the foregoing Scripture: the lamb was to be *roasted*, it was to be *intact*, and it was to be *eaten in its entirety*. This stuff is going to be really good, and I hope that when we're done we have a new and better understanding of Holy Communion, because this is what Passover is really all about, and both are all about (you guessed it) Jesus Christ and His cross. We start tomorrow.

TUESDAY

> And it came to pass, at the *time of the offering of the evening sacrifice*, that Elijah the prophet came near and said, "Lord God of Abraham, Isaac, and Israel, let it be known this day that You are God in Israel and I am your servant, and that I have done all these things at Your Word. Hear me, O Lord, hear me, that this people may know that You are Lord God, and that You have turned their hearts back to You again." Then the *fire* of the Lord fell and *consumed* the *burnt sacrifice*, *and* the wood *and* the stones *and* the dust, *and* it *licked up* the water that was in the trench. (1 Kings 18:36–38; emphasis added)

We now fast-forward almost six hundred years from the first Passover to the time of the kings of Israel and Judah (the two had previously split) and the prophet Elijah. The current king in Israel is the evil Ahab, who married a foreigner by the name of Jezebel, whose name is still synonymous with treachery and dishonor. She was a priestess of the false god Baal, and she seduced Ahab to worship and serve him. God had to discipline His wayward people, who were under the Law, so He ordered His servant Elijah to proclaim a drought over the land, a very long drought of over three years! This was risky business for Elijah as Jezebel had been systematically killing the prophets of the Lord (1 Kings 18:4), and he was the foremost wanted because of this drought thing, but he seemingly fearlessly obeyed. I love his directness. He said only *one sentence*:

"As the Lord God of Israel lives, before whom I stand, there shall not be dew nor rain these years, except at my word" (1 Kings 17:1).

Wow! That's pretty awesome. It's enough to have no rain, but *no dew*?! That's how severe God had to be, but it's not His heart. Here's His heart, painfully expressed by the prophet Hosea one hundred years after Elijah: "Therefore I have hewn them by the prophets, I have slain them by the words of My mouth; and your [Israel's] judgments are like light that goes forth. For I desire *mercy* and not sacrifice, and the *knowledge of God* more than burnt offerings" (Hosea 6:5–6; emphasis added).

This loving God, although I see nothing in Scripture that indicates the children of Israel were even thinking of turning back to Him because of the drought, had seen His children suffer enough, and He was about to bring the drought to a spectacular end. Although I know you're thinking I've lost track of our topic, namely, the body of the Passover lamb, I have certainly not. We will soon see *why* the lamb had to be *roasted* (not boiled) and *completely consumed*—next time.

WEDNESDAY

"The Word of the Lord came to Elijah, in the third year, saying, 'Go, present yourself to Ahab, and I will send rain on the earth'" (1 Kings 18:1).

The prolonged drought was about to end; God would show Himself strong to His people and remind them of His power and goodness. And we are going to see some eternal, profound truths in this showdown on Mount Carmel. All the players will be there: the children of Israel, King Ahab and his false prophets of Baal (450 of them!), and the one lone prophet of the one true God, Elijah. This is the challenge Elijah gives to the people:

"How long will you falter between two opinions? If the Lord is God, follow Him; but if Baal, follow him" (1 Kings 18:21). Wow! That is pretty direct, and still it is the question for every one of us. But look how these clowns answer: "But the people answered him *not a word*" (emphasis added).

So the showdown is on, and it will involve an animal sacrifice, which of course the children of Israel were already very familiar with, but so were the followers of the false religions. But there's an anomaly here, which I've never heard preached, one that seems glaringly obvious to me. Only priests were allowed to offer animal sacrifices to God because they represented humankind to God, but Elijah was *not* a priest; he was a prophet, and prophets represented God to humankind! Something very strange is going on here. God is going to give another glimpse to fallen humankind of His ultimate plan of salvation, which has *nothing* to do with humankind's efforts to reach God and *everything* to do with God's reaching down to save humankind as the apostle Paul would summarize almost nine hundred years later: "But God demonstrates His own love toward us, in that while we were still sinners, Christ died for us" (Romans 5:8).

Scripture is so amazingly deep and complex, and intertwined and perfect. We'll explore it further tomorrow.

THURSDAY

"For our God is a consuming fire" (Hebrews 12:28).

The battle is on, in front of all the children of Israel, as recorded in 1 Kings 18, and this amazing event will answer our queries regarding the Passover lamb: why *roasted*, and why *entirely consumed*? (After this, we'll examine why the lamb was to be eaten *intact*.)

Here's Elijah's challenge: Both parties will offer a bull as a sacrifice to their god. They will cut the animal up (note the difference here versus the lamb) and place it on wood. "But, put no fire under it" (v. 23). Wow, who does that? The children of Israel didn't; they had the fire on the bronze altar in the court of the temple continuously burning, on top of which they placed the animals. Humans were initiating the means of temporary remission of their sins by fueling the fire from below.

But God told Elijah to challenge the false prophets to something completely unheard of. "Then you [the prophets of Baal] call on the name of your gods, and I will call on the name of the Lord; and the God who answers by *fire*, He is God" (v. 24; emphasis added). This time God Himself would initiate the *consuming fire* from *above* to satisfy His righteous judgment on the people. And the people were all in: "It is well spoken," they said.

I think the prophets of Baal knew they were doomed from the start. Their only hope would be if Elijah also failed. But they gave it their best; they leaped and shouted and cried and even cut themselves to the point that "the blood gushed out on them" (v. 28), for a good six hours, from 9:00 a.m. until 3:00 p.m. (trust me), with Elijah making fun of them the whole time. "But there was no voice, no one answered, no one paid attention" (v. 29).

Now it was Elijah's turn, but we're out of time for this morning. We'll end the week in grand fashion tomorrow as what is about to happen will be truly amazing and the key to our healing.

FRIDAY

Hey, it's Friday the thirteenth! *Who cares?* We're not superstitious followers of Baal but redeemed followers of the Most High God, and "This is the day the Lord has made; we will rejoice and be glad in it" (Psalm 118:24).

"Then Elijah said to all the people, 'Come near to me'" (1 Kings 18:30). I just love that short little phrase because Elijah is speaking for God, and He is drawing His wayward children in as their undeserved deliverance from the long drought is near, and what is about to happen on Mount Carmel will be a foreshadowing of all humankind's deliverance from the curse of sin on Mount Calvary more than eight hundred years later. The prophet rebuilds the old stone altar to the Lord that had previously been destroyed by the idol worshippers, but before he places the wood with the cut-up bull on top of it, he does a distinctly unusual thing: he digs out a small trench around the altar, like a moat. It can only hold about four gallons of water, but keep in mind that there has been no rain or even dew for over three years; water is super scarce. Even given that, Elijah orders the people to douse the sacrifice with four waterpots three times so that the sacrifice, wood, and altar are drenched and the trench is filled with water. Wow! Talk about showing up those false prophets. Elijah knew what the apostle

Paul knew, that our God is "able to do exceedingly, abundantly above all that we can ask or think" (Ephesians 3:20).

And then at exactly 3:00 p.m. (trust me), Elijah prays, and God answers spectacularly! We gave the verses, namely, 1 Kings 18:36–38, earlier this week. The *fire* of the Lord comes from on high and absolutely *consumes* the sacrifice, the wood, the altar (remember, it was made of stone), the ground, and all the water that was around it—*all of it*! *That* is why the sacrificial lamb of the first Passover had to be *roasted* and *entirely consumed*.

But there's so much more to this symbolism. Next week we'll contrast Mount Carmel with Mount Calvary and see the major difference in what happened to the sacrifice at the latter and why, because of that difference, healing is part of the atonement. We'll actually prove that next week.

WEEK

MONDAY

Before leaving Mount Carmel, I want to make a couple of observations regarding the Passover lamb and Elijah's sacrifice of the bull. Going back to Exodus 12, we see that the lamb was to be roasted in fire just as the bull was, although with the lamb, the fire was man-made and came from below, whereas with the bull, the fire was God-sent and came from above. For me, this is a beautiful contrast of human effort to please God, which seems so right yet will never succeed, versus God's unmerited favor toward us, known as *grace*, which is all-consuming and relentless.

But I also see another similar type here, and it has to do with the water. Remember this command regarding the Passover lamb? "Do not eat it raw, nor boiled at all with *water*, but roasted in fire" (Exodus 12:9; emphasis added). What's that all about?

Now let me first interject that this entire series, as stated in the title, is based on my *musings*, or interpretations, of scripture—that's all. As stated previously, I'm not a Bible scholar by training; I'm a medical doctor. I may be wrong about a lot of things, but every one of these writings is birthed out of a desire to get it right and be consistent with the "whole counsel of God." I know I'm blessed by these Scriptures. My point? It's perfectly acceptable to disagree with me.

The fact that *water* is specifically mentioned in both Exodus 12 and 1 Kings 18 strikes me as significant. Here's my view: Water is used to symbolize many different things in the Bible, but the symbolism that I think is in play here, which is the most consistent with the rest of the narrative, is that water represents, once again, human effort. To support this view, let's look at the amazing conversation that occurred, interestingly at night, between one of the Pharisees, Nicodemus, and Jesus, recorded for us in John chapter 3. We'll explore that tomorrow morning, and after that we'll get to the promised, and super important, contrast between Mount Carmel and Mount Calvary. You are so patient!

TUESDAY

Nicodemus was an interesting New Testament character, a Pharisee (a devout expert in the Law), and "ruler of the Jews" (John 3:1) who sensed early on that Jesus was no imposter but that His power came from God. Nicodemus had questions for this "teacher," but he didn't want to be associated with Him, at least not yet, so he "came to Jesus by night" (v. 2). In the following Scripture, Jesus is explaining the mystery of salvation, of spiritual rebirth, of reviving that part of us lost in the Fall, and restoring our communion with our Creator God. In short, He's telling Nicodemus he must be "born again" (v. 3). We pick up the narrative there.

"Nicodemus said to Him, 'How can a man be born when he is old? Can he enter a second time into his mother's womb and be born?' Jesus answered, 'Most assuredly, I say to you, unless one is born of *water and the Spirit*, he cannot enter the kingdom of God. That which is born of the flesh is flesh, and that which is born of the Spirit is spirit'" (John 3:5–6; emphasis added).

Jesus is contrasting the water of natural birth, of our carnal nature, with the dormant spiritual nature in every one of us, which can only be "born" when we accept Him as our Savior and our spirit is renewed. Water is associated with human effort here, and I think that's the idea in Exodus 12—the command *not* to boil the lamb with *water*—and in 1 Kings 18, where the water is completely absorbed and consumed by the fire of God from above, as our weak, imperfect human efforts to do right and save ourselves will have *no part* in God's plan of salvation for us! Wow! I think that's pretty neat.

But now we turn our attention to something I think is of paramount importance to our Christian faith, and it has to do with the total *consumption* of the sacrifices in Exodus 12 (the intact lamb) and 1 Kings 18 (the cut up-bull) by the *righteous judgment fire* of God. This is *so* important that we won't race through it this morning, but I will give the key verses for tomorrow: John 19:28–30. Have a great day.

WEDNESDAY

It's 3:00 p.m. on the first Good Friday, and "after this, Jesus, knowing that *all things were now accomplished*, that the Scripture might be fulfilled, said, 'I thirst!' Now a vessel full of sour wine was sitting there; and they filled a sponge with sour wine, put it on hyssop, and put it to His mouth. So when Jesus had received the sour wine, He said, *'It is finished!'* And bowing His head, He gave up His spirit" (John 19:28–30; emphasis added).

Jesus, the sacrificial Lamb of God, was lifted up onto the cross at 9:00 a.m., six hours earlier, the time of the morning sacrifice. Then from 12:00 noon until 3:00 p.m. (the time of the evening sacrifice), he fulfilled His own prophecy, found in John 12:32, which we explained previously: "And if I, if I am lifted up from the earth, will draw all [judgment] to Myself."

And that He did. *All* the *righteous judgment fire* of God, *justly* deserved by the rebellious human race, fell on Jesus Christ over a period of three hours, a scene so horrible that God turned off the lights of the whole earth so no person could see:

"Now it was about the sixth hour [noon], and there was darkness over all the earth until the ninth hour [3:00 p.m.]" (Luke 23:44).

All of our sin and its consequences, such as disease, depression, disability, anxiety, despair, inappropriate anger, poverty, jealousy, and addiction—*all of it*—was *fully absorbed and consumed* bodily by Jesus Christ. It was fully exhausted on Him. And here's the *fact* that you must get, and get deeply: *After this*, Jesus was *still alive*. He wasn't consumed by the judgment fire; the judgment fire was consumed by Him! He had enough strength still in Him to "*cry out in a loud voice*" (Luke 23:46; emphasis added) those three awesome words that we must *never* forget: "*It is finished!*"

Do you realize what that means? Seriously, do you? Previously God's righteous judgment had never even come close to being exhausted on the animal sacrifices; that was obvious as the remission of the sins of His people was only temporary, and just for His chosen people, not the whole human race. But now—*but now*—there is *no more* judgment left for those who believe in Jesus Christ. He took it all upon Him, so you don't have to! The price has been *paid in full*, and not just for forgiveness of sin (as awesome as that is), but also for all healing, as there is another *huge* difference between the Passover lamb and Jesus that we will address tomorrow, which will *seal* this healing thing I've been proclaiming once and for all.

I know I'm way over, but I did not feel led to break this apart; it's simply too important. Thank you.

THURSDAY

We've been dwelling on the first Passover feast, which was to be kept each year as "an everlasting ordinance," just before the enslaved children of Israel left Egypt (the Exodus) and headed toward Mount Sinai on their way to the Promised Land. It was there that a paradigm shift would occur in how God dealt with His lost humans, and although necessary, it would not be pleasant. However, before that, God gave us this beautiful and reassuring glimpse of our final salvation, and it all revolved around an innocent one-year-old lamb. We've seen how the *blood* of that lamb was used to protect and "cover" the sins of the Israelites (an atonement) and how the *body* had to be *roasted in fire* and *entirely consumed*. I tied that into our healing—but you may not be convinced. No worries; I've saved the most compelling and convincing argument for including our physical healing as part of the Atonement of Jesus Christ on the cross for last!

There was one more regulation regarding the preparation of the lamb: it was to be eaten *intact*; it was not to be *broken*. Specifically, there was one part of the body that was involved. Let's go back to Exodus 12: "Nor shall you break one of its *bones*" (v. 46; emphasis added).

Why not? Let's go back now to Mount Calvary:

"But when they came to Jesus and saw that He was already dead, they did not break His legs. … For these things were done that the Scripture should be fulfilled, 'Not one of His bones shall be broken'" (John 19:33, 36).

Wow, what an awesome *comparison* between the Passover lamb and Jesus, and fulfillment of a prophecy made fourteen hundred years earlier. But there's an even more awesome *contrast* we have to acknowledge, because although the innocent baby lamb was not to be broken in any way, our innocent Savior, besides His skeleton, *was to be broken* and terribly so. Look at this revelation Isaiah was given of what the weight of sin had done to our precious Jesus's body:

"Many people were shocked when they saw Him. His appearance was so damaged, He did not look like a man. His form was so changed, they could barely tell He was a human" (Isaiah 52:14 NCV).

Think about that today, if you can. This is why I bristle when I hear folks (especially pastors) refer to "cheap grace," whatever that means. They have no idea.

Tomorrow, what this brokenness means for us.

FRIDAY

"For I received from the Lord that which I also delivered to you; that the Lord Jesus on the same night in which He was betrayed took bread; and when He had given thanks, He *broke* it and said, 'Take, eat; this is *my body* which is *broken* for *you*; do this in remembrance of Me'" (1 Corinthians 11:23–24 NKJV; emphasis added).

Now notice I gave the Bible translation I have been primarily using, namely, the New King James Version, which is basically the King James Version (from the year 1611) in Modern English. Your Bible may say something different. It's very important to get this scripture right. A very commonly used more recent translation of the Bible, the *New International Version* (NIV), puts it this way:

"This is my body, which is for you; do this in remembrance of me."

No "take, eat" and no "broken" (not to mention no capitalization of references to Jesus). This is significant. Why the difference?

The NIV uses the NU-text of the Greek New Testament, which is based on more recently found manuscripts from Alexandria, Egypt, which actually predate the manuscripts used by the King James translators. So the logical conclusion was that the older manuscripts would be more accurate, but that does not appear to me to be the case, and not just in this circumstance. Check out Micah 5:2, a beautiful prophecy of our Savior:

"But you, Bethlehem Ephrathah, though you are little among the thousands of Judah, yet out of you shall come forth to Me the One to be Ruler in Israel, whose goings forth are from of old, from *everlasting*" (NKJV; emphasis added).

But look at how the NIV ends this verse: "whose origins are of old, from *ancient times*" (emphasis added).

Huge difference. Ancient things still have a beginning; Jesus does not. He always has been and always will be—*everlasting*.

Leaving out the very important fact that Jesus's *body* was *broken* for us completely obscures the meaning of Holy Communion. We'll dive deeper into this next week. In the meantime, have a great weekend.

20
WEEK

MONDAY

So this week we will discuss what I truly believe is a super undervalued aspect of our Christian walk, and that is Holy Communion. It has everything to do with our physical healing as believers, and that's why Satan has really tried (and to a large degree has succeeded) in dumbing down the significance and misrepresenting the purpose of one of only two holy sacraments we are asked to observe as believers and the only one we are asked to observe "often." (The other, water baptism, is a onetime event.)

Everything for us, and I mean everything, was accomplished at the cross: our forgiveness from sin, our righteous standing before God, and our physical and emotional healing while alive on this earth. Jesus wanted to make sure we *never* took that for granted, that we never undervalued the cross: "For as often as you eat this bread and drink this cup, you proclaim the Lord's death till He comes" (1 Corinthians 11:26).

We've shown how the old covenant sacrificial animals were effective in the temporary remission of sin for God's people, but they were not made to suffer for the people before being humanely sacrificed. No, they were treated extremely well because they had to be "without blemish" (Exodus 12:5). Not so with Jesus Christ. No, He was to suffer as no other.

"Surely He has born our griefs and carried our sorrows; yet we esteemed Him stricken, smitten by God, and afflicted. But He was wounded for our transgressions, He was bruised for our iniquities, the chastisement for our peace was upon Him, and by His stripes, we are healed" (Isaiah 53:4–5).

There are many more Old Testament prophecies regarding the suffering Messiah, and that suffering, that breaking of the precious body of Jesus

Christ, served *only* one purpose, and it wasn't to blot out our sins. His shed blood accomplished that. If that was all He had to do, there would just be one element in Communion: the cup.

But there are two elements, thank God. The unleavened bread, symbolizing the broken body of Christ, is the one most misunderstood. We'll point out some amazing truths regarding that element this week. Stay tuned. I've come to see 1 Corinthians 11 as the best-kept secret in the Bible.

TUESDAY

The apostle Paul was grieved with the church at Corinth. He had previously instructed them in the proper observation of the Lord's Supper (also known as Holy Communion and the Eucharist), but they were not paying heed; they were abusing it. They were treating it as a meal, and coming to it hungry, and drinking to the point of intoxication (1 Corinthians 11:17–22).

So Paul was determined to make it *clear* to them the absolute importance and significance of this sacrament and the very negative consequences of not observing it properly. That's what he did in verses 23–34 of this amazing chapter.

The problem is (and you'll have to hear me out on this because what I'm going to say will, no doubt, go against what you've been told), this passage of scripture is difficult and, I believe, has been misconstrued such that what is to be a beautiful and affirming ceremony is often viewed as insignificant or, much worse, negative and condemning in nature. And remember this: if you are a believer, a follower of Jesus Christ, you are not *ever* to be under condemnation. It is *never* from the Lord.

"There is therefore now no condemnation to those who are in Christ Jesus, who do not walk according to the flesh, but according to the Spirit" (Romans 8:1).

Remember what we just covered about the *complete* absorption of *all* of God's righteous judgment by Jesus Christ on the cross? What judgment for sin is therefore left for you? This is why this portion of scripture we're about to dissect is so difficult, because it uses the words *judge, judged,* and *judgment* four times. It can give the impression (and this is how I was raised) that a Christian could actually come under the righteous judgment of God once again, to the point of *bringing* disease and even death upon themselves if they take Communion "in an unworthy manner." Not true. Simply not true. Tomorrow I'll give the Scripture in the NKJV. Please read it over—1 Corinthians 11:27–34—and see what you think. Trust me, this is very important stuff. It will forever change the way you take Communion and experience healing.

WEDNESDAY

> Therefore whoever eats this bread or drinks this cup of the Lord in an unworthy manner will be guilty of the body and blood of the Lord. But let a man examine himself, and so let him eat of the bread and drink of the cup. For he who eats and drinks in an unworthy manner eats and drinks *judgment* to himself, *not discerning* the Lord's *body.* For this reason, *many* are weak and sick among you, and many sleep. For if we would *judge* ourselves, we would *not be judged.* But when we *are judged,* we are chastened by the Lord, that we may not be *condemned with the world.* Therefore, my brethren, when you come together to eat, wait for one another. But if anyone is hungry, let him eat at home, lest you come together for *judgment.* And the rest I will set in order when I come. (1 Corinthians 11:27–34; emphasis added)

Wow! There it is. Paul is boldly addressing major errancy in the Corinthian church. And remember, this proclamation of "judgment" is written to Christians, to believers. Kind of scary, isn't it? I used to think so, but I was always unsettled about this portion of Scripture because it just didn't align well with what I knew of the heart of God and His whole counsel, which is, in short, the Gospel.

So I sought the Lord for clarity, and this is what I now know: Paul is showing us that the Christians of this first-century church were *missing out* on all of the benefits and blessings provided already for them in the Atonement by not properly understanding what the *broken body* of Jesus Christ represented for their health and well-being while living on this earth. They were settling for living as nonbelievers, as if they were still under the curse of condemnation brought by original sin. That's why they were sick and weak and dying prematurely! In short, they were not "discerning the Lord's body" (v. 29).

How the Lord led me to that way of thinking was by directing me to look at the original Greek, because remember, the original manuscripts of the Bible, written in Hebrew and Greek, are what were inspired by the Holy Spirit; the translations we use are actually not (although it is right to use them, and they serve us well). Tomorrow we'll explain this further. We'll also look at a guy named Bill Mounce. Have a great day.

THURSDAY

Bill Mounce is a modern Greek scholar and pastor, and he had a novel idea years ago. Instead of the previous "interlinear" word-for-word translations of the Greek New Testament into English with the text in Greek and underneath that text (interlinear) the English translation, he *reversed* that order and had the text in English and the supporting Greek words underneath. The result is called the Mounce Reverse-Interlinear New Testament, and I like it. Here's 1 Corinthians 11:27–32, which we gave in the NKJV yesterday, in this translation:

> Whoever eats this bread and drinks this cup of the Lord in
> an unworthy manner will be guilty of the body and blood
> of the Lord. A person should *examine* (dokimazo) himself,
> then, and *so eat* of the bread and drink of the cup. For the
> one who eats and drinks *without discerning* (diakrino) the
> *body* eats and drinks *judgment* (krima) on himself. That
> is why many of you are weak and sick, and quite a few are
> dead. *But*, if we *had been examining* (diakrino) ourselves,

we would *not* come under *judgment* (krino). But when we are *judged* (krino) by the Lord, we are being corrected by discipline, so that we will *not* be *condemned* (katakrino) *along with the world.* (emphasis added)

This was very helpful to me. Here's what the Lord showed me: We as believers are to do the *examining* or *discerning* of the *meaning* of the Lord's broken body at Communion; we are not to be "judging" ourselves. If we do that "discerning," that is, if we remember that His body was broken exclusively for our healing, then we will *not* be allowing the "judgment" righteously deserved by the nonbelieving world (sickness, weakness, etc.) to come upon us; we will *not* be "condemned" along with the world. If we *don't* do that, we are opening ourselves up to those things. That's where the loving *discipline* of the Lord comes into play, to get us back on track and to refocus us on the cross of Jesus Christ and what He accomplished for us there (the Atonement). The words *diakrino* (to discern/recognize) and *krino* (to judge) are different words, but both translate as "judge[d]" in verse 31 in both the KJV and NKJV. That makes all the difference in the world! Do you see this?

Really chew on this today. Isn't this making Holy Communion more amazing and pertinent?

FRIDAY

So we've really been diving deep into the significance of the Passover lamb, correlating it with the body of Jesus Christ and showing, scripturally, that it was a *preview* of how the suffering and brokenness of His body *purchased* our healing at the cross; it became part of the atonement. This feast of the Passover was observed for fourteen hundred years by the Jews, including Jesus, and it subsequently became known as the Lord's Supper. Jesus bestowed on this observance even greater importance, instituting it as one of our two sacraments as believers and making it *clear* that the bread represents His broken body, given for us. This was now a new covenant as the first Passover lamb was *not* broken and there was no atonement for healing in the old covenant. Jesus expected us to observe this sacrament often, to focus our thoughts and desires on Him and what He accomplished in the Atonement, because that is, in short, what it means to be a Christian—to believe that Jesus Christ was who He said He was and did what He said He did. And there's so much He accomplished at the cross: forgiveness of sin, healing of our physical bodies, our minds, and our emotions, and imparting His righteousness to us. As we read in 2 Corinthians 5:21, "For He [God] made Him [Jesus] who knew no sin to be sin for us, that we might become the *righteousness* of God in Him" (emphasis added).

Satan, the "accuser of the brethren" (Revelation 12:10), *really* doesn't want us to know this. He has managed to distort and twist the truths of Holy Communion such that relatively few Christians fully understand just what it represents. We dutifully observe it, usually once a month in church, and we know it has to do with remembering Jesus's death and our salvation from sin. This in and of itself is truly awesome, but Communion means so much more than that as I've endeavored to show.

Satan accomplishes his goal in two ways, to my way of thinking. In the first circumstance, Holy Communion becomes a ritual; we just go through the motions and don't *discern*, or contemplate, its true meaning. For instance, the last time I had Communion in my own church—and it's a vibrant, Jesus-loving church—absolutely no explanation was given prior to observing it. Time was short, and it had to be accomplished before the second service. I get it, there are practical concerns that come into play, but the *last* thing to short-change is this ceremony that Jesus put such emphasis on and that is crucial to living an abundant Christian life.

The second attack of the enemy on the Lord's Supper is much worse and sinister. We'll address that next time.

WEEK 21

MONDAY

We start a new week; September is over. We will finally end our extended time on the Passover this week and then head out from Egypt to Mount Sinai, but first I want to relate how I was raised to take Communion, as it was distorted and harmful. The Lord's Supper (my favorite term for it) was certainly honored and observed in my church, but it was a very somber and self-reflecting (and therefore self-condemning) "celebration." We were told to "take stock" of our Christian life and "make sure we were worthy" to partake. We had to "make ourselves right with God," whatever that means, or else we would cause sickness, or something even worse, to come upon us. I was always puzzled by this obligation on my part because even as a young boy I knew that if I could actually "make myself right with God," there would be no need for a Savior, no need for the cross, no need for Holy Communion.

But I dutifully tried anyway, and I always realized, of course, that I wasn't "worthy" to partake, yet I did so as not to be embarrassed. I always left church worried that I had done something very wrong. Do you see why Satan is called "the accuser of the brethren"? This was all because of the misinterpretation of 1 Corinthians 11:27–34 as we've attempted to explain previously. What was meant by our Lord to be a beautiful and *affirming* actual *celebration* was a scary and depressing obligation to me. Thank God I've been delivered from that errant thinking. I now absolutely *love* taking the Lord's Supper because I realize (*discern*) its true meaning: that through this sacrament we *remember* what Jesus Christ did *for us* on the cross (forgiveness of sin, righteousness, and *healing*). Just as we couldn't *save* ourselves when we were lost, but had to rely fully on Jesus, we can't *live* an abundant Christian life without fully relying on the cross; we still have to go back to the Atonement every day. That's what Communion reminds us of, and that's why we are to do it often.

I'll disclose something else that you may find sacrilegious: You don't have to wait until the first Sunday to take the Lord's Supper. You don't even have to be in church! Who is Paul writing to in 1 Corinthians 11, pastors? No, he's writing to Christians, and I would point out that the first Lord's Supper wasn't held in a synagogue or the temple but in a private room. And the first Passover was celebrated in the home. Yes, my family and I take Communion at home! Often. And it's a beautiful and empowering thing. We try to be a bit authentic by using kosher grape juice and matzah unleavened flatbread; it's just a really neat family custom. Nothing magical about it, but it is what our Lord asked us to do. I fully believe that frequently reminding ourselves of the healing provided for our physical bodies in the Atonement is worthwhile.

There, we've covered everything I had on my heart regarding Passover. New topic tomorrow.

TUESDAY

So today we start back on the road as we survey God's amazing plan of salvation for the fallen human race. He is working this out through the descendants of believing Abraham, the children of Israel, who are about to bust out from four hundred years of bondage in Egypt. The Passover has been accomplished, and the result is that they (about two million strong) are leaving perfectly healthy and strong and rich (I'm not exaggerating as we'll see). They are about to experience the pure, unmerited grace of God for the next seven weeks or so as they travel to Mount Sinai. This is all described in Exodus 13–17, which presents a beautiful example of how things are supposed to be with our complete dependence on our heavenly Father, just as Adam and Eve related to the Lord God in the garden before the Fall. Hundreds of years later, the psalmist remembered this brief period of time in the history of his people:

"He also brought them out with *silver* and *gold*, and there was *none feeble* among His tribes. Egypt was glad when they departed because the fear of them had fallen upon them. He spread a cloud for a covering, and fire to give light in the night. The people asked, and He brought quail, and satisfied them with the bread of heaven. He opened the rock, and water gushed out; it ran in dry places like a river" (Psalm 105:37–41; emphasis added).

Wow! Isn't that awesome? We'll go more deeply into the details of this fascinating but altogether too brief journey to Mount Sinai over the next few mornings, but first I want to give a few very instructive Scriptures as to why this period of grace and divine intervention all came crashing down just fifty days later:

"Then all the people answered together and said, 'All that the Lord has spoken *we will do*'" (Exodus 19:8; emphasis added).

"And all the people answered with one voice and said, 'All the words which the Lord has said *we will do*'" (Exodus 24:3; emphasis added).

"And they said, 'All that the Lord has said *we will do, and be obedient*'" (Exodus 24:7; emphasis added).

"For it is *God* who *works* in you, both to *will* and to *do* for His good pleasure" (Philippians 2:13; emphasis added).

Hmm, interesting contrast, eh? The first three verses: old covenant; the last one: new covenant. More tomorrow.

WEDNESDAY

O to grace how great a debtor
Daily I'm constrained to be.
Let that goodness, like a fetter,
Bind my wandering heart to Thee.
—"Come Thou Fount of Every Blessing," an eighteenth-
century hymn by Robert Robinson

The verses I gave yesterday morning are to be pondered as we embark on this brief journey of unrestricted grace and mercy experienced by the children of Israel as they leave Egypt and head for the Promised Land via the Sinai Peninsula. They will see unprecedented miracles on their behalf, and supernatural protection and supply, but it will not last. What is to follow will be diametrically opposed.

So we have to ask why. What is this time of unimputed sin and unrestricted grace proving to the universe, intently watching all of this play out on this beautiful orb of ours? It seems as though God is completely ignoring the fact that His children have been separated from Him by sin as if He were going to "look the other way" and bless them anyway, show them unconditional grace. He is showing His heart, His true nature, which is love.

But wait a minute! If He doesn't justly and righteously deal with the sin problem, He is no longer just and righteous and the "foundations of His throne" (Psalm 97:2) are shattered. He knew that, but humankind and the universe had to see that, too. Here's another one of my little foundational sayings (for me) that sums up this part of the journey:

If the sin debt has not been paid, grace is ineffective.

That's what we'll see transpire as the unredeemed children of Israel couldn't respond appropriately to the grace shown them; they would actually clamor to be held responsible for their actions and behaviors, to have *rules* to follow. Sin would start to count again, to show humankind that they couldn't keep the rules and that a Savior was needed to pay the penalty for their sin so they could benefit from God's grace. That's where we are today. *Our* sin debt *has* been paid, and God's reckless grace is sufficient for us and is what keeps us close to Him; it's what restrains us as the foregoing hymn lyrics so beautifully state.

So it is worthwhile to spend some time on this brief grace-filled era because it shows us the heart of our loving God. We'll start that process tomorrow.

THURSDAY

We're about to take off from Egypt and bask in God's unconditional grace for a while, then tackle the genesis of the giving of the Law at Mount Sinai. But first, a little more about this thing called grace, as this is what the Gospel of Jesus Christ is all about; it is the One Gospel. Paul makes that clear in Galatians chapter 1. *Twice* he says, "If anyone preaches any other gospel to you … let him be accursed" (Galatians 1:8, 9). God takes this very seriously. Look at John 1:17: "For the Law was given through Moses, but Grace *and* Truth came through Jesus Christ" (emphasis added).

Note that the word *truth* is intimately associated with grace, not Law. Now the Law (and we're talking about the Ten Commandments) is indeed true, but it doesn't represent ultimate truth, as it actually exists on a carnal level and is base by nature. The grace of God manifested by Jesus Christ and the Atonement fulfilled the Law and superseded it immensely for God was now dealing with us on a spiritual level as the spirit nature of humans was awakened by believing in Jesus. Grace is *so* much higher than Law. This will all be shown scripturally over time. But for now I want to relay a personal story that helped me to understand just what grace does for us as believers if we just let it.

You know, I really do jump around a lot in this little treatise we started back in May. It's not my fault. Here's how I have come to see these writings: there are sometimes seemingly incongruent pieces that we are painting on a big canvas, at different places and different times, but it will all come together when we view it as a whole, like a portrait. I want that portrait to be of a face. And I want the face to be that of Jesus, "for the Light of the Knowledge of the Glory of God … is in the Face of Jesus Christ" (2 Corinthians 4:6). Amen. The story tomorrow.

FRIDAY

"The goodness of God leads you to repentance" (Romans 2:4).

Earlier in my career, I was a navy doctor, stationed at Jacksonville Naval Air Station in Florida. My parents didn't live far. I would take our firstborn young son with me on occasion to see them. The route took me through a couple of very small towns. It was a two-lane highway, 55 mph speed limit, but 35 mph through the towns, which consisted of just two or three houses, it seemed to me. They were that small.

One afternoon I was driving back home with my son and simply wasn't paying attention. I went flying at 55 mph through one of the towns and was pulled over by the state police. No one likes that, but I learned long ago not to make excuses for my own mistakes. I apologized to the trooper and took full responsibility. I was guilty; I hadn't obeyed the rules.

And you know what? He let me go with just a warning. Totally undeserved grace, totally unmerited. I deserved punishment but was shown forgiveness instead.

The "cheap grace" folks make the argument that Christians like me, who are always focused on the grace of God, use that as an excuse to go out and sin like crazy and live just like the world, knowing that we're already forgiven; that we are given over to licentiousness.

But let me tell you what *really* happens when you've truly experienced the overwhelming grace and goodness of God. This was made real to me in the context of the foregoing story. I would pass through that same stretch of road many times since that incident. Want to guess how fast I was driving? The detractors of grace would say I would speed even more since there is no punishment. No, that wasn't the case, even though I never again saw a police car there. No, I would actually drive *less* than the speed limit; I was just so *thankful* I had been forgiven the first time. I was "constrained" by grace, as that old hymn I quoted earlier this week says. That's how it works, at least that's the way it's supposed to work.

I promise to leave Egypt and start our journey next week. But this was a good way to end this week. I leave you with the chorus of a modern good old grace song:

Some may call it foolish and impossible,
But for every heart it rescues, it's a miracle.
It's nothing less than scandalous,
This love that took our place.
Just call it what it is.
Call it grace.
—"Call It Grace," Unspoken

22
WEEK

MONDAY

So, as promised, this week we join the children of Israel as they are miraculously led out of bondage in Egypt, on their way to the Promised Land (Canaan), starting with Exodus 13. But first they must head south to Mount Sinai, also known as the "mountain of God," where God originally spoke to Moses through the burning bush, commanding him to lead His people out of Egypt and back to "this mountain" to worship Him (Exodus 3:12).

The people are basking in God's unrestrained grace. Although previously slaves, they would leave Egypt perfectly healthy and rich. Remember Psalm 105:37? "Then He led the Israelites out; they carried silver and gold, and *all* of them were *healthy* and *strong*" (GNT; emphasis added).

Now think about that. Wouldn't there have been lots of old men and women in that bunch? Wouldn't many of them have been feeble and weak and immobile? Of course, but remember, they had just observed Passover and were allowed to experience what was going to be obtained for all of us at the cross, namely, deliverance from the curse of sin and all its friends, like disease, weakness, and premature aging. The result was perfect health and strength for *all* of them!

That got me thinking, because what they experienced on credit, we now have already paid for! What should that mean for us? As I've already explained, healing of our physical bodies and minds is inherent in the Atonement, but what about this aging thing? This is becoming more relevant for me as I just turned sixty, yet quite honestly I don't feel any differently from when I was eighteen—not physically or mentally. So I researched this topic a bit to get a Biblical point of view. I think you'll find what I learned interesting and encouraging.

Even before we have taken *one step* out of Egypt, we're off on a diversion—and I love it! This will be a good one, and it will even further cement in your mind that I am absolutely crazy! I'll give some verses, and then I'll start my musings about them tomorrow:

"And the Lord said, 'My Spirit shall not strive with man forever, for he is indeed flesh; yet his days shall be one hundred and twenty years'" (Genesis 6:3).

"The days of our lives are seventy years; and if by reason of strength they are eighty years" (Psalm 90:10).

"The older the man, the stronger he is" (Judges 8:21 NIRV).

"For this we say in the word of the Lord, that we who are living—who do remain over to the presence of the Lord—may not precede those asleep" (1 Thessalonians 4:15 YLT).

TUESDAY

Our current topic is the longevity of humankind. In antediluvian times (before the Flood), humans lived a very, very long time, averaging nine hundred years! But remember, we were created, probably, *never* to die. As we know, the Fall of Adam and Eve resulted in immediate spiritual death but gradual physical death (aging), so it would make sense that human beings would live a long time the nearer they were to original sin. The one who lived longest was Methuselah (969 years); he died just as the Flood started. (You could do the math in Genesis chapters 5 and 7. Methuselah was 187 when Noah's father, Lamech, was born to him, and Lamech was 182 when he had Noah, and Noah was 600 when the Flood started.) But men were terribly sinful and suffering greatly, so our merciful God limited their life span to 120 years in Genesis 6:3. This was to be the case *after* the Flood, and as I'll try to show, it is still the case today.

Now certainly after the Flood, some people did live a lot longer than 120 years; for instance, the patriarchs Abraham, Isaac, and Jacob all did. But these guys had an unusually close relationship with the Most High God (nonetheless it was way less intimate of a relationship than we have now as redeemed believers, praise God) and were the exception. Look at these more typical ages at death: Moses, 120; Joshua, 110; and Joseph, 110. Caleb was probably about that old when he died since he was as strong as a 40-year-old when he was 85 years old (see Joshua 14:6–12).

Well, you say, what about Psalm 90:10? Moses wrote that, and he said men were only to expect to live 70 to 80 years, even though he lived to be 120. What's going on there? And what he said was indeed the case. Did you know David lived only to the age of 70? And Solomon, he died at 60! Now I have a theory about that. Solomon had, according to scripture, 700 wives and 300 concubines (1 Kings 11:3). I think the only question we men have regarding that is "How did he last that long?" Just saying.

Here's how I look at that discrepancy between God's one hundred twenty and Moses's seventy to eighty years: God was not holding humankind responsible for sin at the time of His proclamation in Genesis; Moses was dealing with the state of humankind under the Law, which kept humanity in spiritual bondage (Paul called it the "ministry of death" in 2 Corinthians 3:7) and, I believe, shortened their life spans. Does that make sense? The overall life span for all American women is over eighty years now, but I would argue, based on scripture, that Christians living under grace, in whom sin does not have dominion (Romans 6:14), *should* expect a life span of around one hundred twenty years!

I know what you're thinking: (1) he's crazy, and (2) who'd want to live that long? I can't argue the former, but I will the latter…tomorrow morning.

WEDNESDAY

"Moses was one hundred and twenty years old when he died. His eyes were not dim nor his natural vigor diminished" (Deuteronomy 34:7).

Moses indeed lived under the Law; he is actually known as the Lawgiver, but of course he was just the messenger, and the Law did not limit his access to the grace of God. Look at Exodus 33:11: "So, the Lord spoke to Moses *face to face*, as a man speaks to his friend." And "the skin of his face shone while he talked with Him" (Exodus 34:29). He experienced the very presence of God, which is why he was so strong and vigorous and full of life at the age of 120 years. We don't have to settle with getting feeble and weak as we age; we can age *gracefully* (literally). Remember that Judges 8:21 verse from Monday? According to that, humans should actually get stronger as they age!

Here's why none of this is crazy: it is entirely thanks to Jesus Christ, His sacrifice on the cross, and His resurrection from the dead—His victory over sin and death. This next verse says it all:

"But if the Spirit of Him who raised Jesus from the dead *dwells in you*, He who raised Christ from the dead will also give *life to your mortal bodies* through His Spirit, who *dwells in you*" (Romans 8:11; emphasis added).

Do you see what I'm saying? Because the Holy Spirit *lives* in us, we should not fear living as long as the Lord wants us to in order to fulfill His purpose for our lives on this earth. And we should enjoy good health along the way. The point is not how long we can live; the point is that death and disease have *no grip* on us. We are to have an abundant life (John 10:10).

If you think these views of mine are extreme, just wait until tomorrow morning! It's going to get a lot more interesting as we dissect that other verse from Monday, 1 Thessalonians 4:15. And we'll take a look at an interesting New Testament character, mentioned only by Dr. Luke, who may have blown that 120 number right out of the water!

I just love this stuff.

THURSDAY

"And behold, there was a man in Jerusalem whose name was Simeon, and this man was just and devout, *waiting* for the Consolation of Israel, and the Holy Spirit was *upon* him. And it had been revealed to him by the Holy

Spirit that he would not see death before he had seen the Lord's Christ"
(Luke 2:25–26; emphasis added).

He's mentioned only here, this Simeon character, and there are some
notable things about him. For one thing, he was *old*; he is known in Latin
as Simeon senex (old Simeon) and is referred to in early Christian poetry
and hymns as Aged Simeon. He may have been super old! Remember the
Septuagint we had mentioned earlier, the first translation of the Hebrew
Old Testament into Greek? Tradition holds that Simeon was one of the
seventy-two Jewish scholars who worked on this, and it was completed well
over a hundred years before the birth of Christ! He may have been close
to two hundred years old.

Stop! Before you delete this email, hear me out. Notice another thing Luke
tells us about Simeon: the Holy Spirit was *upon* him. *That's* the difference,
and it's why his life could have been extended, awaiting the First Coming
(Advent) of our Lord, which was so important to him.

This brings me to a pertinent aside: In the Old Testament, the Holy
Spirit could not *indwell*, or *live in*, believers like Simeon. He had not been
given to us yet; that would occur in Acts chapter 2 (also written by Luke).
So, He (the Spirit) would come and go. This is why David pleads, after
committing adultery with Bathsheba and having her husband killed, in
Psalm 51:11: "Do not cast me away from Your presence, and do not take
Your Holy Spirit from me."

But there seems to have been a more pervasive influence of the Holy Spirit
on Simeon, as was the case with our other long-living Old Testament saints
like Moses, Joshua, and Joseph. Is it now more plausible that he might have
been miraculously old? I see another awesome thing here: he was totally
focused on the coming of Jesus, His First Coming as a human baby, His
coming to be one of us and dwell with us and suffer and die for us. Simeon
had died to himself a long time earlier, I think, and had lost himself in our
Lord, and the years just flew by.

Wow! I'm so over this morning, but I've got more about Simeon, and
this beautiful woman named Anna who comes on scene just as Simeon is

leaving, and how all this ties in with us twenty-first-century believers who are looking for the *Second* Coming of our Lord. We will push on tomorrow.

FRIDAY

Surprisingly, we've spent the entire week on the topic of Christian longevity—what the Bible has to say about it. This started as an offshoot of the discussion about the supernatural vitality and health that *all* the children of Israel had at the time they left Egypt, and I'm arguing that this blessing is available to *all* believers today who have the Holy Spirit living in them. I honestly believe the Lord has ordained around 120 years for us—healthy years. But that may be the lower limit in this particular time that we are privileged to live in along the road of God's great plan of salvation. I have more explaining to do, and we won't finish this topic this week, but I'm pretty confident we'll finally get out of Egypt next week. It's all good. I, at least, am really enjoying this miniseries.

Let's finish Simeon first. Although he was really old, he was still in possession of a beautiful mind. Look at this amazing prophecy he gave to Mary regarding her six-week-old baby boy:

"Behold, this Child is destined for the fall and rising of many in Israel, and for a sign which will be spoken against (yes, a sword will pierce through your own soul also), that the thoughts of many hearts will be revealed" (Luke 2:34–35).

Wow! We still quote that. Simeon now exits the story, but one more caveat about him, regarding his name. The Hebrew root word for the name Simeon is *shama*, which means "to hear." Every Jew would have known exactly what Simeon's name meant. It was a reference to the Shema, Deuteronomy 6:4, which is their confession of faith, which they were to recite twice daily. It goes like this:

"Hear, O Israel: The Lord our God, the Lord is one! You shall love the Lord your God with all your heart, with all your soul, and with all your strength."

This was considered the greatest commandment in the Law according to Jesus (Matthew 22:35–37), and it represented the Law very well (note the prominence of "You shall"), but it was not representative of the heart of God. This way of thinking would be superseded by grace, which is all about what He *did* at the cross, not what we do to please Him on our own.

I say all that because as soon as Simeon leaves the Christ child in the temple, a woman named Anna comes in. There are some really neat things about her, not the least of which is her name. "Anna" is a derivative of the Hebrew name Hannah, which means—you guessed it—*grace*! This is a picture of grace supplanting Law. Don't you just love this Bible of ours? We will never be able to even scratch the surface of it.

We'll find out more about this woman next week, and at some point we'll leave Egypt. You might want to pack this weekend for the trip, which took only seven weeks in real time but which might take us a lot longer.

23
WEEK

MONDAY

"Now there was one, Anna, a prophetess, the daughter of Phanuel, of the tribe of Asher. She was of great age, and had lived with a husband seven years from her virginity; and this woman was a widow of eighty-four years, who did not depart from the Temple, but served God with fastings and prayers night and day. And coming in that instant she gave thanks to the Lord, and spoke of Him to all those who looked for redemption in Jerusalem" (Luke 2:36–38 NKJV).

"She was very old, having lived with her husband for seven years after her marriage, then as a widow for eighty-four years" (Luke 2:36–37 ISV).

"She was very old; she had lived with her husband seven years after her marriage, and then was a widow *until* she was eighty-four" (Luke 2:36–37 NIV; emphasis added).

Happy Columbus Day! (Is that still politically correct?) We are back to Anna and her blessing of the baby Jesus, and we have a discrepancy. Was she eighty-four or at least one hundred seven? I've been postulating that Simeon and Anna, both close to the Holy Spirit and looking eagerly forward to the First Coming of the Messiah, lived an unusually long time, and I'm about to compare that to our current day and age, but our good friend the *New International Version* of the Bible is again making things challenging, apparently because its translators didn't think Dr. Luke had his facts straight, as it would have been very unlikely that ninety-one years of Anna's life were accounted for *after* she got married, which would have probably made her at least one hundred seven at the time of Jesus's birth. So, instead of eighty-four years of widowhood, the NIV translators changed it to eighty-four years of life.

To my "whole counsel of God" way of thinking, an unusually old Anna fits *perfectly* with the narrative, which is that a Spirit-filled, Jesus-focused life can be very long—at least one hundred twenty years. As I've pointed out, Simeon and Anna were living under the Law and didn't have the benefit of *being* the "righteousness of God in Christ Jesus" (2 Corinthians 2:21). Yet they "remained" until their Lord came to earth.

So what does all this mean for us? We'll look at 1 Thessalonians 4:15–18 tomorrow morning. It's very interesting. And what it references could actually occur at any time!

TUESDAY

"Our beloved brother Paul, according to the wisdom given to him, has written to you, as also in all his epistles, speaking in them of these things, in which are some things *hard to understand*" (2 Peter 3:15–16; emphasis added).

It was the apostle Paul, a former expert in the Law and former Christian killer, whom Jesus chose to explain the full Gospel to, and he was tasked to present it to us in his letters to the church. Paul taught things previously unknown—"mysteries" (1 Corinthians 15:51). What we'll focus on now, as we finish up with examining the quality and longevity of the life we can expect as Christians, is one of those difficult to understand teachings, but it is scriptural and true and fits with the "whole counsel of God." It is also very exciting and encouraging. Here it is:

> For this we say to you by the word of the Lord, that we who are alive *and remain* until the coming of the Lord will by no means precede those who are asleep. For the Lord Himself will descend from heaven with a shout, with the voice of an archangel, and with the trumpet of God. And the dead in Christ will rise first. Then we who are alive *and remain* shall be caught up together with them in the clouds to meet the Lord in the air. And thus we shall always be with the Lord. Therefore comfort one another with these words. (1 Thessalonians 4:15–18; emphasis added)

This passage is *not* referring to the Second Coming of the Lord, when Jesus Christ returns to planet Earth, along *with* us (believers), to save His people and set up His kingdom on earth (see Zechariah 14). This event occurs before that, before the "great and awesome Day of the Lord" (Joel 2:31). Jesus Himself referenced it in John 14:2–3:

"In My Father's house are many mansions; if it were not so, I would have told you. I go to prepare a place for you. And if I go to prepare a place for you, *I will come again and receive you to Myself*; that where I am, there you may be also" (emphasis added).

Paul gave further details of this awesome event in 1 Corinthians 15:51–55. We refer to it as the Rapture, and although that word is not in the Bible, I like it because it emphasizes the joyous, ecstatic nature of this event when our Lord comes *for us* to pull us out of this earth and to Him, saving us from the righteous judgment that will follow on this earth. We are not to endure the Tribulation. Romans 5:9 makes that very clear:

"Much more then, having now been justified by His blood, we shall be *saved from wrath* through Him" (emphasis added).

So we've established today that this Rapture thing will occur at some point in human history, right? What it all means … tomorrow.

WEDNESDAY

We're discussing Paul's description of the Rapture given in 1 Thessalonians 4 and 1 Corinthians 15. It is then that the believers who have already died and whose spirits are already with the Lord in heaven ("absent from the body, present with the Lord" [2 Corinthians 5:8]) will receive their new, glorified, incorruptible bodies (1 Corinthians 15:52). Then those believers who are still alive on earth, who are seemingly differentiated into two groups, those who are *alive* and those who are *remaining*, will "be changed" in the "twinkling of an eye" and be simultaneously raised up from the earth and given their glorified bodies, to meet Jesus "in the air" and subsequently "always be with the Lord"! Wow!

But note that *"remain"* designation, which the *New International Version* translates as those "who are *left till the coming*" (yes, I do like the NIV at times). To me, that implies something unusual, as if these believers have been given a promise of an extension of their lives on this earth until Jesus Christ comes for them. Where did we see this sort of thing before? Yep, good *old* Simeon and Anna in Luke chapter 2, both close to the Holy Spirit and both *remaining* alive until they physically see their Savior in bodily form. And *so is it with us now*! From what I know of Bible prophecy and eschatology, I am confident that some of us believers alive today will not taste death until the Rapture. What an awesome thought!

So here's why I think that all this stuff I've gone over about *age* is *relevant*: I want us to see that *age* is *irrelevant*. Sure, we are going to get older each year, but we don't have to ever *be old* in the sense of being weak and incapable of doing all that our Lord has purposed for us to do; that is simply not scriptural and denies the power of the atonement. I mean that. I think we simply talk ourselves into "getting old" as if it's a foregone conclusion that one has to slow down and take it easy, etc. As a matter of fact, the concept of retirement is nowhere in scripture.

I hope this diversion hasn't offended you; that's not the purpose. And you don't have to believe any of it. You can choose to get old; that's very popular. It doesn't affect your position in Christ. But I do think of this gently sobering verse toward the very end of this great canon of Scripture we call the Bible, in Revelation 21:4, when we are forever reunited with our Lord: "And God will wipe away every tear from their eyes." I think we'll all have momentary tears when we realize just what *could* have been ours in Christ during our lives on this earth, but those tears will be very temporary. Amen.

I went on very long this morning, but I had to finish. Tomorrow morning, the train out of Egypt leaves the station.

THURSDAY

Now we continue on our journey through God's plan of salvation for humanity. We join the children of Israel, His chosen people, as they leave the bondage of Egypt and head for the Promised Land of Canaan, called that because it was the promise of God to believing Abraham that his descendants would possess that land. We've just observed the first Passover, and we have seen how the sacrificial lamb served as a beautiful, but imperfect, representation of our perfect sacrificial Lamb, Jesus Christ, on the cross.

Here's what we're going to concentrate on now: both these events, separated by fourteen hundred years, were followed by a fifty-day period that ushered in two of the most significant events in human history, the former full of condemnation and death, and the latter full of power and life. I want to start with three verses that, at first glance, may seem very disparate in nature because the first and second are separated by eight hundred years, and the second and third by six hundred years, and they are written by three different authors. The first was Moses, the *Law*giver. The second was Jeremiah, a great *prophet* of God. And the third was Dr. Luke, a *grace*-filled Gentile believer in Jesus Christ. But as a testimony to the complexity and beauty of the Word of God, they are actually all very related and complementary to each other. We'll start weaving them together tomorrow morning. Here's the verses; meditate on them today:

> And the Lord went before them by day in a pillar of cloud to lead the way, and by night in a pillar of fire to give them light, so as to go by day and night. (Exodus 13:21)

> Behold, the days are coming, says the Lord, when I will make a new covenant with the house of Israel and with the house of Judah—not according to the covenant that I made with their fathers in the day that I took them by the hand to lead them out of the land of Egypt, My covenant which they broke, though I was a husband to them, says the Lord. But this is the covenant that I will make with the house of Israel *after* those days, says the Lord: I will put My law in their minds, and write it on their hearts; and I will be their God, and they shall be My people. (Jeremiah 31:31–33; emphasis added)

When the Day of Pentecost had fully come. (Acts 2:1)

Have a great day.

FRIDAY

> You go before I know
> That You've gone to win my war.
> You come back with the head of my enemy.
> You come back and You call it my victory.
> Hallelujah, great Defender,
> So much better Your way.
> —"Defender," Rita Springer

This song captures the heart of God, and this was manifest in the pillar of cloud by day and the pillar of fire by night as the Lord went ahead of His people to provide for them and protect them from the enemy. It is a beautiful picture of the Father's love, but it is still so inferior to what we have today because, you see, the people were sinful; they were spiritually dead to God. He could not dwell *in* them because he is *righteous* and *just*. And God is Spirit, whereas humankind was entirely carnal. They weren't sinning *against* God as there were no subsequent rules from Him to break since the garden, but they were sinning. And remember, the whole universe was watching intently because these humans were still *lost*. I believe that only the Godhead knew the ultimate plan, and were executing it perfectly to maximize the final harvest of human souls.

So God could only be *physically* present with His people at this point in human history, not *spiritually*. Hence the great physical manifestations of His love that we will see on this fifty-day sojourn, like the pillars.

But God yearned for a better way, a new covenant. That's where the incredible prophecy of Jeremiah 31 comes in. He will live *in* our hearts and *in* our minds. And why would He be able to do that? Because, "I will forgive their iniquity, and their sin I will remember no more" (Jeremiah 31:34). Wow! The sacrifice of Jesus Christ on the cross allows for *complete* remission of sin as if it never existed, as if "everything sad has been made untrue." We can now directly commune with God. This was finalized fifty days *after* the Crucifixion. That's our last verse from yesterday, but it will have to wait until next week. I love this stuff!

24
WEEK

MONDAY

"When the Day of Pentecost had fully come" (Acts 2:1).

It's a new week. We're focused on the number fifty—two fifty-day periods of time separated by fourteen hundred years, both hugely important. They both start at Passover. We spent a good amount of time studying the significance of the first celebration, occurring on the night of the tenth plague on Egypt, followed immediately by the Exodus out of bondage. We will look closely at the fifty-day journey to Mount Sinai and at the significance of what happened there because it would go on to change how God would deal with humankind.

But first we're going to look at the realization of the promise Passover represented because Jesus Christ was crucified on Passover, AD 33, and something significant was going to happen fifty days later that would *allow* the victory Jesus won on Mount Calvary to be manifest in us believers. But here's something interesting that I puzzled over for years. Look at this verse:

"Until the day in which He was taken up, after He, through the Holy Spirit, had given commandments to the apostles whom He had chosen, to whom He also presented Himself alive after His suffering by many infallible proofs, being seen by them during *forty days* and speaking of the things pertaining to the kingdom of God" (Acts 1:2–3; emphasis added).

Yes, Jesus Christ in His resurrected, glorified body stayed on this earth for some forty days after Passover, ministering to His disciples. Wonderful! But why did He leave ten days (some say nine days) *before* Pentecost, at which time the promised Holy Spirit would come to indwell and empower the believers? Why leave them on their own without the Holy Spirit and without Him? For days! Why? Jesus was obviously concerned about what might happen during that time as He "commanded them not to depart from Jerusalem, but to wait for the Promise of the Father" (Acts 1:4).

The pat answers I found regarding this time difference didn't ring true to me; they weren't consistent with what I knew of the "whole counsel of God" (Acts 20:27), so I pushed the Lord further for an answer. And you know what? *Rats!* We're out of time. Tomorrow I'll share what He showed me.

TUESDAY

As we've discussed before, nothing in Holy Scripture is insignificant, and I wanted to know why Jesus Christ left His believers alone on earth for about ten days before the giving of the Holy Spirit on Pentecost. Why the delay between the Ascension of Jesus and the arrival of the Spirit? Every time in the past that I've sought the Lord (through the guidance of the Holy Spirit) for answers to these seemingly insignificant questions, the answer has been awesome. That was the case this time also as we shall presently see.

The reasons I had been told for this timing are as follows: (1) The number forty is of great significance in the Bible, so it is symbolic. And indeed the number is used a lot: forty days and nights of rain during the Great Flood; forty years of wandering in the wilderness for the children of Israel; forty days and nights of temptation for Jesus; etc. But these were all periods of trial or testing, and we're talking about the victorious, risen Christ. What was He being tested for at this point? He already passed all the tests with flying colors! And it may not have been exactly forty days anyway. Not a good explanation. (2) The disciples needed to spend time in fasting and prayer so as to take stock of themselves before they would be able to be filled with the Spirit. *Seriously?* The whole point of pretty much everything we've shown thus far is that human beings simply *cannot* "take stock" of themselves or prepare spiritually for anything. Remember, they didn't have the Holy Spirit yet, and now they didn't even have Jesus with them. They were vulnerable, and the Lord knew that. Therefore He had them "shelter in place" until "Pentecost had fully come."

So those explanations didn't sit right with me. I knew the fifty days were very important as it was the plan of this very ordered God of ours that the Spirit would be given the same day the Law was given, as a stark contrast. I didn't think the forty days was significant. Could it be that the original intent was for Jesus to stay with His followers the full fifty days, but something compelled Him to leave sooner? I knew He did not want to leave His beloved flock at all, so it must have been something pressing.

Now don't get me wrong; I wasn't fretting over this day and night, or anything like that, as it's not a foundational sort of thing, but I was perplexed. And then one day I found my wife's Bible lying randomly (yeah, right) open on the kitchen table, and I looked to see what she had been reading. It was Revelation chapter 12, which is a really neat chapter. I've read it lots before, but one verse just jumped out at me this time, and it was …

Wow! Where does the time go? See if you can guess which verse I'm talking about for tomorrow morning. Here's a hint: it has to do with the Ascension.

WEDNESDAY

"She bore a Child who was to rule all nations with a *rod of iron*. And her Child was *caught up* to God and His throne" (Revelation 12:5; emphasis added).

This is the verse that caught my eye. Immediately I thought of the Ascension of Jesus Christ. So, I thought, maybe what follows will shed some light onto why this Ascension event occurred when it did, several days before the Comforter would be sent.

First of all, is this verse actually referring to Jesus? As always, if we let the Holy Spirit guide us, the Bible will actually interpret itself. Look at this messianic psalm:

"I will declare the decree: the Lord has said to Me, You are My Son, today I have begotten You. Ask of Me, and I will give You the nations for your inheritance, and the nations of the earth for your possession. You shall break them with a *rod of iron*" (Psalm 2:7–8).

So, yep, this child is Jesus. The woman is Israel, as becomes obvious later in the chapter. Don't let this "ruling with a rod of iron" thing scare you; it's a good thing. When Jesus comes back the second time, it will be as righteous Judge and Ruler, and He will rule with His Word, which is strong (iron was the strongest known substance in Bible times) and immutable/unbending. Remember, God is righteous and just always. This righteous rule will be nothing like the heavy-handed unrighteous rule of today's tyrants and dictators. As you may have gathered, I am a fan of Bob Dylan (who, by the way, will be in heaven for sure; he's saved and a Jew). He wrote an awesome song entitled "When He Returns," and it starts like this: "The iron hand, it ain't no match for the iron rod." That's what he's talking about. Check out the rest of the lyrics. They are astounding.

But back to the narrative as we're getting to something even more astounding. The verse right after the Ascension verse in Revelation 12, verse 6, refers to persecuted Israel being divinely protected for forty-two months, which is three and a half years or one thousand two hundred sixty days. That's an obvious reference to the Great Tribulation, which has not occurred yet. But the Ascension has already occurred. So what gives? This is important, but we can't squeeze it in today. Next time.

THURSDAY

You know, I love how the Holy Spirit directs these musings in such a fresh way, like the wind blowing where it wishes as Jesus stated in John 3:8, but it may be confusing at times. So here's where we are: We are surveying the plan of salvation, setting a "sure foundation" for the cross and the Atonement, so that we can be more convinced of the need for the Atonement and believe more perfectly in the reality of what that Atonement accomplished for us, namely, remission of our sins, healing of our physical bodies and minds, and the gift of righteousness bestowed upon us as believers. We've worked

our way up to about twenty-six hundred years after Creation; the children
of Israel are just leaving Egypt and embarking on a fifty-day journey to
Mount Sinai. We're currently contrasting that fifty-day period with the
fifty days between the crucifixion of Jesus Christ and the arrival of the
Holy Spirit, our Comforter, on Pentecost in the year AD 33. We've noticed
that there is a ten-day gap in time between the Ascension of Jesus to heaven
and the arrival of the Holy Spirit on earth, and our inquiring hearts and
minds want to know why that is. We found a possible clue in Revelation
12, verse 5, where a woman gives birth to a child, and the child is caught up
to God. But the next verse doesn't follow chronologically; it jumps ahead
to a time still in the future even for us, when Israel (the woman) is facing
fierce tribulation and sees its need for God's protection over a forty-two-
month period of time.

The pressing question is this: Does God do that in His Word? Does
He take things out of order and juxtapose something in the past with
something in the future, or something present now with something very
ancient?

The answer is: yep! He sure does. I'll give some examples, but I first
want to point out that God's view and interactions with "time" are very
different from ours since time seems to be, from my reading of Scripture,
a very artificial and temporary construct to accommodate our carnal
nature. It is not an eternal thing. God exists beyond and above time,
and that's evident in the name that He wanted Moses to refer to Him
as, at the burning bush in Exodus 3: "I AM WHO I AM." He is eternal and
not constrained by time. The Bible states that there was a beginning of
time ("According to His own purpose and grace which was given to us
in Christ Jesus *before time began*" [2 Timothy 1:9; emphasis added]) and
there will be an end to time ("And he swore by Him that liveth for ever
and ever ... that there should be *time no longer*" [Revelation 10:6 KJV;
emphasis added]; God supersedes time. We'll look at some really neat
examples of that tomorrow, and then, once we've dispensed with verse 6
of Revelation 12, we'll see the *really awesome* stuff going on in verses 7–9.
Then maybe, just maybe, we'll have an answer to Jesus's abrupt departure
from this earth.

FRIDAY

In Revelation 12:5 we have an obvious allusion to the Ascension of Jesus Christ, which occurred almost two thousand years ago, and in the very next verse there is an equally obvious allusion to a time still in our future, during the Great Tribulation. The verses are linked by the word *then* as if the events occurred consecutively, but they did not. Is this consistent with the Word of God? Are there other examples of such?

There are. The first that comes to my mind is the prophecy of the seventy weeks in Daniel chapter 9, which is an amazingly accurate prediction of the time from the rebuilding of Jerusalem (at the time of the prophecy, the children of Israel were captive in Babylon, but they would soon be allowed to return to their land and rebuild) to the time of the Messiah, Jesus Christ. It was no doubt this prophecy that prompted the Three Wise Men from the East to set off to find this "newborn King," and they were spot-on, arriving when He was very young (no, they weren't there at His birth). The seventy "weeks" were actually seventy weeks of years, or four hundred ninety years, but only "seven weeks and sixty-two weeks" (verse 25) were accounted for at that time. The seventieth week was very different, and not addressed until verse 27, which is clearly alluding to the Great Tribulation, to that seven-year period. So there was a gap there, and that's what we're seeing in Revelation 12 also.

I think there's an even more interesting gap between two consecutive verses in the Bible, and it occurs right at the *very* beginning, between Genesis 1:1 and Genesis 1:2. Yes, it's actually called the "gap theory," and I happen to believe it. It is certainly not a foundational sort of thing, and it's perfectly okay to believe that the earth is very young, created at the time of the creation of humankind. That doesn't make you a bad person. But I think the earth itself is old and that stuff happened here before Genesis 1:2, and it wasn't good. It directly led to this great, awesome drama (actually a love story—the greatest love story ever told) currently playing out on planet Earth. As always, I base this on Scripture, which is purposely not conclusive on this matter. That would make it too easy. But I think it provides enough hints that the awesome Creation of Genesis 1 was a redo for the most part. Except for one notable difference: humankind. I do believe human history is only six thousand years old; there were no humans before Adam and Eve, but it is very possible, to my crazy way of thinking, that what was here before them necessitated their creation, created in the "image of God" with a free will, able to determine their own course.

We'll look a bit at the Scripture I'm alluding to next week. We will eventually get back to the Ascension / Holy Spirit gap after we cover the beginning of humankind gap, I promise, but there is really no hurry. Any time we spend meditating on this awesome Word of God is good. Have a great weekend.

MONDAY

We start this week with Scripture:

"In the beginning God created the heavens and the earth. The earth was without form, and void; and darkness was on the face of the deep. And the Spirit of God was hovering over the face of the waters" (Genesis 1:1–2 NKJV).

"Now the earth was formless and empty, darkness was over the surface of the deep, and the Spirit of God was hovering over the waters" (Genesis 1:2 NIV).

"The earth hath existed waste and void, and darkness is on the face of the deep, and the Spirit of God fluttering over the waters" (Genesis 1:2 YLT).

Hmm, interesting verbiage in these verses. Wouldn't it seem odd that God would create the earth to look like this? Look at the words: *empty*, *waste*, *void*, especially prominent in that last-mentioned translation, the YLT, which is from the 1800s and which strove to stay as faithful to the original manuscripts as possible. You know, *void* is also used as a verb, and it means to nullify or cancel something already there. Seems to me that the earth was formed along with all the rest of the physical universe "in the beginning," but then something cataclysmic happened and it was destroyed, but interestingly not annihilated; it was still there. That's where verse 3 kicks in. But what happened? Look at this portion of scripture, and note the similar phrases when compared to Genesis chapter 1, albeit in the reverse. These verses strike me as portraying a *decreation*. What do you think?

"I beheld the earth, and indeed it was without form, and void; and the heavens, they had no light. I beheld the mountains, and indeed they trembled, and all the hills moved back and forth. I beheld, and indeed there was no man, and all the birds of the heavens had fled. I beheld, and indeed the fruitful land was a wilderness, and all its cities were broken down at the presence of the Lord, and by His fierce anger. For thus says the Lord: 'The whole land shall be desolate; yet *I will not make a full end*'" (Jeremiah 4:23–26; emphasis added).

Doesn't that last verse describe the state of earth in Genesis 1:2? Now, as I've pointed out previously, I'm not a Bible scholar or a minister, just a layperson trying to sincerely understand Scripture via the enlightenment of the Holy Spirit, but I don't think this detailed description of destruction fits with anything that's occurred yet since Adam and Eve. The next questions are, "What was here before this desolation?" and "What did this previous civilization (cities broken down) do to warrant this display of the fierce, righteous anger of the Lord?"

For that, we go to two chapters we've covered before, namely, Isaiah 14 and Ezekiel 28. And you know whom those chapters talk about, don't you?

TUESDAY

You might be wondering why we're spending time on something the Bible doesn't spend a lot of time on and doesn't explain clearly. If you're thinking that, then good for you. Indeed, I believe one of the main tactics of the enemy, besides accusing Christians and making us question our position in Christ, is to get us focused on things extraneous to the true Gospel, even though they are "religious" things. Two of these areas are cosmology and eschatology. Very smart people spend a lot of time debating how the universe started and how it will end, but if the ultimate outcome of these endeavors is not glorifying to Jesus Christ and His cross, then they are futile. The apostle Paul was as well versed in Holy Scripture as anyone who ever lived, yet he said in 1 Corinthians 2:1–2: "And I, brethren, when I came to you, did not come with excellence of speech or of wisdom declaring to you the testimony of God. For I determined not to know anything among you except Jesus Christ and Him crucified."

I want everything I'm saying in this series to ultimately point to the cross. I'm going to repeat here a short and simple statement of truth that I gave earlier, one that is very important to remember:

The cross is the sign of the ransom paid by the *love* of God to satisfy the *justice* of God and secure the *righteousness* of God.

That's not Scripture; that's just me, but it has helped me to keep in focus the important things of this Christian faith of ours. That's why I'm spending a little time on *why* and *how* this current earth and humankind came to be, because it has everything to do with that foregoing statement. You'll see.

So we left God mulling over an empty, void, wasted earth in Genesis 1:2, and we're wondering what happened. What and who led to the cataclysm described in Jeremiah 4? I'd like us to think over these verses for tomorrow:

"How you are fallen from heaven, O Lucifer, son of the morning! How you are cut down to the ground, you who weakened the nations! … Those who see you will gaze at you, and consider you, saying: 'Is this the man who made the earth tremble, who shook the kingdoms, who made the world as a wilderness and destroyed its cities?'" (Isaiah 14:12, 16–17).

"Therefore I cast you as a profane thing out of the mountain of God; and I destroyed you, O covering cherub, from the midst of the fiery stones. … I cast you to the ground, I laid you before kings, that they might gaze at you. … And I turned you to ashes upon the earth in the sight of all who saw you" (Ezekiel 28:16–18).

WEDNESDAY

Here's how I like to think of what transpired between Genesis 1:1 and Genesis 1:2 and why it matters to our salvation and healing today.

Back at the start of this series, this past spring, we looked at Satan—Lucifer—and saw that he was one of the highest-ranking angels, if not the highest-ranking angel, and he was given much authority such that he purposed to become God. He started a campaign of slandering God's goodness, of lying about God, and I believe his base, the part of the universe God had given him authority over, was planet Earth.

What was he ruling over here on the pre-Adamic earth? I don't know, of course, but I suspect other, lower-ranking angels. I know they weren't humans, not in the sense of what Adam and Eve were created to be, triune in nature with a spirit, a soul, and a body. But whatever they were, they bought into Satan's lies and joined him in the rebellion against God's authority and sovereignty. The great God of heaven couldn't allow this assault on his nature and rule, so He threw Satan and his fallen angel followers *out* of heaven as seen in yesterday's Scripture. I believe He destroyed Satan's base, planet Earth, by His "fierce anger" (Jeremiah 4:26).

And here's something interesting: This would not be the last time Satan had to be thrown out of heaven, removed from God's presence. We'll address that when we get back to the Ascension–Holy Spirit gap that prompted this recent discussion.

So the planet was "voided," or nullified, but not the perpetrators; they—Satan and one-third of the angels—were still alive and functioning (Revelation 12:4). As I've postulated before, the rest of the universe, still in God's camp, were questioning things. Surely God had shown His power by squelching the rebellion, but that didn't *prove* that He was always *just* and *righteous* or that His nature was *love*. It just showed He was stronger than Satan. In short, the universe was unsettled.

That's the state of things in Genesis 1:2, and here's the point I've been working up to: the Godhead had a plan, an awesomely wise and beautiful and loving plan, to *prove* to the universe that He was all of the above and that He was the God of *restoration* as He would take this totally messed-up planet, ruined by sin, and bring forth a new creation, formed in His very image, given free choice (which, by the way, if the angels had free choice, they had only one choice), and set free in an idyllic world to see whom they would choose to follow and to demonstrate to all the universe that even if they did not choose Him, He would not abandon them but would provide a *way* to save them, all who would allow Him to, while preserving His holy attributes of *justice* and *righteousness* and magnifying His lavish *love*.

And *that*, my dear readers is why there's a gap between Genesis 1:1 and 1:2, and why indeed there actually had to be. We'll get back to Revelation 12 tomorrow. Sorry for the length; this stuff is pretty deep and takes time to explain.

THURSDAY

Okay, I really want to get back to Revelation 12, but I would be remiss not to comment on today. I debated, as it's not really worthy of our time, but I think a Christian perspective of this "holiday," Halloween, is in order. I don't like it—it's dark and grotesque and base and twisted—but it's a big deal in our society, and Satan, I'm sure, revels in it. That's my main problem with it; Satan gets a lot of attention, and he deserves none because he has been defeated and he knows it.

But here's an honest question: "Why, if Satan has been completely defeated at the cross, is he still around and seemingly functioning quite well?" Colossians 2:15 makes it very clear that Satan and all his followers were "made a public spectacle" of to the universe, which had just witnessed Jesus's "triumphing over them." The enemy was "disarmed," so why all the evil present today, to the point that it has its own "holiday"? Well, I saw something on TV just this week that helped me understand, and I'll pass it on to you. First let's look again at the ancient prophecy given by God to the serpent (Satan) at the Fall of Man:

"I will make you and the woman hostile toward each other. I will make your descendants and her Descendant hostile toward each other. He will *crush* your head, and you will bruise His heel" (Genesis 3:15 GW; emphasis added).

I was watching a survival show (on the Weather Channel), and these people were lost in the desert and starving. The survival specialist was demonstrating how to kill a rattlesnake for food. After pinning it down with a stick, you are to crush its head with the heel of your boot. Neat, right? So that pricked my theological ears. What the specialist said next really got me because he said you have to be very cautious after seemingly killing the snake by crushing its head as the snake will still react "instinctively and reflexively" by thrashing about and even biting, such that it could still envenomate (i.e., inject its poison into) a person. Wow! I immediately thought that is a very good portrayal of how Satan is functioning now. Indeed his head has been crushed and he has been defeated (and has *no* power over us as believers), but he is still allowed to thrash about and practice his evil until "He [Jesus] has put all enemies under His feet" (1 Corinthians 15:25). And that won't be for a while. Actually, it won't be until after the thousand-year reign of Jesus Christ on this earth that Satan is completely and forever destroyed, never to raise his ugly head again (Revelation 20:10).

Here's the take-home points for today, as Satan seems to win the day: (1) He has already been defeated, and his days are numbered. (2) This "holiday" is also doomed. I guarantee there will be no Halloween during the millennial reign or in heaven. (3) The candy is still okay: "Don't call anything impure that God has made clean" (Acts 11:9 NIV).

Have a great day in the Lord.

FRIDAY

The risen Jesus Christ, in His glorified body, walked this earth for some forty days after His resurrection, then ascended to His Father in heaven, where He has remained since. He has not been back to planet Earth. But He did promise to send the Holy Spirit. "And I will pray the Father, and He will give you another Helper, that He may abide with you forever—the Spirit of truth, whom the world cannot receive, because it neither sees Him nor knows Him; but you know Him, for He dwells with you and will be in you" (John 14:16–17).

That would occur on Pentecost, fifty days after the Crucifixion, fifty days after Passover, and so we are left with several days devoid of the presence of Jesus or the Holy Spirit on this earth, between the Ascension and the giving of the Holy Spirit. I think that's significant as God is a God of details and perfect plans; His timing is never off. In looking for the deeper meaning for this gap, I was led to Revelation chapter 12. We've already discussed verse 5, which clearly refers to the Ascension, and the next verse, which refers to a future event. Now we finally get to the crux of the matter:

> And war broke out in heaven: Michael and his angels fought with the dragon; and the dragon and his angels fought, but they did not prevail, nor was a place found for them in heaven any longer. So, the great dragon was cast out, that serpent of old, called the Devil and Satan, who deceives the whole world; he was cast out to the earth, and his angels were cast out with him. … Woe to the inhabitants of the earth and the sea! For the devil has come down to you, having great wrath, because he knows that he has a short time. (Revelation 12:7–9, 12)

Wow! So this begs two huge questions: (1) Why is Satan in heaven? Wasn't he thrown out a long time previously, at the time of his rebellion, before human history? (2) When did this expulsion occur, or has it occurred yet? Most likely your Bible's footnotes suggest this will occur at the time of the Great Tribulation, but I beg to differ. I'm going to put out two statements this morning that I believe are true, and then I'll spend next week defending them from scripture:

1. We (*humans*) allowed Satan to have access back into heaven.
2. This casting out occurred sometime between the resurrection of Jesus Christ and Pentecost, and it is why our Lord had to leave His beloved followers on this earth prematurely.

Have a great weekend.

26
WEEK

MONDAY

We start the week with Scripture:

"Now there was a day when the sons of God came to present themselves before the Lord, and Satan also came among them" (Job 1:6).

"Again there was a day when the sons of God came to present themselves before the Lord, and Satan came also among them to present himself before the Lord" (Job 2:1).

"Then he showed me Joshua, the high priest standing before the Angel of the Lord, and Satan standing at his right hand to oppose him. And the Lord said to Satan, 'The Lord rebuke you, Satan! The Lord who has chosen Jerusalem rebuke you! Is this not a brand plucked from the fire?'" (Zechariah 3:1–2).

So there you have it. In the Old Testament, Satan, although fallen and previously thrown out of heaven, is obviously there, and he's up to no good. In Job, the events of which probably took place around the time of Abraham, he came to the celestial meeting of the "sons of God" (the term for other celestial beings, including angels, but not *the* Son of God) directly from our earth, where he was "going to and fro … and walking back and forth," looking for humans to mess with. It should be noted that he had to get permission from God, even though human beings were spiritually dead and separated from their Creator and Father. You see, although Adam and Eve succumbed to Satan's temptation and sinned against God, no subsequent human being had sinned *against* God as He had not given them rules to keep—not yet at least. They were sinning and reaping the consequences of their sin, but they weren't under God's judgment, because

He was not *imputing* their sins to them (we covered all of this previously). Humankind was on their own, floundering about, spiritually dead, not capable of full communion with their God, and the universe was intently watching. To my little layperson's mind, *that's* the whole point of the book of Job, as even a moral, good, upright, God-fearing man (and Job was all of those) whose spirit person had not been renewed and made perfect, which would only become possible in the Atonement two thousand years into the future, *could not please God fully*, as Job's righteousness was a self-righteousness and Satan could be given license to hurt him. And, boy, did he.

You see, humankind had a conscience, which I believe was either acquired or revived when Adam and Eve ate of the tree of the knowledge of good and evil. Job listened to his conscience and was intent on living right ("one who feared God and shunned evil" [Job 1:1]) and on making sure his many children were living right by offering burnt sacrifices for them *every day* (Job 1:5)!

Really good, right? Do good, get good, right?

Well, that thinking didn't work too well for old Job. I know what I'm going to expound on tomorrow is not conventional, and I've not heard it preached, but remember, I'm not a preacher, I'm not a theologian, and I haven't read Christian commentaries. But I have read the Bible with the desire to know it well and see everything through the prism of Jesus and the cross and grace. If that's not good enough, then so be it. More tomorrow.

TUESDAY

We've established that Satan had access to heaven and could present himself before God in the Old Testament. That was the case at the time of the Crucifixion and resurrection of Jesus Christ too. We'll soon see how that came about as that wasn't the case at the time of the six-day Creation of Genesis 1. Satan was still banned from heaven and the presence of God at that time.

But first, what was Satan using that access for? We must realize that he absolutely hates us. He knows that we humans are the apple of the Godhead's eye, created in His image and chosen to be the vehicle that would ultimately prove the goodness and righteousness and justice of God. Satan wants to deceive us and hurt us and keep us separated from God's love. The Bible says that Satan "deceives the whole world" and is "the accuser of our brethren, who accused them before our God day and night" (Revelation 12:9–10).

The nearer we are to the Lord, the more Satan is going to hate us, and the more he is going to go after us (it's okay, though. He's simply not smart enough to know he actually has no power over us believers, for "greater is He that is in you, than he who is in the world" [1 John 4:4]). That's where we left off yesterday in Job. Job was a good man. Satan saw that. And he saw how God has blessed Job. His assumption was that the one leads to the other: If these little humans do right by God, He'll bless them abundantly; that's the incentive. Humans like Job didn't love God out of pure motives, just because He is God; they loved Him to benefit themselves. Satan wanted to demonstrate that to the watching universe. He wanted to show that God's precious little humans were no better than him, that they also simply wanted to get everything for themselves that they could. It was all about them, that "boastful pride of life" thing.

And you know what? Satan was actually right. Unredeemed humans—and Job was that—are exactly that way, and that's why the book of Job is so perplexing and kind of unsatisfying and not very uplifting, as Job was not functioning at all in the spiritual realm, and "God is Spirit" (John 4:24). Job and his friends were trying to intellectualize what happened. The only true light that I see in any of the arguments made by them is Job's beautiful and unexpected exclamation in chapter 19, verses 25–27 (emphasis added):

"For I know that my Redeemer lives, and He shall stand at last on the earth; and after my skin is destroyed, *this I know*, that in my flesh *I shall see God*, Whom I shall see for myself, and my eyes shall behold, and not another. How my heart *yearns* within me!"

Wow! He was foreseeing Jesus, and a new incorruptible body, and being physically with Him at the Second Coming! Is that amazing or what? Satan was so arrogant and sure of himself that he missed it! As I've said before, he never saw the cross coming, and it was too late when he realized what was going on. Praise God. More tomorrow.

WEDNESDAY

> Rudolph the Red-Nosed Reindeer had a very shiny nose,
> And if you ever saw it, you would even say it glows.
> All of the other reindeer used to laugh and call him names.
> They never let poor Rudolph join in any reindeer games.

I know what you're thinking: *He's finally lost it. I knew he wasn't quite right.* But trust me, there is a deep theological concept in this song, a song that has always bothered me since I first heard it as a little kid. You see, Rudolph's acceptance by his fellow reindeer was dependent on *what he did* (guided Santa's sleigh), not on *who he was*. They couldn't care less about him until he saved Christmas, and I'm sure they all quickly lost interest in him afterward (well, maybe not Clarice).

My point is, that's how so many people, Christian and non-Christian alike, and I think Job, view God - as the great rewarder of our good actions. He's not loved for who He is—our loving Father, all-powerful, all-knowing, and always good all the time—but for what He can do for *us*. Wasn't this exemplified by Job in chapter 1, who daily went through his rituals of offerings to ensure divine protection over his children and his possessions? That's why he was so upset about losing everything, because he was *righteous* and *upright*, and God couldn't allow these catastrophes to happen to him! Bob Dylan put it this way, in "When You Gonna Wake Up?": "Do you ever wonder just what God requires? You think He's just an errand boy to satisfy your wandering desires."

I'll finish my take on Job and his book and the role of Satan tomorrow, but I leave you with these beautiful words from Natalie Grant's "More Than Anything" for today. May it be our prayer:

Help me want the Healer more than the healing.
Help me want the Savior more than the saving.
Help me want the Giver more than the giving.
O help me want You, Jesus, more than anything!

THURSDAY

So here's how I see the interplay of God, Satan, and Job, which reveals more of how God was dealing with humankind during these patriarchal times, before the Law was given:

1. The book of Job highlights the futility of humankind's self-righteous acts. Job was a good, upright, conscientious man, but he couldn't even come close to satisfying God's requirements of perfect holiness. Isaiah put it well: "But we are all like an unclean thing, and all our righteousnesses are like filthy rags" (Isaiah 64:6). This was something human beings had to come to terms with; they needed God.

2. Satan just loves to hurt humans; as Jesus said, he came "to steal, and to kill, and to destroy" (John 10:10). If it were up to Satan, all human life would be obliterated.

3. But Satan was on a tight leash in Old Testament times; he was restrained from exerting his full power over humans. He had access to the great God of heaven and could come before Him to ask permission to harm humans, but I think the case of Job was the exception rather than the rule because, again, humankind was not sinning against God at this time. Humankind was in a kind of limbo because their salvation had not yet appeared, and they weren't even aware of the standards they were to meet as we hadn't yet reached either Mount Sinai or Mount Calvary.

4. However, the time would come when Satan's full evil power would be unleashed on humankind. That is what we're working toward. It's described in Revelation 12, where we find the following verse: "Woe to the inhabitants of the earth and the sea! For the devil has come down to you, having great wrath, because he knows that he has a short time" (v. 12).

I think that purging of Satan from heaven occurred way before the Great Tribulation. It occurred when Jesus ascended to heaven, before Pentecost, almost two thousand years ago. We'll provide the rationale for that view soon, but first another fascinating glimpse of Satan in heaven, showing him doing what he does best—tomorrow.

FRIDAY

It's Friday! Time for a recap. The premise we have previously established—that healing is part of the Atonement of Jesus Christ for believers—took four thousand years of human history to occur, and we've embarked on a tour of God's plan of salvation to show why it took that long to come to fulfillment, as seeing the beauty and complexity of this plan, set before the "foundation of the world" (Revelation 13:8), will bolster our belief that all of this is actually true, more so than anything you can physically see or feel. We've traversed twenty-six hundred years thus far, and the children of Israel are setting off on a fifty-day journey from Egypt to Mount Sinai. We're contrasting that period of time with the fifty-day interval between the Crucifixion and Pentecost in the New Testament. Most recently, we've been dissecting this peculiar gap of nine or ten days between the Ascension of Jesus Christ to heaven and the giving of the Helper—the Holy Spirit—to indwell believers on this earth. I believe the answer to this is something of great significance to us as believers, but it is rather hidden in Scripture; I've never heard it discussed or preached. I believe it has to do with Satan and his access to heaven, his ability to come into the very presence of God and accuse us before our Father.

We've seen that Satan indeed does show up in heaven in the Old Testament. We've looked at Job, and next we'll look at Zechariah. After that, we'll explain how Satan got that access since he had previously been thrown out from the presence of God at the time of his rebellion. After that we'll finally get to the main points here: how and when and why he was expelled the second and final time from heaven. Here's the really good news for us: That liar is no longer in heaven. He's not allowed. His previous position has been *replaced*!

But before all that, I want to say one more thing about the book of Job. In short, God allowed Satan to do a lot of bad things to this good but unredeemed human, and in a sense I think what Job experienced was what all lost and fallen humans actually deserved but were spared from by the "compassion and mercy" of our loving Father. God was demonstrating for the watching universe the total depravity of human beings, how even their most righteous and upright acts fell very short of His requirements.

But look how the story ends: "And the Lord restored Job's losses. ... Indeed, the Lord gave Job twice as much as he had before. ... The Lord blessed the latter days of Job *more* than his beginning. ... Job lived 140 years, and ... died, old and full of days" (Job chapter 42). Wow, what a good, good God! This is the true take-home message from the story of Job. Look at this New Testament verse in James: "You have heard of the perseverance of Job and seen the end *intended* by the Lord—that the Lord is compassionate and merciful" (James 5:11; emphasis added). Praise God! We look at Zechariah next week. Have a great weekend.

27
WEEK

MONDAY

Happy Veterans Day! It is a holiday near and dear to my heart. I was a navy pediatrician for six years and absolutely loved my time in the military. There is something very special about a uniformed doctor attending to the needs of the children of our soldiers and sailors (we navy docs take care of the US Marine Corps kids also). I'll never forget the feeling of pride when standing at attention in my dress whites for inspection early in the morning as the sun was just rising on the grounds of the old Balboa Naval Hospital located right in beautiful Balboa Park in San Diego. I was "just" a doctor, but every one of us standing there would have done anything we could to defend our awesome country without any concern for our own well-being. We would have sacrificed for the higher cause. There's a beautiful Christian principle wrapped up in that idea of sacrifice, fully exemplified by our Lord Jesus Christ. One of my heroes is the Civil War general Joshua Lawrence Chamberlain, of Gettysburg fame, a wonderful Christian citizen soldier. He wrote beautifully (as most people of that era did). I have memorized several of his quotes. Here's one of them:

"This is the great reward of *service* ... to live far out and on in the lives of others. This is the mystery of the Christ: to give life's best, for such high sake, that it shall be found again unto life eternal" (emphasis added).

Wow! Remember those who have served and are currently serving our country today, and express your gratitude directly if possible. It is their sacrifice that has ensured the freedom of speech that allows even this blatantly Christian series to be shared without compromise and without fear.

We're now moving to the prophet Zechariah's vision of Satan in heaven. Some background is in order. Job's story took place hundreds of years before the Law was given on Mount Sinai, and Zechariah was on the scene hundreds of years after; the two were separated by close to fifteen hundred years! Satan had access to heaven all throughout the Old Testament, but since Mount Sinai, his role there was distinctly different from what we saw in Job as now humankind's sins were being counted. There were now rules, and they were being broken. Satan wanted to make sure God knew it and did something about it, for God had to be just and He had to be righteous, or else the foundations of His rule would be knocked out (Psalm 89:14). We'll pick it up right here tomorrow. Have a great holiday.

TUESDAY

"Then he showed me Joshua the high priest standing before the Angel of the Lord, and Satan standing at his right hand *to oppose Him*. And the Lord said to Satan, 'The Lord rebuke you, Satan! The Lord who has chosen Jerusalem rebuke you! Is this not a brand plucked from the fire?'" (Zechariah 3:1–2; emphasis added).

Now for our second example of Satan in heaven in the Old Testament, and it's taking place around five hundred years before Jesus. Much has happened since the time of Job. God has entrusted believing Abraham and his descendants with shining the light of the Gospel, God's plan of salvation for the human race, upon the earth. The children of Israel would soon go into bondage in Egypt, be miraculously delivered, be given the Law at Mount Sinai, which was actually the "ministry of death" (2 Corinthians 3:7), which required institution of the Levitical system of priests and sacrifices for the temporary atonement of their now imputed sins, and wander through the wilderness for forty years, before finally mustering enough faith in God to overtake the enemy and possess their Promised Land, Canaan. They would be overseen by "judges" for a while but then clamor for a king (like the other nations), and God would honor their request. Kings would come and go, some really good (David, Solomon, Josiah), most really bad, and the kingdom would split into the separate kingdoms of Judah (comprised of the tribes of Judah and Benjamin) and Israel (the other ten tribes). The two kingdoms would be taken into captivity as a consequence of their failure to obey their God. The Jews (from the kingdom of Judah) would be conquered by Babylon, which itself would be conquered by Persia, and King Cyrus (a heathen, but absolutely used mightily by the Lord) would decide to let the Jews go back to Israel and rebuild the walls of Jerusalem and the temple.

The priests would go back also. The high priest at the time of Zechariah was named Joshua (obviously not the Joshua of Moses's time), and he represented the people to God, which is the role of the priest. Zechariah was given this intriguing glimpse into heaven, showing us "behind the scenes" events occurring on a celestial/spiritual level that the subjects here on earth (Joshua and the children of Israel he represents) had no idea were going on. Awesome!

That's the background. We'll look at what it all means for us tomorrow.

WEDNESDAY

The prophet Zechariah vividly portrays a celestial scene composed of three players: the Angel of the Lord (this is the preincarnate Jesus), Satan, and Joshua the high priest, who represents the children of Israel, God's chosen people. It is a courtroom scene with Joshua and Satan standing before the Lord, who is the Judge. Satan is positioned to the right of Joshua, the traditional position of the prosecutor, or "accuser" as seen in Psalm 109:6: "Let an accuser stand at his right hand when he is judged." *That's* what Satan was doing over and over again in heaven since the institution of the Law—*accusing* God's chosen people of not being worthy of God's favor, protection, and love. Remember Revelation 12:10? Satan is described as "the accuser of the brethren, who accused them before our God day and night."

And Satan had *every* legal right to do that! Joshua and all the rest of humankind were sinners as Zechariah documents clearly: "Now Joshua was clothed with filthy garments" (Zechariah 3:3). Joshua was *guilty* of sinning before God and had to be punished or else God would not be righteous and just.

But just look how our Lord responded to Satan's accusations (the passion and intensity in this response is amazing to me): "The Lord said to Satan, 'The Lord says *no* to you, Satan! The Lord who has chosen Jerusalem says *no* to you! This man was like a burning stick *pulled from the fire*'" (Zechariah 3:2 NCV; emphasis added).

Wow! Do you realize what's going on here? Jesus was overruling Satan, not giving any credence to his true accusations and likening His chosen people (which indeed includes all of us believers) to a stick in a raging fire of destruction that is rescued, pulled out, *saved*! Jesus is looking way into the future, five hundred years down the road of God's plan of salvation, to His cross and the atonement. Wow!

I think He was looking a little beyond that, too, to the time shortly after His resurrection, when He would once and for all rid heaven of this horrible affliction known as Satan, such that he would no longer be able to accuse us before God. We're working toward that, but first I promised to look at how Satan ever got back into the presence of God to start with. We'll tackle that next time.

THURSDAY

"Then God said, 'Let Us make man in Our image, according to Our likeness; let them have *dominion* over the fish of the sea, over the birds of the air, and over the cattle, *over all the earth*.' ... Then God blessed them and God said to them, 'Be fruitful and multiply; fill the earth and *subdue* it; have *dominion* over the fish of the sea, over the birds of the air, and over every living thing that moves on the earth'" (Genesis 1:26, 28; emphasis added).

"And now I have told you before it comes, that when it does come to pass, you may believe. I will no longer talk much with you, for the *ruler of this world* is coming, and he has nothing in Me" (John 14:29–30; emphasis added).

"And you He made alive, who were dead in trespasses and sins, in which you once walked according to the course of this world, according to *the prince of the power of the air*, the spirit who now works in the sons of disobedience" (Ephesians 2:2; emphasis added).

Adam and Eve, created in the image of God, were given authority over the earth. *They* were to represent this planet and all humans in front of God in heaven when He held council with His subjects as seen in Job 1:6 and 2:1. That was the plan. But look at the two New Testament verses from above. Who's the ruler/prince of this earth in those passages? Yep, Satan! And he *legally* obtained that right when Adam and Eve abdicated their throne at the Fall, yielding to Satan and giving him *their* authority.

Here's the amazing thing to me: God *honored* it. It was the *just* and *righteous* thing to do because the authority and rule over earth was stolen not from God but from humankind. God would not go back on His word, so what He had promised to humankind was now Satan's. Remember, the whole universe was intently watching this drama of the ages play out. Would God just up and destroy Satan and His fallen angels *and* humankind? That would have left lots of questions about God's integrity and love.

No, God had to put up with evil Satan's coming before Him in heaven and *accusing* His own chosen people "night and day" because He did not have the *legal* authority to expel him. Only a man could have that authority—and not just any man, but a *sinless, perfect man*. That's what we've been working toward. Jesus refers to this very time in the second verse, above, when He says, "The ruler of this world is coming." Coming to what? From where?

This is all getting very interesting, I think. More tomorrow.

FRIDAY

So it's Friday, and we've spent the last two weeks showing how Satan gained access to heaven and the presence of God after his initial fall from heaven, and just what he was doing with that access in Old Testament times. It wasn't good for us humans, because he would constantly *accuse* us, rightfully, of being unworthy sinners and *remind* God of our fallen status. So it is *huge*, to my way of thinking, to know that Satan is *not* there anymore. Here's what I've been shown as to how this all came about:

1. The expulsion had to be accomplished by Jesus Christ, and Him alone, as He was the only perfect, sinless human, and therefore He could rightfully and justly retake the position of the first Adam.

2. The event had to occur sometime *after* the defeat of Satan at the cross and the subsequent resurrection of Jesus, and *before* the sending of the Holy Spirit to dwell within us believers on earth.

3. Jesus had to be *physically* present in heaven (specifically, the most holy place of the heavenly tabernacle) to accomplish this task.

4. It was not an easy task as an all-out *war* took place in heaven between the archangel Michael and all God's loyal angels, and Satan and all his fallen angels.

5. The Holy Spirit *had* to be given to indwell and empower human believers at the time of this expulsion because the consequence of not having Satan in heaven, although awesome for believers, spelled catastrophic trouble for earth and nonbelievers. How Satan interacted with humans would be changed as he would be unrestrained.

Wow! That's a lot to digest, isn't it? We'll start next week looking at the scriptures to support all these premises, but I want to end this week with just a reminder to you that these views I have of this Christian faith of ours come solely from reading, meditating on, and pondering God's Word, and fully relying on the Holy Spirit within me to illuminate what scripture means. If I can do this, believe me, any believer can. I leave you with a beautiful portion of Scripture from the apostle Paul, which explains this better than I can. Have a great weekend.

"For the Spirit searches all things, yes, the deep things of God. For what man knows the things of a man except the spirit of the man which is in him? Even so, no one knows the things of God except the Spirit of God. Now we have received, not the spirit of the world, but the Spirit who is from God, *that we might know* the things that have been freely given to us by God" (1 Corinthians 2:10–12).

28
WEEK

MONDAY

It's Monday; another beautiful week in the Lord begins. We're pondering why our Lord ascended to the Father, leaving His followers alone on planet Earth at the time that He did, days before the Comforter was given. I believe this had to do with Satan's legal but unwanted presence in heaven and what it would take to oust him once and for all. This week we turn to the fascinating book of Hebrews, which I believe will clarify my arguments and demonstrate once again just what an awesome Lord we have and how much He loves us.

No one is certain who wrote the New Testament book of Hebrews, although we do know that ultimately the Author was the Holy Spirit (2 Timothy 3:16), but I like to think the Gentile physician Luke (who wrote the Gospel of Luke and the Acts of the Apostles) wrote it. It's that doctor bond thing, I guess. But Luke was from Antioch, which was a center of both Greek culture and Jewish culture, and I think Dr. Luke was drawn to Judaism and had a deep understanding of the Old Testament and Levitical law, which is demonstrated so well in this book. Yet he wasn't a Jew, and he wasn't as biased toward the Law as a Jewish Christian would be, and thus he could more clearly see the superiority of Jesus's atoning sacrifice and work on the cross over the Old Testament system of priests and sacrifices, which is what the book of Hebrews is all about. What the writer is showing is that the Levitical system served merely as a "copy and a shadow of the heavenly things" (Hebrews 8:5) and that Jesus is the "real thing" and would now become our one High Priest, forever doing away with the old sacrificial system. By the way, that indeed did happen. The Roman sacking of Jerusalem and destruction of the temple in AD 70 put an end to the service of the Jewish priests and the animal sacrifices, not to be revived through to this present age.

This morning we're setting the stage for this week. Here are the two portions of Hebrews to mull over for tomorrow:

"Now this is the main point of the things we are saying: We have such a High Priest, who is seated at the right hand of the throne of the Majesty in the heavens, a Minister of the sanctuary and of the true tabernacle which the Lord erected, and not man" (Hebrews 8:1–2).

"But Christ came as a High Priest of the good things to come, with the greater and more perfect tabernacle not made with hands, that is, not of this creation. Not with the blood of goats and calves, but with His own blood *He entered the holy place once for all*, having obtained eternal redemption" (Hebrews 9:11–12).

Have a great day.

TUESDAY

The book of Hebrews is dealing with something we haven't reached yet in our journey through God's plan of salvation, namely, the giving of the Law via Moses on Mount Sinai and all that went along with that. We'll eventually get there, but you know how this treatise jumps around a lot, and the Word of God is so beautifully interwoven that there is no problem doing that. Remember, my goal is to paint a portrait, when all is said and done, of the Gospel—the good news—of Jesus Christ and His cross, and what that means for us. As you might recall, we're still just embarking on our trip from Egypt to Mount Sinai, but we have camped out on that fifty-day interval and are contrasting that with the fifty days from the Crucifixion to Pentecost in the New Testament. We're working toward something that I think is really neat and affirming. It has to do with Satan in heaven and, believe it or not, the earthly Old Testament tabernacle and the eternal heavenly tabernacle. That's where we are now.

So with the Law (rules) came the knowledge of *sin*, and now humankind was going to be held accountable for their sins. Our loving, merciful God gave plans for the temporary atonement, or covering, for their sins at the same time that He gave the Law. The Law had to do with priests and animal sacrifices and the earthly temporary dwelling place for the Lord, known as the tabernacle. There are whole chapters on this in the Old Testament, which may seem peculiar and tedious, but every part of that tabernacle was a foreshadowing of Jesus Christ and His Atonement, as that's what all of scripture is really about (remember the road to Emmaus?). The author of Hebrews gives a concise summary of what we are going to focus on now, namely, the earthly tabernacle. We'll end this morning with that picture, found in Hebrews 9:1–5:

> Then indeed, even the first covenant had ordinances of divine service and the earthly sanctuary. For a tabernacle was prepared: the first part, in which was the lampstand, the table, and the showbread, which is called the sanctuary; and behind the second veil, the part of the tabernacle which is called the Holiest of All, which had the golden censer and the ark of the covenant overlaid on all sides with gold, in which were the golden pot that had the manna, Aaron's rod that budded, and the tablets of the covenant; and above it were the cherubim of glory overshadowing the mercy seat.

Have a great day.

WEDNESDAY

Yesterday we referenced a brief description of the Old Testament tabernacle, which consisted of an outer court (not mentioned) and two enclosed areas that could be entered only by going through a veil; these were off-limits to the people. Only the priests could enter the first chamber, called the sanctuary, where there were the pieces of furniture mentioned yesterday, namely, the lampstand (also known as the menorah), the table that held the showbread, and the incense altar (also not mentioned). Only the high priest could enter the innermost chamber, separated by another very thick veil, and only once a year (the Day of Atonement). This chamber was known as the holy of holies, and it contained only the Ark of the Covenant. The verse yesterday described what was *inside* and what was *on top of* that ark. This is something we just can't skip over as it provides a neat little synopsis of God's plan of salvation and makes clear again His true nature, shown by His mercy, forgiveness, and grace.

But first let me point out that the earthly tabernacle was simply a copy, given on Mount Sinai, of the true, actual, physical heavenly tabernacle that will be the scene of what we're ultimately working toward here. There *is* a heavenly sanctuary; look at the verses I gave two days ago, Hebrews 8:1–2. Jesus is called the Minister of the *Sanctuary* and the *true tabernacle*, which the Lord erected, not humans. And there *is* a heavenly holy of holies; look at the second Hebrews quote from two days ago, Hebrews 9:11–12. Jesus actually entered it (and, even more, He provided the way for us believers to enter it too—Hebrews 10:19–22). Just as there is an actual throne in heaven, there's an actual tabernacle. But *when* did Jesus enter it and for what purpose? That's what we're going to answer shortly, but we really have to look at this ark thing first.

Remember what was in the ark? Three items: the actual tablets of stone containing the Law, the budding rod of Aaron, and a sample of manna, contained in a golden pot. Remember what overlaid the ark? The mercy seat and two cherubim (representations of angels), one on each end. And the whole thing was amazingly hammered out from one solid slab of pure gold. Those two cherubim were facing each other and *looking* down at the mercy seat. Can you picture this? They were looking at a solid piece of gold; they couldn't "see" what was *in* the ark. And that's important. We'll pick up right here tomorrow morning.

THURSDAY

Much is made of the Ark of the Covenant. Remember the movie *Raiders of the Lost Ark*? The focus is usually on those fascinating articles *in* the ark and their great significance, but what they really represent are the *failures* of humankind and our unrighteous, fickle nature. Those items are a reminder of God's efforts to reform and save humanity based on humankind's ability to respond and how disastrous that strategy was. In short, the articles prove the futility of humankind and our need for a Savior. That's why they were *hidden in* the ark, because they were not to be the focal point; what was *on top* of the ark was to be.

Consider the tablets of stone with the Law engraved on them. By the way, you might think that anything actually touched by God Himself would not even be able to be handled by humans, but here's something not widely known: indeed, the Law was given *through* Moses, as John 1:17 says, but it was done *via* angels; God Himself wasn't physically present on Mount Sinai. He used angels as the intermediaries. Look at Acts 7:37–38: "This is that Moses … who was in the congregation in the wilderness with the angel who spoke to him on Mount Sinai." And this awesome verse: "What purpose then does the Law serve? It was added because of transgressions, until the Seed should come to whom the promise was made, and it [the Law] was appointed through angels by the hand of a mediator" (Galatians 3:19).

Wow! Do you know what that tells me? Indeed the Law was important; it was essential to prove the sinfulness of humankind and the righteousness of God, but it wasn't where God's heart is. He wasn't even there when it was given.

But now just think of this: Where was God at the cross? *He was on it!* That's what the universe saw; that's what proved His overwhelming, inexplicable *love* for us; that's what settled the issue once and for all that God is *good* and that Satan is a liar!

I wasn't planning any of this today. I love being led of the Spirit because He is always right on and beautiful, and He *always* points us to Jesus and His cross. More on the contents of the ark tomorrow.

FRIDAY

The Ten Commandments have been such a revered part of Judeo-Christian thought through the ages, but their position in the Ark of the Covenant is telling. The tablets of stone on which they are engraved are hidden in the ark, under the mercy seat. There is something that supersedes them, something that is above them.

Do you remember the Ten Commandments? I memorized a lot of stuff growing up, and the commandments were included, but they actually aren't that easy to recall. John 3:16 is, and the song "Amazing Grace" is, but those ten "rules" don't lend themselves easily to memory. Why is that?

There is a phrase in Psalm 42:7, written by David, "deep calls unto deep." I think that's what's going on here. David says this after he exclaims in verse 1, "As the deer pants for the water brooks, so pants my soul for You, O God." Isn't that beautiful? I think the true, deep nature of God, that He is love, is recognized by the deepest part of our souls, and we are all aching to know Him; it's just that many of us suppress that need. The Ten Commandments are not on that very deep level; they certainly served a necessary purpose, but they were *fulfilled* by Jesus Christ (Romans 8:3–4), and we as believers no longer live under bondage to them. We aren't restrained by "Thou shall not!" but by the *goodness* of God, which leads to repentance (Romans 2:4). We are actually held to a much higher standard of conduct than what was required under the Law. Look at the words of Jesus in Matthew 5:27–28: "You have heard that it was said to those of old, 'You shall not commit adultery.' But I say to you that whoever looks at a woman to lust for her has already committed adultery with her in his heart." Wow! In short, Jesus made the already impossible requirements of the Law (who could keep the tenth commandment, about not being jealous of anybody?) much, much more impossible, making it clear that we could only be acceptable to God by appropriating the righteousness of Jesus Christ, freely given to us as believers (2 Corinthians 5:21).

So the Law was a failure insofar as the redemption of humankind is concerned. It's "in the box." What about the budding rod and pot of manna? They will have to wait until next week, but maybe you could look at chapters 11 and 17 of the book of Numbers in preparation. Have a great weekend.

29
WEEK

MONDAY

It's another Monday. Thanksgiving is just a few days away, and Christmas Day is just a month away. We're really close to seeing Satan get kicked out of heaven, but the scene for such is, I believe, the celestial tabernacle. We're focused on the earthly copy of such. In that tabernacle is the holy of holies, and in the holy of holies is the Ark of the Covenant, and in the ark are three items, all representing the fragility and weakness of humankind. We've already examined the tablets of stone and see how they represent humankind's inability to become holy by obeying God's rules. Now we'll look at the budding rod of Aaron and discuss how this is a reminder of humankind's questioning and defiance of God's authority.

The background story is found in Numbers. The children of Israel left Mount Sinai and were brought to the door of the Promised Land, but they didn't *believe* that God would give them the land as He had promised, because there were *giants* in the land. They gave in to unbelief, except for Joshua and Caleb. Their punishment for this unbelief was to wander through the wilderness for forty years, one year for each day the twelve Israeli spies had been scoping out the Promised Land, and there they would all die; God's righteous judgment (of course, not yet being absorbed by Jesus Christ on the cross) was severe and harsh. "But as for you, your carcasses shall fall in this wilderness" (Numbers 14:22). Their children, led by Joshua and Caleb, would enter the land.

So, as one would imagine, the accursed men of Israel were not happy with that verdict, and they weren't happy with their leadership, namely, Moses and Aaron, so they mounted a challenge. They were not willing to accept the will of God as He was the one who appointed Moses and Aaron. A lot of really dramatic things happened in Numbers 16 and 17. I mean *really* dramatic things. Think of this next time you're contemplating defying God's will: "The ground split apart under them [the rebels], and the earth opened its mouth and swallowed them up, with their households ... with all their goods. So they and all those with them went down alive into the pit; the earth closed over them, and they perished from among the assembly" (Numbers 16:31–33). Wow! Such is the legitimate, righteous wrath of God, but we believers will *never* face that. Look at Romans 8:9, which is another really good verse to memorize: "Much more then, having now been justified by His blood, we shall be *saved from wrath* through Him" (emphasis added). Amen.

Now here's an amazing tidbit, illustrative of the boastful pride of humankind. Even after seeing all that, the people were still questioning Aaron's authority as high priest. That's where the rod came in, which we'll discuss next time. Nothing boring about this Old Testament stuff, is there?

TUESDAY

"And the Lord spoke to Moses, saying, 'Speak to the children of Israel, and get from them a rod from each father's house ... twelve rods. Write each man's name on his rod. And you shall write Aaron's name on the rod of Levi. Then you shall place them in the tabernacle ... and it shall be that the rod of the man whom I choose will *blossom*'" (Numbers 17:1–5; emphasis added).

The "rod" is simply a walking stick made of deadwood. There is no life in it. Thus to have something green and alive emerge from one would be truly miraculous. God had to resort to the miraculous with his ever-unbelieving and always contentious people, now questioning Aaron's God-given authority. And here's an important life lesson: God would rather us *not* rely on miracles, on the spectacular, but continue daily in communion and harmony with Him, to *rest* in Him and His perfect will for us, such that the *norm* is a victorious, impactful, bountiful life. As my Bob Dylan put it, in the song "Pressing On":

Many try to stop me, shake me up in my mind,
Saying, "Prove to me that He's the Lord; show me a sign!"
What kind of sign do they need, when it all comes from within?
What's been lost has been found. What's to come has already been.

But back to our story. "Now it came to pass on the next day that Moses went into the tabernacle of witness, and behold, the rod of Aaron … had *sprouted* and *put forth buds*, had *produced blossoms*, and *yielded ripe almonds*" (Numbers 17:8; emphasis added). Wow! Just how extravagant is this God of ours? I love it. It's a beautiful picture of renewal, of resurrection, of "making everything sad to be untrue." But for the purposes of the ark, it's a reminder of humankind's rejection of God, just like in the garden, and therefore that rod has to be *hidden inside* the box.

One more item: the golden pot of manna. It's appropriate to talk food tomorrow, the day before your Thanksgiving feast, and even more appropriate to discuss *thankfulness*, or more specifically, the lack of it, because that's why the manna is in that box. Can't wait.

WEDNESDAY

"Then the Lord said to Moses, 'Behold, I will rain bread from heaven for you … and the people'" (Exodus 16:4). "And when the layer of dew lifted, there, on the surface of the wilderness, was a small round substance, as fine as frost on the ground. … And Moses said to them, 'This is the bread which the Lord has given you to eat'" (Exodus 16:14, 15). "And the house of Israel called its name Manna … and the taste of it was like wafers made with honey" (Exodus 16:31).

The children of Israel, two million strong, are marching from Egypt to Mount Sinai, and God initiates the forty-year miracle of manna (which literally means, "What is this stuff?"), prepared fresh six days a week, every morning, for His children to feast on. What a God! Remember, this is occurring *before* the Law, and the Israelites are the recipients of God's unmerited grace. But do you recall one of my little sayings from several weeks ago: *If the sin debt has not been paid, grace is ineffective.* That is certainly the case here. Look at this response of the people, now *after* the Law and marching to Canaan:

"So the children of Israel also wept again and said, 'Who will give us meat to eat? We remember the fish which we ate freely in Egypt, the cucumbers, the melons, the leeks, the onions, and the garlic; but now our whole being is dried up; *there is nothing at all except this manna* before our eyes!'" (Numbers 11:4–6; emphasis added).

Wow! You know, I may have a bit of an overactive imagination, but previously I had put some thought into what I would want to eat and drink for *every* meal if I were stranded on a deserted island, all by myself, for years. The meal would be a ham and swiss cheese sub with everything on it (this gives the requisite vegetables and fruit), except onion (I know I'm alone; I just don't like onions). The drink would be Gatorade (G2) Glacier Cherry since I drink that pretty much exclusively now, and the dessert would be (this was tough as I could have done better in the fruit department than a tomato on the sub, but I went with my heart) a Kit-Kat bar, especially appealing since I would not have to share. And don't question the "tomato is a fruit" thing. It is a legitimate fruit, and also allows a comparison of knowledge and wisdom. Knowledge is knowing the tomato is a fruit; wisdom is not putting it in your fruit salad.

I honestly think I would *not ever* complain about this diet plan (and, after rescue, I could star on the show *My 600-lb Life*), but I bet the *manna* stuff was every bit as good. Yet the Israelites complained—they weren't *thankful* at all—and that's a big deal in God's eyes. In Romans chapter 1, Paul gives a vivid description of how human beings could turn their backs on God. This is part of that process: "Although they knew God, they did not glorify Him as God, *nor where thankful*" (Romans 1:21). That's what that pot of manna in the ark represented: humankind's *thanklessness*.

So we have the tablets of stone, demonstrating humankind's inability to keep the rules and be holy; the budding rod, demonstrating humankind's defiance of God's authority and will; and the pot of manna, demonstrating humankind's thanklessness. All these "treasured" items are hidden in the ark. Tomorrow we'll look at what *overlies* the ark, and that will reveal the most awesome thing to be *thankful* for this Thanksgiving season. It has everything to do with that golden mercy seat and those two cherubim, and it will come to life *on* Thanksgiving Day, which is why I had to make today's entry so long. Thanks for understanding, and don't miss tomorrow's!

THURSDAY

> Then Bezalel made ... the mercy seat of pure gold; two and a half cubits was its length and a cubit and a half its width. He made two cherubim of beaten gold; he made them of one piece at the two ends of the mercy seat: one cherub at one end on this side, and the other cherub at the other end on that side. He made the cherubim at the two ends of one piece with the mercy seat. The cherubim spread out their wings above, and covered the mercy seat with their wings. *They faced one another; the faces of the cherubim were toward the mercy seat.* (Exodus 37:6–9; emphasis added)

Happy Thanksgiving Day! We're going to uncover something this morning that I hope will make this Thanksgiving even more special. It has to do with the Day of Atonement, described in Leviticus 16, and the mercy seat, described in the foregoing Scripture. The high priest would be allowed to "atone for" or "cover" the sins of all the children of Israel during one special ceremony one day a year, and that ceremony included this: "He [the high priest] shall take some of the blood of the bull and sprinkle it with his finger on the mercy seat" (Leviticus 16:14). God would see that blood of atonement and forgive their sins, as "according to the Law, almost all things are purified with blood, and without shedding of blood there is no remission (of sin)" (Hebrews 9:22).

God would see the blood on the mercy seat, *between* the cherubim, who were positioned such that they were looking right down at that blood-covered mercy seat, but He would not see all the failures of humankind housed *in* the ark. That sacrifice would allow the children of Israel to be right with their God for a year—but only for a year. This ceremony had to be repeated over and over again, year after year.

As awesome as this Day of Atonement was, it was just a "shadow" of something greater, something final. Here's the fulfillment, and this is what's going to make your day:

"But Mary stood outside by the tomb weeping, and as she wept she stooped down and looked into the tomb. And she saw *two angels* in white, *sitting, one at the head and the other at the feet*, where the body of Jesus *had* lain" (John 11:11–12; emphasis added).

Wow! Just picture that beautiful scene. Two white-robed angels staring at the very spot where the perfect sacrifice was, one on each end, just like the angelic cherubim were positioned to stare at the blood on the mercy seat! But there was one *huge* difference. Do you see it?

The sacrifice *wasn't there!* For this sacrifice was no bull or lamb, but Jesus Christ, and He defeated sin and death, and rose from the dead, as those two angels said to Mary in Luke 24:5–6 (emphasis added): "Why do you seek the living among the dead? He is not here, but is *risen!*"

That should be the ultimate object of our thanksgiving today and every day. Right? Amen. Have a blessed holiday.

FRIDAY

It's Friday, and we're drawing close to the climax of our recent ponderings of how Satan was forever kicked out of heaven. We've set the scene by revealing the construct of the earthly and heavenly tabernacles, and we have shown that the former was simply a temporary "copy" of the latter. Since it was "earthly" and constructed by sinful humans, the items in the tabernacle had to be "purified." This was accomplished with the blood of the sacrificial animals. Leviticus chapter 16 goes into great detail regarding that, and Hebrews chapter 9 summarizes this as follows: "Then likewise he [Moses] sprinkled with blood both the tabernacle and all the vessels of the ministry. And according to the law almost all things are purified with blood, and without the shedding of blood there is no remission (of sin)." (vv. 21–22).

Understood. It makes sense, this purification of the earthly sanctuary. But here's the truly amazing thing that is not so obvious: the celestial, heavenly sanctuary *also* needed to be purified! Look at this:

"Therefore it was necessary that the *copies* of the things in heaven (the earthly sanctuary) should be purified with these (the blood of animals), but the *heavenly things themselves* with *better sacrifices* than these" (Hebrews 9:23; emphasis added).

Wow, think of that! Why would *heavenly* things need to be purified from sin? What in heaven is not holy? Isn't everything in heaven perfect and true and good?

Nope. Remember who's there? Who *we* put there legally?

Yep, Satan is there, and he had been since the Fall of Man, a constant reminder of our sin and rebellion. This is why God's many attempts to win us back to Him via grace in the Old Testament were fruitless. We couldn't receive that grace because we were sinful, the Savior hadn't come, and Satan was contaminating the heavenly tabernacle.

But that all changed at the cross, and the resurrection sealed the deal. Now one thing remained: the heavenly tabernacle had to be *purified*. And who could do that? We end this week with these beautiful Scriptures, and we'll wrap this topic up next week. Have a great weekend!

"Not with the blood of goats and calves, but with His own blood He entered the Most Holy Place once and for all, having obtained eternal redemption" (Hebrews 9:12).

"For Christ has not entered the holy places made with hands, which are copies of the true, but into Heaven itself, now to appear in the presence of God" (Hebrews 9:24).

30
WEEK

MONDAY

It's Monday, it's December, and we've set the scene (the heavenly sanctuary) for the final expulsion of Satan from heaven, from the presence of God. We closed last week with Hebrews 9, which clearly showed that Jesus Himself would enter the most holy place with His own blood to purify it. And *that*, my friends, is when the following happened:

> And war broke out in heaven: Michael and his angels fought with the dragon; and the dragon and his angels fought, but they did not prevail, nor was a place found for them in heaven any longer. So the great dragon was cast out, that serpent of old, called the Devil and Satan, who deceives the whole world; he was cast to the earth, and his angels were cast out with him. ... Therefore, rejoice, O heavens, and you who dwell in them! Woe to the inhabitants of the earth and the sea! For the devil has come down to you, having great wrath, because he knows that he has a short time. (Revelation 12:7–9, 12)

We gave these Scriptures previously, but they bear repeating because this stuff is really important and, I believe, not widely taught, if taught at all. For instance, the footnotes in your Bible probably state that this expulsion will take place at the time of the Great Tribulation. That is, it hasn't even happened yet. But that doesn't make sense to me. I've been endeavoring to show that it took place right after the Ascension of our Lord to heaven—and here's why: How could evil (Satan and his fallen angels) coexist with Jesus in heaven now that Jesus, as 100 percent God and 100 percent man, defeated him, obliterating Satan's legal standing before God as the rightful representative of planet Earth? Couldn't happen.

Here's why it was so important to get all evil and condemnation out of the celestial sanctuary *before* the Holy Spirit was given to indwell believers on earth: *We* believers are now the earthly sanctuary ("Do you not know that you are the temple of God and that the Spirit of God dwells in you?" [1 Corinthians 3:16]). *We* are where God, as the Holy Spirit, resides on earth, and that residence had to be purified before He could be sent to indwell us permanently. For us to be completely righteous and holy before God (and we actually are exactly that if our faith is in Jesus Christ and His cross), there could be no accusing/condemning entity in the heavenly sanctuary, nor the earthly sanctuary. Do you see that? This is why Satan was not going to give up this position easily, because he would no longer have any power over us—not legally, not justly—if he were banned from the throne of God. He is powerless in regard to us because "He who is in you is greater than he who is in the world" (1 John 4:4). Amen!

Hence the great war, which would not be won until our victorious Lord and Savior arrived on the scene *physically* bearing the permanent scars of redemption. That's why He left us when He did. He demonstrated yet again His overwhelming love for us by making absolutely sure that Satan could never hurt us again.

Wow! That's a lot to consider on a Monday morning, but I'm not done. There's still a lot of truth—deep, granted, but nonetheless super important—wrapped up in Hebrews 9 and Revelation 12. More tomorrow.

TUESDAY

Before the throne of God above
I have a strong, a perfect plea,
A great High Priest, whose name is Love,
Who ever lives and pleads for me.
My name is graven on His hands.
My name is written on His heart.
I know that while in heaven He stands,
No tongue may bid me thence depart.
When Satan tempts me with despair

And tells me of the guilt within,
Upwards I look … and see Him there
Who made an end to all my sin.
Because a sinless Savior died,
My sinful soul is counted free.
For God the Just is satisfied
To look at Him … and pardon me.
—"Before the Throne of God Above," 1863

Charitie Bancroft was twenty-two years old when she wrote this song; she initially entitled it "The Advocate," and she beautifully captures in word and song what we've been studying. Notice that Satan is not in heaven accusing us and reminding God of our sin and worthlessness; only our Advocate, our one High Priest, is before the throne of God, and because of His righteousness, we are seen as flawless, perfect, in God's eyes! This young woman's spiritual insight floors me; I wasn't thinking of these things at the age of twenty-two!

But Satan is still active, isn't he? Look what he's doing in the song: he is trying to cause despair and condemnation in the believer. But here's an important distinction that you just have to see, and this is why I've been spending so much time on this topic: Satan is attacking us human believers *here* on planet Earth and on a carnal level, playing to our emotions, intellect, and physical senses. He is opposing us directly; he is *not* making a case against us in heaven before God on a spiritual level, because *He is no longer there*! So God will *always* see us *only* as righteous and holy and flawless and perfect, for such is the nature of our Holy Spirit–filled spirit person. Get this now: God is *never* against us; He is *always* for us, and the only power Satan has over believers, over us, is what *we* give him! I'm serious. He has zero power otherwise. Even when we give in to his temptation (and we all do), he cannot negatively affect our position in Christ. We are always sons and daughters of the Most High God, perfect in His eyes.

If this sounds just too good to be true, well, then that's exactly what the Gospel is. I've learned to stop questioning it and just thankfully accept it and look forward to every day in our Lord. Back to Revelation 12 tomorrow.

WEDNESDAY

More dramatic excerpts from Revelation 12, and remember, this is not the Revelation of John, but the Revelation of Jesus Christ to His followers (believers) via the apostle John:

"Rejoice, O heavens, and you who dwell in them. ... Woe to the inhabitants of the Earth and the sea. For the Devil has come down to you, having great wrath. ... Now when the dragon saw that he had been cast to the Earth, he persecuted the woman who gave birth to the male Child. ... And the dragon was enraged with the woman, and he went to make war with the rest of her offspring, who keep the commandments of God and have the testimony of Jesus Christ" (vv. 12–17).

We really deal with the hard questions in this series, don't we? We've already established why we can "come boldly to the throne of grace, that we may obtain mercy and find grace in time of need" (Hebrews 4:16), because we have a High Priest over the house of God to whom we can "draw near with a true heart in full assurance of faith" (Hebrews 10:21–22). This is all because Satan has been permanently expelled from heaven.

Now we tackle that age-old question, "Why is there so much evil in this world?" Now, again, I had been taught growing up that this woeful time for the earth, when Satan comes down to us, occurs at the time of the Great Tribulation, after the Rapture of the believers, but I don't buy that. It seems to me he's already been here, wreaking all kinds of havoc and causing us plenty of woe.

But hasn't that been the case since the Fall of Man in the garden? Yes, to a degree, but before the way of escape from sin and death came about (occurring at the Crucifixion; sealed at the resurrection), there was not nearly as much satanic activity on this earth. Just look at any Bible concordance and see how many times the name Satan and the word *devil* are used in the Old Testament compared to the New. It's astonishing. Satan was on a tight leash as we saw in Job. There was plenty of misery, heartache, sickness, and death among humans, for sure, but I think primarily because of the natural consequences of our sinful nature and separation from God, rather than because of concerted attacks from Satan and his demons.

The way I look at the history of humankind, things dramatically changed shortly after the time of Jesus Christ, as we went from BC to AD. We'll explore examples of this dark menace and how it negatively affected Jews (the woman), Christians (the rest of her offspring), and the human race in general, starting tomorrow.

THURSDAY

The Jews are God's chosen people; Satan was God's chosen archangel. He was originally named "Lucifer, son of the morning" (Isaiah 14:12), but he turned against God's love and led one-third of the angels in a rebellion, which failed, causing the rebels to be thrown out of heaven. "Therefore I cast you as a profane thing out of the mountain of God" (Ezekiel 28:16). But Satan wasn't destroyed—not yet. We previously saw why: because the universe had been rocked by these accusations against God; there were questions. In response, the Godhead ordained a beautiful plan to prove, once and for all of eternity, that God is *love* and, at the same time, *just* and *righteous*. That plan revolved around a new creation, humans, made in the "image of God." They were given the awesome responsibility of *freedom*, that is, a free will, and they quickly fell from the spiritual to the carnal realm, enticed by "the lust of the flesh, and the lust of the eyes, and the boastful pride of life" (1 John 2:16), thereby giving the authority they had been given over this earth to Satan, allowing him access to heaven once again, legally. And God honored that.

But there would be a plan in place, formed "before the foundation of the world" (Ephesians 1:4), to save these humans, and God would choose the children of a man named Abraham to shine His light of redemption on planet Earth. There was a prophesied Messiah, a Savior, and He would come through these "children of Israel." Satan knew that. His plans to keep the Messiah from coming were foiled, and the Messiah came, fully God and fully man. He would righteously and justly free humans from the bondage of Satan, from sin, and from death and disease for all who would believe. He would defeat Satan at the cross, and the whole universe would see, beyond any doubt, that God was *love* as He Himself would take the punishment of sin, meant for sinful humankind, fully upon Himself. The ransom for humans was paid. As I like to say, the cross is the sign of the ransom paid by the love of God to satisfy the justice of God and secure the righteousness of God.

Because of this victory, Jesus Christ could ascend to heaven and once again, this time permanently, kick Satan out. Where would Satan go? Yep, back to planet Earth, knowing he was defeated, knowing his ultimate outcome (the lake of fire and brimstone [Revelation 20:10]), yet knowing the end for him was not yet, but soon. He was *really angry* (Revelation 12:12). The first target of his great wrath would be the Jews (the woman in Revelation 12). He would hit them hard—very hard. History proves it; this isn't make-believe stuff. We'll start looking at this historical evidence tomorrow; covering the theological history of humankind in three paragraphs was enough for this morning!

FRIDAY

"Alas! For that day is great, so that none is like it; and it is the time of Jacob's trouble, but he shall be saved out of it" (Jeremiah 30:7).

This is a prophecy regarding the Great Tribulation, a time of unprecedented travail for the Jewish people. There's a reason why Satan will be able to unleash his wrath on Israel like never before at that time. We'll get to that later. My point this morning is that Satan has already been attacking the Jews severely, starting shortly after the Ascension of Jesus Christ to heaven and the simultaneous casting out of Satan to earth.

During Jesus's time on earth, Israel was a nation, subdued and under the authority of the Roman Empire, of course, but still allowed to practice their religion and sacrifice in their temple. Within just one generation (thirty-seven years) of Jesus's death, the Roman general Titus (later the emperor) sacked Jerusalem in AD 70 and utterly destroyed the temple (just as Jesus predicted in all three synoptic Gospels—Matthew 24, Mark

13, and Luke 21), and the Jews were dispersed. This time, their sojourn in faraway places would not be just for a generation or two, as was the case with the Assyrian and Babylonian captivities, but for a very, very long time. They would not have a nation again until 1948! And to this day, there has been no further institution of the sacrificial system. This was unprecedented in Old Testament times.

Need I mention the Holocaust? There were approximately nine million Jews living in Europe before World War II; six million lost their lives. Does that sound like "great wrath" to you? Two out of three Jews were exterminated, willfully and purposely. This number represented two out of five Jews worldwide! What if the United States were to suffer that sort of mortality? Satan has been intent on wiping out the Jews, and it's still the case. He'll never be successful, but he'll come very close in the Tribulation. Second Thessalonians 2:7–9 reveals why he'll be so successful then:

"For the mystery of lawlessness is already at work; only He *who now restrains* will do so until He *is taken out of the way*. And then the lawless one will be revealed … the coming of the lawless one is according to the working of Satan" (emphasis added).

I'm out of time this morning. We'll look a little more at this portion of scripture next week, then we'll look at how Satan's wrath has been directed against the Church and humanity in general. Have a great weekend.

WEEK 31

MONDAY

"And Jesus came and spoke to them, saying, 'All authority has been given to Me in Heaven and on Earth … and, lo, I am with you always, even to the end of the age'" (Matthew 28:18, 20).

Our Lord uttered these words just before His ascension to heaven, just before He left the planet and His believers. Yet He said that He would *always* be with us. And He said that all power was given to Him, not just in heaven but also on earth. What? Didn't He actually leave, not yet to return? And isn't this earth under the dominion of Satan? It sure seems like it.

Happy Monday. We've been searching out scripture regarding what I believe to be super-important events that happened after the Ascension of Jesus and before the Day of Pentecost. We know the Crucifixion of Jesus Christ is the focal point for the entire universe; everything else is relative to that, and not just here on earth, as it was there that the universe settled the questions regarding God's character and nature once and for all. As a consequence of that victory, the environments of heaven and earth abruptly changed; everything would be different now. Satan lost his standing in heaven and was cast out forever. This is huge for believers as there is no longer an accuser in heaven. The earth is now the domain of Satan because, although he is completely defeated, his end is not yet; he has not been put under Jesus's feet yet ("The Lord said to my Lord, 'Sit at my right hand till I make Your enemies Your footstool'" [Psalm 110:1]). Satan is very angry, full of wrath, and that anger is especially hot against the Jews and the Church. That's our latest topic.

But something else also happened at this time, and it is the most significant of all as the presence of God came to planet Earth to *indwell* believers, to actually live inside them, never to leave them. This is unprecedented. In the old covenant, Jesus would show up in preincarnate form (referred to as the Angel of the Lord) on occasion, but He would always leave. The same could be said of the Holy Spirit. "Do not take Your Holy Spirit from me" (Psalm 51:11). There was no permanent presence of God on this fallen, rebellious earth. Isn't that crazy? And if that arrangement had been allowed to continue once Satan and his demons were unleashed on this planet, we would all be doomed. But we're exactly the opposite; actually we are "more than conquerors" (Romans 8:37). On that positive note we will end today.

TUESDAY

"You are the salt of the earth ... you are the light of the world" (Matthew 5:13, 14).

These are the words of Jesus, given in the Sermon on the Mount. He's talking about believers. The reason we are the "salt and light" of this world is that the presence of God, the Holy Spirit, dwells within us, and empowers us and guides us, and illuminates our minds. It is this power of God, manifest through us in this world, that *restrains* the evil of Satan from completely destroying humans; it is keeping him in check to a degree. Here's what I think: Just looking at world history, we find that the more the Gospel is manifest in this world, the more Satan is restrained. We're going to flesh this out later, but the point I want to make this morning is that the reason there will be so much unrestrained evil against the Jews during the Great Tribulation, the time of Jacob's trouble, is not because Satan is thrown out of heaven to come down to earth at that point—he's already here, obviously—but because the restraining Holy Spirit is *taken out* of the earth via the Rapture of believers. That's why I believe the Rapture will take place at the very start of the seven-year Tribulation time. Doesn't this make sense? It does to me, and I think it also explains why the United States doesn't seem to play a restraining force for good in end-times prophecy as our population will be decimated after the Rapture.

Isn't this stuff interesting? Now this doesn't mean the Holy Spirit will have no activity on this earth during the Great Tribulation, as many humans will be saved during this time (and martyred), and the Holy Spirit is necessary for salvation to occur; He "baptizes" us in Christ (Romans 6:3). However, His presence will be a fraction of what it is now as seen in those verses we gave last week, 2 Thessalonians 2:5–10, a portion of which says, "He who now restrains will do so until He is taken out of the way."

But even before that time, Satan has been actively wreaking havoc on the earth. We've briefly looked at his manifest anger against the Jews; next we'll look at how he has persecuted the Church, identified in Revelation 12:17 as "the rest of her [Israel's] offspring, who keep the commandments of God, and have the testimony of Jesus Christ." Have a great day.

WEDNESDAY

"I tell you the truth, when you were younger, you tied your own belt, and went where you wanted. But when you are old, you will put out your hands and someone else will tie you and take you where you don't want to go" (John 21:18 NCV).

There is no doubt that the wrathful, hateful, vengeful Satan and his friends "went to make war" (Revelation 12:17) with the early Church, and by that I mean the body of believers in Jesus Christ, whether Jew or Gentile. Let's start with the disciples: of the eleven remaining, ten would die a martyr's death. None would fall away from the faith, but only one, John, would die of old age.

The question comes up here, and it's a good one, "What about Judas Iscariot?" Didn't he repent after betraying Jesus? Wasn't he ultimately saved?

The answer is an emphatic *no*! Jesus made it very clear the night of his betrayal: "Those whom You gave Me I have kept; and none of them is lost *except* the son of perdition, that the Scripture might be fulfilled" (John 17:12). Judas was *remorseful*, not *repentant*. There's a huge difference between the two. Repentance is not dependent on "regretting" that you have sinned, which Judas clearly did as seen in Matthew 27:3–4: "Then

Judas, His betrayer, seeing that he had been condemned, was *remorseful* and brought back the thirty pieces of silver to the chief priests and elders, saying, 'I have sinned by betraying innocent blood'" (emphasis added). Repentance (the Greek word is *metanoia*) literally means to "change your direction 180 degrees," to turn from your way of thinking to Jesus's way of thinking; it is a metamorphosis from a self-centered life to a Jesus-centered life. To accomplish that, one has to die to one's sinful, carnal nature; one's sins have to be forgiven and blotted out. Our Lord accomplished that at the cross. No matter how sorry, or remorseful, we are for our sins, they are still *our sins* until we give our life to Jesus, and then they are remitted (canceled), to be remembered no more (Jeremiah 31:34)!

Wow, I don't really know where all that came from. I wasn't planning any of that, but I think it's revealing to see that even one of the twelve chosen disciples of Jesus Christ, who spent over three years with Him, was not saved. Don't beat yourself up if you aren't successful in "converting" your loved ones, no matter how good a witness you have been. It's not your fault. Not all will be saved; there are some who are so self-proud that they will "neglect so great a salvation" (Hebrews 2:3).

We didn't have a chance to explain the opening verse today. It's about the disciple Peter. We'll pick it up here tomorrow.

THURSDAY

Our current topic is the persecution of the early Church by an incensed Satan, recently banished from heaven by our Lord Jesus Christ. The verse we gave yesterday morning, John 21:18, is a prophecy of the risen Jesus about the apostle Peter and "by what death he would glorify God" (v. 19). In fact, Peter would be crucified as his Lord was, but with one difference: Peter would request to be crucified upside down, not considering himself worthy to die in the same manner as Jesus.

Peter seemed to know exactly what Jesus was referring to, but his response was most unusual: He looked over to the apostle John, who wrote this account, and said to Jesus, "'But Lord, what about this man?' Jesus said to him, 'If I will that he remain until I come, what is that to you? *You follow Me*'" (John 21:21–22; emphasis added).

I have some thoughts about what this was all about, but first let's be clear that the early Church faced a ton of persecution, and not just regarding the ten martyred disciples. We know of the horrendous oppression Christians suffered under the Roman Empire, but it was even worse for the very small number of true believers after "Christianity" gradually became the official religion of Rome under Emperor Constantine in the fourth century AD. The atrocities of the Roman Catholic Church against believers during the Middle Ages are chronicled in Foxe's *Book of Martyrs*. I wouldn't recommend this book for bedtime reading with the kids. In truth, early Christians seemed to be anything but "more than conquerors," and they suffered greatly. We are allowed to honestly ponder *why*. If the scripture is absolutely true, and if Satan has no power over believers since the Holy Spirit indwelling us is so much greater than the evil spirit of this world (1 John 4:4), then why all the carnage in the Church, even to this day? Why is Satan seemingly winning?

You know, I think it's neat that we can honestly question this great God of ours without fear. "'Come now and let us reason together,' says the Lord" (Isaiah 1:18). A function of the Holy Spirit in us is to help answer these questions, "for the Spirit searches all things, yes, the deep things of God" (2 Corinthians 2:10). These questions are deep, and I love to ponder them. Tomorrow morning I'll give you what answers I've been given regarding the persecution of Christians, all from simply meditating on God's Word and making sure my thoughts align with the "whole counsel of God" (Acts 20:27). I certainly don't have all the answers, and that's okay, because we won't understand things fully until we see Him face-to-face. And then I don't think it will even matter.

FRIDAY

That Satan and his demons have been attacking the Church—and by that I mean the body of believers in Jesus Christ, also known as the "Bride of Christ" (Revelation 19:7–9)—with a vengeance since the very start, when Satan was expelled completely from the presence of God in heaven and the Church was born on the Day of Pentecost, when the Holy Spirit came to earth to indwell and remain in believers, is obvious. But why has he been so successful in persecuting the Church, especially in the first fifteen hundred years of its existence? Aren't we more powerful than he? What follows are some observations of mine, couched in scripture, but nonetheless just my musings. We'll start today and finish this up next week.

I mentioned previously that the Holy Spirit, dwelling in all true believers, is the restraining force against the unleashed power of Satan on this earth. Just think how few believers there were on this earth right after Jesus left and the Holy Spirit came. There were just one hundred twenty believers in the Upper Room when the Holy Spirit was given. Although miraculously three thousand more responded to Peter's sermon on the Day of Pentecost, there was still just a limited presence of the Holy Spirit on earth. And how many demons (fallen angels) were there? We don't actually have any idea; there could have been one hundred, or one hundred million, or one hundred million billion. We just don't know. But I do know this: there were twice as many good angels, and whatever the number was then is the same number now. That's kind of an intriguing thought. Angels, good or fallen, can't reproduce, but we believers can! Just think of it. Let's say there were initially five thousand believers in the very early church and one hundred million demons. Now I know it's like comparing apples and oranges, because we as believers can "do all things through Christ, who strengthens us" (Philippians 4:13), but the numbers are still impressively in Satan's favor. However, there are probably hundreds of millions, if not billions, of believers today, and there's not a single new demon. I find that encouraging. You see, things that are evil and of Satan are *finite*; there are limitations on numbers and time because Satan has a beginning and an end (that is, his influence on the universe has an end; he himself will be *forever* tormented in a lake of fire and brimstone. I hope he's reading this!). But the things of God are eternal and limitless. Amen!

My point is that Satan's limited power was relatively unrestrained in the time of the early Church, and it makes sense to me that this contributed to the intense persecution they endured. And not only the church but also humanity in general as Satan absolutely hates all humans since they were created in the image of God and he was not. A very *dark* era in human history, actually often called by even non-Christians the Dark Ages, was about to become manifest. More on the church and human history next week. Have a great weekend.

32
WEEK

MONDAY

It's Monday. We haven't taken time for an overview of where we are and how we got here for many weeks, so let's do that now. If you can remember all the way back to the start of these writings seven months ago, you'll recall we had three goals. We're still on the first of these, namely, showing what is available to believers regarding healing, focusing on the Atonement of Jesus Christ on the cross. We still have the topics of the role of modern medical science in healing and the healing of nonbelievers to cover, but these writings are to span a full year, so we have time. No worries.

We have already meticulously set the foundation for claiming that physical/mental healing is part of the Atonement, but we wondered why it took four thousand years of human existence for that to take place. That brought us to examine God's plan of salvation. We've progressed from the Fall of Man in the garden to the children of Israel's miraculous delivery out of their Egyptian bondage, but we stalled over this amazing fifty day period of time between the Exodus and Mount Sinai, contrasting that with the equally amazing time between the Crucifixion and the Day of Pentecost. Most recently we have become even more focused on the nine- or ten-day (depending on whether you count the day of the Ascension as Day 1, or the day after that) period of time during which there was no apparent presence of God on this earth since Jesus had ascended (left), and the Comforter, the Holy Spirit, had not been given to indwell and empower believers, as Jesus walked this earth for forty days after the resurrection, and Pentecost occurred fifty days after the Passover (Good Friday). I have postulated that this period of time was when Jesus purified the celestial sanctuary by casting Satan out of heaven, and he was cast fully to this earth. He has been tormenting humankind, and especially the Jews and the church, to a greater degree than he was ever allowed to before. We've looked briefly at the Jewish persecution, and now we're dealing with the wiles of the enemy against the Church. Got it?

We're questioning why the Church hasn't been more victorious, why almost all of the disciples died a martyr's death, and why the early believers were subject to the cruel whims of the Roman emperors, like being killed by wild beasts as a public spectacle. The first reason I gave last time had to do with the scarcity of the presence of the Holy Spirit (because of the scarcity of believers), compared to the widespread presence of evil manifest by Satan and all the fallen angels (demons). This would have a negative impact not only on Christians but also on humankind in general. I think this is very obvious from history, at least the history I was taught in school. Before I enumerate the other thoughts I have regarding the trials of the early Church, I want to say more about what the relative lack of restraint on Satan and his friends meant for the world during what is known as the Middle Ages, tomorrow.

TUESDAY

"You, O king, were watching; and behold, a great image! This great image, whose splendor was excellent, stood before you; and its form was awesome. This image's head was of fine gold, and its chest and arms of silver, its belly and thighs of bronze, its legs of iron, its feet partly of iron and partly of clay" (Daniel 2:31–33).

It's around 600 BC, and the Babylonian Empire, under King Nebuchadnezzar, rules the known world. The Jews are captive in Babylon, and Daniel has found favor and is an adviser to the king. The king has a troubling dream, even more troubling because he can't remember it! All he knows is that it was very important, and he has to recall it and find its meaning. We all know the story: Nebuchadnezzar orders his sorcerers, astrologers, and magicians to tell him the dream and the interpretation, but they, of course, cannot fulfill this seemingly impossible request. Remember, they are empowered by Satan and his demons, and Satan is *not* omniscient; only God is. They are overwhelmed by this ridiculously unreasonable request and are obviously upset with the king. Look at their response:

"There is not a man on Earth who can tell the king's matter, therefore no king, lord, or ruler has *ever* asked such things. ... It is a difficult thing that the king requests, and there is no other who can tell it to the king, *except the gods*, whose dwelling is not in flesh" (Daniel 2:10, 11; emphasis added).

They got that right! But the request finally comes to Daniel. He inquires of the Lord and is told the dream and the interpretation. Then he makes this *awesome* statement when explaining to the king why he has the answer to the king's request and the pagan magicians and sorcerers did not. *"But there is a God in heaven"* (Daniel 2:28; emphasis added). Whenever you're feeling overwhelmed or down or defeated, just remember that! And this God *does* dwell with flesh! He is all-knowing and ever-present and all-powerful, and He absolutely *loves* you!

Wow! This is a great way to start our day! Tomorrow morning we'll explain the vision and see how this is all related to the order and rule of the ancient world. We'll discuss how it all changed for the worse, starting just after the time of Jesus Christ, at which time Satan became fully engaged with this earth, having been cast out of heaven. Have a great day.

WEDNESDAY

Are you ready for some ancient history? Did you know that the Bible, especially the Old Testament, is an awesome history book? It's a history book like no other as it often foretells (through prophecy) what is going to happen centuries before it happens, then it accurately describes it when it happens. What history book does that? One written by God does that. The most obvious example of this are the more than three hundred specific prophecies about Jesus Christ in the Old Testament, all of which came to pass. But this dream of King Nebuchadnezzar is pretty awesome itself as it will lay out about a thousand years of the rule of successive earthly empires, all of them clearly heathen but also obviously used by God to help fulfill His plan of salvation for the human race. We'll spend some time showing that because I think it reveals the heart of our loving God by establishing some sort of order and sense in an unredeemed world, pending the arrival of the ultimate solution to humankind's dilemma, Jesus Christ. I want to point out again how dramatically different things would become shortly after the time of Jesus, and not for the better, as Satan and his demons were unleashed on the earth as we've shown and went after the Jews and the Church with a great vengeance, but also caused unprecedented suffering in the whole world. The age of the great empires would be no more, and things would become *very* dark until two new, and this time Christian, empires would rise up and usher in a period of relative order and peace, namely, the Pax Britannica (British Peace) and Pax Americana (American Peace).

I know, this all sounds interesting (and it actually is), but what does any of this have to do, even remotely, with healing? It's not obvious, but there is a reason I've been told to set all this foundation for what we believe. It has to do with this verse:

"Always be ready to give a defense to everyone who asks you a reason for the hope that is in you" (1 Peter 3:15).

Christianity is intelligent and beautiful and, I think, easily defended, but we need to know the foundation of our beliefs to mount such a defense. And such knowledge only comes through studying Scripture and seeing *why* we can truly believe and know that healing for believers is in the Atonement, and then being able to show that, from Adam and Eve on, there has been an actual plan in place to save us and reunite us with God and restore what the enemy took. That's why we are so meticulously dissecting Scripture and attempting to have an explanation for every argument that comes up against what we believe. Seeing the heart of God in all of human history is such an awesome thing; it strengthens our faith. It's called a Christian worldview, and that's what I'm trying to paint a portrait of in this treatise. We'll paint some more tomorrow as we start examining the Great Image of Daniel 2.

THURSDAY

So back to Daniel 2 and the awesome image of King Nebuchadnezzar's dream. The head of fine gold represented Nebuchadnezzar's own empire, Babylon, the dominant power in the world at that time (around 600 BC).

Now it should be noted that before Babylon was Assyria, the capital of which was Nineveh, the wicked city Jonah was told to go and preach repentance to, a concept so disgusting to Jonah (as the Assyrian Empire was very wicked and cruel) that he, of course, refused to go. But God would win that little battle, and the reluctant prophet went and preached. And guess what? "So the people of Nineveh believed God" (Jonah 3:5), and repented bigtime, and God, for the time, spared them, a city of probably over half a million people. Again this shows the heart of God as the Assyrians were not even His chosen people, yet He showed such mercy and long-suffering toward them. Jesus Himself pointed out the irony of the repentance of evil Nineveh versus the lack of repentance of the Jews of His time: "The men of Nineveh will rise up in the judgement with this generation and condemn it, for they repented at the preaching of Jonah; and indeed a greater than Jonah is here" (Luke 11:32).

My point is that God used Assyria for His glory, and He would have used them more had their repentance been sustained, but it was not. Therefore Babylon, under King Nebuchadnezzar, would subsequently be the dominant power—the "head of fine gold." It is obvious that God would work through this heathen ruler. Look at what God says about him via the prophet Jeremiah: "I have made the earth, the man and the beast that are on the ground, by My great power and by My outstretched arm, and have given it to whom it seemed proper to Me. And now I have given all these lands into the hand of Nebuchadnezzar the king of Babylon, *My servant* ... so all the nations shall serve him and his son" (Jeremiah 27:5–7; emphasis added).

Wow! This is a heathen king, but he would see over and over again the deliverance of Daniel and his friends and come to recognize the superiority of their God. "Now I, Nebuchadnezzar, praise and extol and honor the King of heaven, all of whose works are truth, and His ways justice" (Daniel 4:37).

So we have the great empire of Assyria then Babylon, and then the "chest and arms of silver." The anatomy is significant as it implies two entities joined in the middle. Daniel sees this empire to come after Babylon in his own vision, described in Daniel chapter 8: "Then I lifted my eyes and saw, and there, standing beside the river, was a *ram* with two horns … the *ram* that you saw, having the two horns—they are the kings of Media and Persia" (Daniel 8:3, 20; emphasis added). So this is clearly the Medo-Persian Empire, one of whose emperors in particular, Cyrus, was mightily used by God. What Cyrus would be led by the Lord to do would be prophesied by Isaiah, who would mention him *by name* a good one hundred years prior to the event! "Who says of Cyrus, 'He is My shepherd, and he shall perform all My pleasure, saying to Jerusalem, "You shall be built," and to the temple, "Your foundation shall be laid"?'" (Isaiah 44:23).

Yes, Cyrus the Persian king would allow the captive Jews to return to the Promised Land and rebuild Jerusalem and the temple, and God's plan of salvation for the human race would stay on track, soldiering on. But there are three more empires composing that Great Image. Tomorrow.

FRIDAY

> This great image, whose splendor was excellent … its belly and thighs of bronze. (Daniel 2:31, 32)

> But after you shall arise another kingdom, inferior to yours; then another, a third kingdom of bronze, which shall rule over of all the earth. (Daniel 2:39)

> I saw the ram [the kingdom of Medo-Persia] pushing westward, northward, and southward, so that no animal could withstand him. … He did according to his will, and became great. And … suddenly a male goat came from the west … and the goat had a notable horn between his eyes. Then he came to the ram … and ran at him with furious power. And I saw him confronting the ram; he was moved with rage against him, attacked the ram, and broke his two horns. … The male goat is the kingdom of Greece. The large horn that is between its eyes is the first king. (Daniel 8:4–7, 21)

The third great empire found in the Great Image is Greece, and its king is Alexander the Great, who lived in the fourth century BC. Isn't the Bible amazing? The book of Daniel was written two hundred years before all of this, yet the prophecy is right on. There's an interesting account by the Jewish historian Josephus of how this impacted Alexander the Great himself. The king, in his conquest of the known world, was marching to Jerusalem, and the high priest met with him before his arrival and showed him these very prophecies in Daniel, written centuries earlier, of Alexander's victory over Persia. This so impressed Alexander that he showed favor to the Jews, and Jerusalem was not destroyed. But Alexander was destroyed. At the young age of just thirty-two (younger than Jesus Christ at His death), he succumbed to a febrile illness, either infectious or the result of intentional poisoning.

My point: This was another purely heathen empire, but the great God of heaven interacted with its ruler, orchestrating things to accomplish His will and purpose. That would also be the case with the next great empire, the greatest of them all, but to a lesser degree. And then the age of the Great Empires will come to a temporary end, coinciding with the increased evil of an unleashed Satan. The fifth and final earthly empire of the Great Image is yet to come to fruition. Here's what I think about that one: (1) God will have no such influence or interactions with this one as it will be entirely evil, and (2) the ingredients for its formation are already here.

Wow! The Word of God illuminates truth like nothing else. I love studying it. We'll finish up with the third empire, that of Greece, next week, and then move on to the fourth empire, one as strong as iron, one that would be chosen to rule the word at the time of the incarnation of Jesus Christ, which we celebrate next week: the Roman Empire. Have a great weekend.

33
WEEK

MONDAY

What an exciting week we commence. It's the eve of Christmas Eve, which reminds me of the origin of Christmas Eve as told to me when I was a young, impressionable boy. It goes back to the garden, and it was the day before the first Christmas, but Adam, as usual, was confused and exclaimed to his wife, "It's Christmas, Eve!" She pointed out the error, but the name stuck.

So we're appropriately looking at how God was paving the way for the birth of His only Son on this earth, to fulfill His plan of salvation by working through the great empires of Assyria, Babylon, Medo-Persia, Greece, and Rome, the last of which would be in power when the Savior arrived. We'll finish Alexander the Great and Greece today.

"Suddenly, a male goat came from the west, across the surface of the whole earth, *without touching the ground*" (Daniel 8:5; emphasis added).

Last week we saw that the goat is Greece, under their great leader Alexander, whose army was relatively small but superfast. The rapidity of Alexander's conquests was such that Daniel saw the goat in his vision as basically flying, not even touching the ground! There was something very important being spread throughout the known world with this army, namely, their language, Greek. It would become the universal language on earth, much as English is today. This would be the case even in the Roman Empire, where Latin was the formal official language, but Greek was the practical, day-to-day language.

This is significant because the Gospel of Jesus Christ would be revealed in this language; the New Testament was written in Greek. And as we pointed out previously, the Old Testament was also translated into Greek from Hebrew even before Jesus (the Septuagint). This is so interesting to me, that the greatest story ever told, that of the Jewish Messiah, was not revealed in Hebrew but in a Gentile language. Now Jesus didn't speak Greek, nor exclusively Hebrew, but a combination of Hebrew and Aramaic. Why was that? What happened to the Hebrew language?

Well, here's my musings on this. Firstly, the Jewish people, in general, had greatly strayed from God's Word, such that they completely missed the obvious, that Jesus Christ was their Messiah, thus opening up the Gospel to the Gentiles, whose language was Greek. Secondly, and I think more importantly, the Greek language is beautifully deep and complex, able to convey subtleties in thought and intent, which was necessary because the Word of God is, as I think we've shown already, incredibly deep and complex yet, at the same time, very simple and direct. It all depends how deep you want to go. Lastly, Greek was the common, universal language, facilitating distribution much more so than if the Bible had been written in Hebrew. To me, it's a tragic commentary on the Jews and their wandering from their God and rejection of their Savior. But it's not the end of the story! They'll be "grafted" back in (Romans 11). I'm just thinking, if there is one common language during Jesus Christ's rule on this earth, it will be Hebrew.

We start the Roman Empire tomorrow.

TUESDAY

"And the fourth kingdom shall be as strong as iron, inasmuch as iron breaks in pieces and shatters everything" (Daniel 2:40).

It's Christmas Eve. We now reveal the empire chosen to play host to the incarnation of the great God of heaven on earth. The Son would humble Himself, divest Himself of all His glory, power, and honor, and be born as a defenseless, helpless baby human. All the universe was dumbfounded because it is an inconceivable thing that God would become man! They marveled at the thought that the Ruler of the universe would subject Himself to the rule of a base, ruthless, but very strong earthly empire whose crushing of dissent would ensure a period of world "peace" not previously seem—the Pax Romana, Roman Peace. The world would not be free, but it would be ordered under Roman rule, allowing for the proclamation of the truths of the only truly liberating message for humankind, the Gospel of Jesus Christ. This is another beautiful example of God's intricate plan of salvation as He chose just the right time in human history for Jesus to come, maximizing the harvest of souls for the kingdom.

It's interesting that the first three empires in the Great Image were symbolized by precious metals—gold, silver, bronze—but not this one, not the Roman Empire. There's nothing flashy or beautiful about iron, but it was the strongest material known to humankind at that time, and it could destroy the softer precious metals. Rome would rule with an iron hand and maintain the peace, but not righteously or justly. That little baby, however, would one day, many, many years later, rule with a *rod* of *iron*, justly and righteously, as seen in Revelation 19:15: "And He Himself will rule them with a rod of iron."

But not *this* time. That's not why He came this first time, the First Advent. He came to deal with *sin*. He came to *die*. He came to *suffer* and *die*. This innocent baby boy, the first human *ever* to be born sinless, was *born* to *die*! Remember that today.

Wow! You know, I'm just so in love with the Holy Spirit; I just have to say that. I don't plan the order of these writings; He does. I couldn't have foreseen that we would be studying the Roman Empire at just the right time of year to tie it in with Christmas, but here we are! I love it.

Hey, kids, try to get some sleep tonight, this night before Christmas. Tomorrow's a big day.

WEDNESDAY

"And it came to pass in those days that a decree went out from Caesar Augustus that all the world should be registered ... this census. So, all went to be registered, everyone to his own city" (Luke 2:1–3).

Merry Christmas! We're seeing how God the Father so beautifully orchestrated the birth of His Son, working through the secular Roman Empire as Mary and Joseph lived in Nazareth, but the Messiah was to be born in Bethlehem (Micah 5:2). *Both* Mary and Joseph were descendants of King David (different sons of David; Joseph from Solomon and Mary from Nathan), and David's hometown was Bethlehem, so by order of the Roman emperor, they had to go to Bethlehem to be counted. That's where the Christ child would be born. Amazing, isn't it?

He would be born in the dark of night, but that night sky lit up like the Fourth of July when the Savior of the world entered:

"Now there were in the same country shepherds living out in the fields, keeping watch over their flock by night. And behold, an angel of the Lord stood before them and the *glory of the Lord shone around them*" (Luke 2:8–9; emphasis added).

Then a whole bunch of angels showed up, and this is what they proclaimed: "Glory to God in the highest, and on earth peace, goodwill toward men!" (Luke 2:14 NKJV).

As much as I like the NKJV, this particular translation is misleading. Think about it. Did the arrival of the Messiah actually usher in an age of peace and goodwill among humans on this earth? Actually, quite the contrary. Circumstances on planet Earth are going to get a lot worse soon after Jesus, as we will presently show. What the angels are actually saying is "peace toward men of goodwill." I like the New Century Version translation of this:

"Give glory to God in Heaven, and on Earth let there be peace among the people who please God" (Luke 2:14).

Makes more sense, doesn't it? How do we please God? We *accept* the free gift of salvation through His Son. Only then will we be at peace! God is not mad at us anymore, we're not estranged from Him anymore, once we put our faith in Jesus Christ!

And that's what Christmas is all about. Have a great day in the Lord!

THURSDAY

"But we were hoping that it was He who was going to redeem Israel" (Luke 24:21).

The fourth great empire of King Nebuchadnezzar's vision in Daniel 2, the Roman Empire, was in power during the entire length of our Lord's time on this earth. He was subject to its authority, and He didn't contest it. This was problematic for His followers, those who did believe in Him, because they thought the Messiah would come to liberate them from Roman oppression; they didn't understand that the Holy Scripture described two very different scenarios for the Messiah, the Suffering Servant and the Conquering King, because their eyes had not been opened to the mystery of *two* separate advents of our Lord. They didn't comprehend that *this* advent was all about *sin*, and it had to happen to allow for the *second* advent, yet to come, which would be all about *righteous rule*. Jesus never went against the secular authority over Him, but He did frequently go against the *religious* authority over Him, composed of the scribes and Pharisees, as He was all about His Father's business, about showing the world, and indeed the closely watching universe, what His Father was really like, where His heart was, namely, centered on uncompromised *love*. He seemed to me to be rather disinterested in the rule of Rome all around Him as this strong-as-iron, crushing power would not crush Him, would not keep Him from fulfilling His purpose. That would be obvious. But here's the amazing thing: He didn't crush it either! It's almost as if the civil government in place over Him existed at a much lower level than He; it was neither here nor there. The Pharisees noticed this and planned to call Him out on that. Here's the account Matthew gives, and it is beautiful:

> Then the Pharisees went and plotted how they might entangle Him in His talk … saying, "Teacher, we know that You are true, and teach the way of God in truth; nor do You care about anyone, for You do not regard the person of men. Tell us, therefore, what do You think? Is it lawful to pay taxes to Caesar, or not?" But Jesus perceived their wickedness, and said, "Why do you test Me, you

hypocrites? Show Me the tax money." So they brought
Him a denarius. And He said to them, "Whose image and
inscription is this?" They said to Him, "Caesar's." And
He said to them, "Render therefore to Caesar the things
that are Caesar's, and to God the things that are God's."
(Matthew 22:15–21)

Wow! What an awesome answer, and so very appropriate still, some two
thousand years later. Jesus was no activist, not in the sense of what that
means today, as there are whole groups of religious folk who make it seem
that the thrust of Jesus's ministry was social justice, equality, ending
poverty, and saving the planet from the excesses of humankind, that He
was all about these tangible, earthly things. Nothing could be further from
the truth, as all those things I just mentioned, although not inherently
bad, are *carnal*, and the Word of God, the Gospel, Jesus Christ, is *Spirit*.
He was and still is all about that part of humanity that was killed at the
Fall, our spiritual dimension, because without that being restored and
renewed, all else is ultimately futile. Wow! A lot to ponder today, this day
after Christmas.

FRIDAY

"Christ has redeemed us from the curse of the law, having become a curse
for us (for it is written, '*Cursed is everyone who hangs on a tree*')" (Galatians
3:13; emphasis added).

Jesus Christ is fulfilling the Godhead's perfect plan of salvation right under
the nose of the powerful Roman Empire, and they certainly play a role in
that plan. For one, Jesus is allowed to preach and teach throughout the
land without a ton of resistance because He was no threat to Roman rule;
He was not trying to overthrow the government of Rome, just the kingdom
of evil. To my way of thinking, the Roman soldiers probably found Him
refreshing and intriguing. He was strong and bold and straightforward and
very sophisticated. And He really rattled the religious system of the Jews.
I think the Roman military loved that. I think Jesus interacted a lot with
the Roman soldiers. Remember the centurion (commander of one hundred

soldiers) in Matthew chapter 8 and Luke chapter 7 who had a very sick servant and *believed* that Jesus could heal him with just His *word* ("But only speak a word, and my servant will be healed" [Matthew 8:8])? And remember the centurion at the Crucifixion ("Truly this Man was the Son of God!" [Mark 15:39]). Remember him?

It was the unbelieving Jews who condemned Jesus to crucifixion, not the Romans. Remember how tormented Pilate was about the whole thing? But it did fall to the Roman soldiers to actually do the deed, and they were experts at this particularly cruel form of execution—crucifixion. It's not that it didn't exist before, but Rome perfected it, and it was very significant that Jesus Christ was to suffer and give up His life in this manner. Please see the opening verse. He had to be suspended between heaven and earth on a *tree* to absorb all the righteous judgment of God deserved by humankind, to reverse the curse.

Where have we seen a *tree* be of such importance before? Where? Could it have been at the very start, when the curse was first incurred? And where was that?

So many questions as we go into this holiday season weekend, but it's all good. Have a great weekend.

34
WEEK

MONDAY

Good Monday morning! Today we'll give quite a bit of scripture that we'll examine tomorrow, wrapping up this discussion on the interplay between Jesus Christ and the Roman Empire, thereby also wrapping up this calendar year. On New Year's Day, we'll look back at what we've covered so far in this series and then look forward to what we still have left. We'll give an outline for such (which we'll probably not follow) as we head for the home stretch of this yearlong series on the physical and spiritual healing of humankind. Sound good?

> And the Lord God commanded the man, saying, "Of every *tree* of the garden you may freely *eat*; but of the Tree of the Knowledge of Good and Evil, you shall not *eat*, for in the day that you *eat* of it, you shall surely *die*." (Genesis 2:15–16; emphasis added)

> So when the woman saw that the *tree* was good for food, and that it was pleasant to the eyes, and a *tree* desirable to make one wise, she *took* of its fruit, and *ate*. She also gave to her husband with her, and he *ate*. (Genesis 3:6; emphasis added)

> I am the bread of life. … This is the bread which comes down from Heaven, that one may *eat* of it and *not die*. … Most assuredly, I say to you, unless you *eat* the flesh of the Son of Man and *drink* His blood, you have no life in you. … Whoever *eats* My flesh and *drinks* My blood has eternal life. … He who *eats* My flesh and *drinks* My blood abides in Me, and I in Him. … He who *feeds* on Me will

live because of Me. … He who *eats* this bread will *live forever.* (John 6:48–58; emphasis added)

The Lord Jesus Christ on the same night in which He was betrayed *took* bread; and when He had given thanks, He *broke* it and said, "*Take, eat*; this is My *body* which is *broken* for you; do this in remembrance of Me." In the same manner He also took the cup after supper, saying, "This cup is the new covenant in My blood. This do, as often as you *drink* it, in remembrance of Me." (1 Corinthians 11:23–24; emphasis added)

Moses, the disciple John, and the Apostle Paul, respectively, wrote these portions of Scripture, but the Holy Spirit was the inspiration. These verses are all related and super significant—which we'll discuss tomorrow.

TUESDAY

New Year's Eve is here, and no matter what your resolutions are for the next year, I promise that if you resolve to meditate on what we're going to discuss today, over and over and over, you will be blessed as it will bring life and joy. And it's all *true*.

Humankind, in the persons of the first Adam and his wife, fell by *eating* of a forbidden fruit, hanging from a forbidden (cursed) *tree*. They were not forbidden from looking at it, examining it, or even touching it, but they were commanded not to *eat* it.

Humankind's *redemption* came in the person of the second Adam, Jesus Christ, hanging from a cursed *tree* in the form of a cruel cross, absorbing *all* of the curse of sin meant for humankind into Himself, yelling out with "a *loud* voice" (Luke 23:46; emphasis added), "*It is finished!*" (John 19:30; emphasis added). With that, all the sins of every human ever born were *forgiven* and *remitted* (as if they never had happened). All our names were written in the book of life, and they will remain there for eternity *if* we *believe* in Jesus and *accept* the gift of salvation freely given—that is called being saved by *grace* through *faith* (Ephesians 2:8).

So we *partake* of the person of Jesus Christ at salvation. The Holy Spirit baptizes us into Jesus Christ (1 Corinthians 12:13) and comes to live within us (John 14:16–17) as soon as we confess Jesus as our Lord and *believe* in Him (Romans 10:9). Salvation is a *belief* thing, not an action.

So what is Jesus getting at in John 6 by repeatedly (and I mean repeatedly) talking about *eating* His flesh and *drinking* His blood, which are actions?

I think the answer is twofold: (1) We are to *abide* in the Lord and be conformed to Him by *eating* His Word (Scripture), that is, reading it *and* meditating on it to see Jesus in all of it (John 8:31), as we discussed at length way at the start, on the road to Emmaus. (2) We are to *constantly* be cognizant of the cross, of the Atonement, as that one event is what everything else in the universe revolves around. One way we effectively do that is to observe Holy Communion. That's why it was instituted and why we devoted so much time to it in this series. We are not actually eating our Lord's physical body and drinking His physical blood. It is symbolic. But it is nonetheless very powerful as we meditate on His sacrifice and what it means for us as believers.

That's my prayer for all of us this coming year, to get so focused on Jesus that nothing else even comes close, for "of Him and through Him and to Him are all things, to whom be glory forever. Amen!" (Romans 11:36). Wow!

WEDNESDAY

> Faith indeed tells us what the senses do not; but not the contrary of what they see. Faith is above them, not against them.
> Apart from Jesus Christ, we do not know what is our life, nor our death, nor God, nor ourselves.
> —Blaise Pascal, seventeenth-century French mathematician and theologian

Happy New Year! I love that Blaise Pascal guy. These two quotes, in particular, summarize the goals of this treatise, namely, to examine the spiritual aspects of physical healing and, through that, paint a portrait of Jesus Christ. We've progressed along nicely through the last seven and a half months, but now we commence a new calendar year, so I thought it best to spend a little time highlighting what we've covered thus far, and what we intend to cover the first four and a half months of this year, bringing to a conclusion fifty-two weeks of weekday postings, each one building upon the one prior and leading to the one to come and telling a continuous story along the way. I hope that's acceptable.

In the introduction to this series, I stated three areas we were to cover, and we're *still* on the first one, namely, proving that healing is part of the Atonement of Jesus Christ on the cross. This is a hugely important concept and one that is multifaceted. I wanted to leave no doubt that it is true. Also, we've set this reality in the context of the amazing drama that played out on planet Earth involving humankind, God, and Satan, in which it was shown conclusively, for the whole questioning universe to see, that God is love but is also completely righteous and just. This happened two thousand years ago, and since then there's been a settled universe but not a settled earth.

We started with discriminating between the spiritual and the carnal, discussing that we were created with *both* natures. Adam and Eve were spiritual beings able to communicate directly with God, but they were also equipped with a soul, comprised of intellect, emotions, and imagination, and a physical body, equipped with the five senses of seeing, hearing, smelling, tasting, and touching the things of this physical world. In truth, we were created to be *triune* beings as we were, after all, made in the image of God.

All of that included something else, something both liberating and terrifying at the same time: *free will*. For that to be operative, we had to be given a choice. God did give us a choice, and surely these "fearfully and wonderfully made" (Psalm 114:39) humans would choose in favor of their lavishly loving Father and *choose* to obey the *one* rule He gave them. The watching universe waited in anticipation. Would the humans be able to continue to function in the spiritual realm, allowing that aspect to inform and empower their souls and minds and bodies, or would they *fall* from the superior spiritual realm and come to rely instead on their carnal attributes?

We know the answer, don't we? But we have much more to review, much to meditate on, reflect on, ponder over—and that's a very good thing. We'll end today with this verse, and continue first thing tomorrow:

"Whatever things are true, whatever things are noble, whatever things are just, whatever things are pure, whatever things are lovely, whatever things are of good report, if there is any virtue and if there is anything praiseworthy—*meditate* on these things" (Philippians 4:8; emphasis added)

THURSDAY.

We continue our review. Satan is in the garden with Adam and Eve because God must allow His children to face opposition and hopefully overcome it, which He had equipped them to do. All they had to do was to *trust* Him and *believe* Him, but Satan was so very good at what he has always done best—*lying*—that he twisted the Word of God and got Adam and Eve to *question* whether God really had their best interests in mind. Did God *really* say, "You shall not eat of *every* tree of the Garden" (Genesis 3:1; emphasis added) and "You will not surely die" (Genesis 3:4), both lies from Satan?

Adam and Eve fell for it. They broke the intimate spiritual connection to their Father, and that part of them *did* surely die—not their souls or physical bodies, but their spirits. That death was immediate, and it triggered the gradual process of aging, disease, anxiety/stress, and poverty that all subsequent humans would be born into as they would all be born spiritually dead. That's why we're even having this series, because of what happened that fateful day in the garden.

Here's the point: humankind fell from the spiritual realm to the carnal realm, a much more inferior realm, and that's where every unredeemed human functions. The human mind, as awesome as it is, and the human body, as "fearfully and wonderfully made" as it is, are both *finite*; they are *limited*. They are not informed or illuminated or empowered by the Holy Spirit as they were created to be. That's what Pascal sensed: faith (spiritual things) is *above* carnal things, not opposed to them. This is a simply *huge* concept to grasp.

So when we do put our faith in Jesus Christ, and our spirits are awakened and made perfect, we are immediately 100 percent acceptable and flawless in God's eyes. But what about our carnal souls and bodies? Well, the renewing of those aspects is a gradual process (the theological term is *sanctification*) as we allow the perfect spiritual realm to infiltrate and change (renew) our minds, our emotions, and *our bodies*! We showed on the road to Emmaus how Jesus Himself instructed us to do that. We are to "see" Him in all of scripture and meditate on such, thus becoming more drawn to Him and more like Him. This is what that great scripture Romans 12:2 is all about:

"And do not be *conformed* to this world, but be *transformed* by the renewing of your mind, that you may prove what is that good and acceptable and perfect will of God" (emphasis added).

That "renewing of the mind" requires faith and belief. I put forth that there is a difference between the two. We'll review that tomorrow.

FRIDAY

We're summarizing the beautiful, life-changing truths we discussed last year in this treatise and then charting a course for the New Year. We've come to the super important topics of *faith* and *belief,* which are fundamental to the Christian faith.

"For God so loved the world that He gave His only begotten Son, that whoever *believes* in Him should not perish, but have everlasting life" (John 3:16; emphasis added).

There's a reason this is the most memorized verse in the Bible: it succinctly summarizes God's plan of salvation for the human race. Note that there is no mention of what one must *do*, just what one must *believe*. The *works* will follow, not precede, our righteous standing before God. We can't *earn* our salvation; it's a gift to those who *believe*.

Now I also ask you to note the phrase *everlasting life*. What exactly does that phrase mean? Seems obvious, right? We'll live forever since our eternal spirits have been revived. That's what it must mean, right?

Yep, it means that, but it also means *so* much more. We'll let Jesus Christ define eternal (everlasting) life. These are His Words in the prayer to His Father on the night of the Last Supper: "And *this* is eternal life, that they [believers] *may know You*, the only true God, and Jesus Christ whom You have sent" (John 17:3; emphasis added).

Wow! Do you realize what that means? We have "eternal life" right here and now on this planet; we don't have to wait for some future time! That is just overwhelming to me. What a God!

But back to this subtle distinction I see between faith and belief. Remember my definitions?

Faith is the *confident expectation*, based on scripture, that what you're praying for will come to pass. Every believer, by definition, has faith because it is the act of putting your hope in Jesus Christ. Romans 12:3, as we pointed out, indicates every believer actually has *the same* measure of faith! Remember, the KJV and NIV have that subtlety right; the NKJV does not.

Belief is the *unwavering conviction* that what you're praying for *has already* come to pass. It's on a deeper level, and it will *grow* over time as our minds become more transformed to be like the mind of Christ (1 Corinthians 2:16).

Great stuff to mull over this weekend. Enjoy.

WEEK 35

MONDAY

Happy Monday! We pick up the narrative in our review. We spent a good amount of time on the importance of belief and provided examples of both belief and unbelief in the Bible, but we really focused in on Abraham and his offering up of Isaac in Genesis 22 in the land of Moriah. What an awesome *act* of obedience on Abraham's part, but the underlying belief that allowed for this visible action went back way before, to Genesis 15, when God took His friend Abraham outside and told him that his descendants would be as numerous as the stars of heaven, even though Abraham was already at that time an old man, and childless. We saw the importance of this verse:

"And he [Abraham] believed in the Lord, and He accounted it to him for righteousness" (Genesis 15:6).

That is the key to our salvation even now and is why we, as modern-day believers, are considered the descendants of Abraham. We have to really get this because it has everything to do with our physical healing. Look at this portion of scripture:

"He [Abraham] did not *waver* at the promise of God through *unbelief* … and being fully *convinced* that what He had promised He was also able to perform. And therefore, it was accounted to him for righteousness. Now it was not written for his [Abraham's] sake alone that it was imputed to him, *but also for us*. It [righteousness] was imputed to us who *believe* in Him [God] who raised up Jesus our Lord from the dead" (Romans 4:20–24; emphasis added).

Wow! Remember my definition of *belief*, that *unwavering conviction* part? That's what Abraham had then *and* on Mount Moriah, where he absolutely *knew* he would come back down that mount with Isaac intact, even if he did have to kill his son! Hebrews 11:17–19 makes that very clear. This just inspires and moves me. That's the kind of *confidence* we can have in our God! And it takes on even more importance as we review the amazing healing and forgiving of the paralytic, which we'll do tomorrow.

TUESDAY

"For which is easier to say, 'Your sins are forgiven you', or to say, 'Arise and walk'? But that you may know that the Son of Man has power on earth to forgive sins"—then He said to the paralytic, "Arise, take up your bed, and go to your house" (Matthew 9:5–6).

We spent some time on this crucial story, found almost identically worded in all three synoptic Gospels. I call it "The Forgiving *and* Healing of the Paralytic." Jesus Christ was foreshadowing the soon-to-be Atonement and making it crystal clear that it would not be solely for the remission of sin but would also provide for our physical and emotional healing! That's why I gave this shocking, but completely true, statement:

If you are saved, then you are healed!

Now understand, although the healing of the saints (that's us, believers) was fully provided for at the cross (and to be frequently celebrated through Holy Communion), the *manifestation* (physical, visible reality) of such has to be *approximated* by us. That has everything to do with *belief.* I call this "seeing the unseen." It has to do with the *renewing* of our carnal minds so we can be *transformed* more and more into the image of Christ and allow the righteousness of our perfect spirit person to permeate our mind *and* body. So physical healing may be immediate, but more often it is a gradual process, to my way of thinking, since we are still "in the flesh" as long as we are stuck in these mortal bodies on this fallen earth. It's a constant battle. I compared this to Michelangelo's unfinished sculptures, our carnal minds and bodies being progressively liberated and brought into the light from the dark granite of our fallen state.

But remember, we fight that battle from a position of *victory* because the war has already been won! Satan doesn't want anyone to know this, that he's already been thoroughly defeated. He loves to see Christians sick and weak and poor because that limits their ability to spread the Gospel and bring others into the kingdom. We need to constantly remind ourselves that we *are* the *righteousness* of God in Christ Jesus (2 Corinthians 5:21).

So the next thing we set out to do, having seen that healing is in the Atonement, was to explain why it took four thousand years of human history for that atonement to be provided, going back to the garden to further build our faith by seeing the beauty and perfection of God's plan of salvation. We'll start reviewing that tomorrow, but isn't this review neat? I don't think I'll ever tire of hearing these truths.

WEDNESDAY

"And always be ready to give a defense to everyone who asks you a reason for the Hope that is in you" (1 Peter 3:15).

This verse is probably referring to other people who question us as believers as to why we believe what we do, but I think it also applies to our own carnal nature (intellect/mind) questioning the same thing. It's a subconscious, nagging questioning of our own beliefs. Has anyone besides me experienced this, even after giving your life to Christ? That's why we next endeavored, in this healing series, to go back to the beginning—to the garden—and establish God's amazing plan of salvation, culminating in the sacrifice of Jesus Christ on the cross, as we sought to understand why it took four thousand years to get there, to further bolster our confidence in the absolute truth of the Word of God and *know* the power of the Atonement.

Adam and Eve, created *without* a sin nature, sinned. There was absolutely no rational reason for this, for this going directly against God's authority (and that's all sin is). Those two had *everything* given freely to them, and they functioned in a spiritual realm, and they communed *directly* with God on a daily basis. Can you imagine? Why would they risk all of this?

Just think of all the heartache and devastation they inflicted on the human race.

I know what you're thinking as I was told the same: any one of us would have fallen just like they did. I'm not so sure. Now realize this: they had *no sin* in them, whereas we're "born already ruined" as Bob Dylan says. As a redeemed believer, I think I can honestly say that I am just so grateful to my Redeemer that I would not *willfully* sin against Him. Maybe that's the key thing here. Adam and Eve had never experienced *forgiveness* because they had never required it, and that wonderfulness of undeserved forgiveness is the essence of the Gospel. Remember the story of the sinful woman forever changed by the message of forgiveness, who washed Jesus feet with her *tears* and dried them with her long *hair,* and kissed His feet, anointing them with expensive oil? This beautiful and moving story is recounted in Luke 7:36–50 (you just *have* to read it). Jesus said this of that demonstration of her *love* for Him:

"Therefore I say to you, her sins, which are *many,* are *forgiven,* for *she loved much.* But, to whom *little* is *forgiven,* the same *loves little*" (Luke 7:47; emphasis added).

So maybe we could give Adam and Eve a little break here. Nonetheless, I do wonder (here I go again) whether those two ever repented (turned toward God). We'll end today with this question, which perhaps you've never thought of before: Are Adam and Eve in heaven? Hmm. We'll talk this over tomorrow morning.

THURSDAY

Adam and Eve. I find them fascinating. I do imagine them quite a bit, how they interacted with Creation and God and each other. But, you know, the more I think *about* them, the less I think *of* them. Here's why:

Adam is mentioned in the Bible way more than Eve, even though she was the one deceived by Satan. Look at these amazing verses in 1 Timothy 2:13–14:

"For Adam was formed first, then Eve. And Adam was *not* deceived, but the woman, being deceived, fell into transgression" (emphasis added).

Wow! Now just think about what this means. I suspect the impression most guys would have here is that Adam was stronger than Eve and would not have ever been deceived; the mess of the Fall of Man was all Eve's fault!

Not to my way of thinking. There's something way deeper going on here, and you already know how I love to see the Gospel in everything, especially scripture. Here's what I think: The fault here lies *way more* with Adam than with Eve. She was *deceived*; she *thought* she was doing the right thing by eating of the forbidden fruit. Adam was *not deceived*; he *knew* it was the wrong thing to do, yet he *willfully* did it anyway! I liken this to involuntary manslaughter vs. first-degree murder. In both cases, death of an innocent party occurs, but in the former, there is no willful *intent*, whereas in the latter there is. We have every reason to think Adam *knew* the consequences of disobeying God and viewed them less important than his carnal desires. And that is *sin*.

Where's the Gospel in this? It's at the cross, where it always is. Look at this:

"Then Jesus said, 'Father, forgive them, for they do not know what they do.'"

Wow! Just realize this: We humans *did know* what we were doing when we sinned against God, setting in place the plan of salvation that would culminate in the cross, but Jesus Christ Himself, while enduring inconceivable suffering on the cross, lowered our guilt from first-degree murder to involuntary manslaughter! He said we were deceived and that we didn't mean to put Him on that cross! What a Savior! This ought to really make your day.

We'll finish Adam and Eve tomorrow.

We're ending this week musing over the fates of the first man and woman. Here's what the apostle Paul has to say about Adam, whom he refers to as the "one man":

"Through one man sin entered the world, and death through sin ... by the one man's offense many died ... the judgement which came from one man's offense resulted in condemnation ... through one man's offense judgement came to all men, resulting in condemnation ... by one man's disobedience many were made sinners" (Romans 5:12–19).

Wow! Paul is really trying to get a point across here. Adam is guilty as—no pun intended—*sin*, right? Scripture clearly puts the blame for the fallen human condition on him, and nowhere in Scripture is there any indication that he ever repented. Nowhere. But I do want to emphasize that the picture Paul is painting in Romans chapter 5 is actually one of Jesus, not Adam. He's contrasting the "first Adam" with the Second Adam, Jesus Christ, and pointing out how He "reversed the curse." Here's the key verse, worthy of memorization:

"For if by the one man's offense death reigned through the one, *much more* those who receive an abundance of Grace and the gift of Righteousness will *reign* in life through the One, Jesus Christ" (Romans 5:17; emphasis added).

Amen! But what about Eve? Did she turn back to the Lord and become obedient to Him? I don't think so, and here's why. Look at these two verses:

"Now Adam knew Eve his wife, and she conceived and bore Cain, and said, 'I have acquired a man from the Lord'" (Genesis 4:1). "And Adam knew his wife again, and she bore a son and named him Seth, 'For God has appointed another seed for *me* instead of Abel, whom Cain killed'" (Genesis 4:25; emphasis added).

Do you see the emphasis on *I* and *me*? I don't think she ever bowed her will to that of the Father. Just my thinking. But look also at the legacy of her mothering. One of her first two children (they may have been twins) killed the other! And by the end of just seven generations, her offspring were so messed up (evil continually) that God saw that He had to actually destroy everyone except Noah and his family if He were to have any chance of saving the human race. Not a good track record for humankind.

There's one more piece of evidence that Adam and Eve remained lost. I find this one quite intriguing, not because of what's *in* scripture regarding them, but because of what's not. But that will have to wait until Monday (I know you hate it when I do this, but we really are out of time this morning). Here's a hint for the weekend: it has to do with a Hall of Fame.

36
WEEK

MONDAY

Happy Monday! This week we'll finish the review of the material we covered last year (I think. But that's the problem; I'm not really calling the shots) and provide a proposed plan going forward as we enter the home stretch of this treatise, but first we have to finish this diversion focused on Adam and Eve.

Hebrews chapter 11 is known as the "Hall of Faith," and in it the author gives examples of various men *and* women who gained the approval of God in Old Testament times by seeing the unseen as we've spent a good deal of time explaining previously. The author of Hebrews sets the stage with this description of faith in the opening verse (and it's a description, not a definition):

"Now faith is the substance of things hoped for, the evidence of things not seen."

Just a quick word of clarification as I see both faith and belief, which I have proposed are actually *not* the same thing, described in this verse, faith being the "confident expectation" or "hope" (something we modern-day believers all have, and in the same measure), and belief being the "unwavering conviction" or "reality" (which is a work in progress for believers, and which grows as our minds become more and more renewed and like that of Jesus). This construct is, to my way of reading Scripture, consistent with the "whole counsel of God," and it works nicely for me.

The expected players are listed: Noah, Abraham, Sarah, Isaac, Jacob, Joseph, Moses, David, et al. But there are two names conspicuously absent.

Yep, Adam and Eve. Abel, their second son, who was killed by Cain, is the first person mentioned. I find that telling, don't you?

Here's what's really neat. Look who else is included: the prostitute Rahab, pitiful little Gideon (see Judges 6:15), hedonistic Samson, and a weak-kneed guy by the name of Barak (I'm not making this up; see Judges chapter 4), who was too afraid to go into battle by himself. Why? Why are they there?

Because all of these people, including the ones I mentioned first, were *flawed* and they *knew it.* They realized they couldn't accomplish anything on their own strength but had to rely on the Lord. That's an essential element of faith/belief. I don't think that was *ever* the case with Adam and Eve. I think they stayed proud and self-serving and did not humble themselves before God. I could, of course, be wrong. Scripture is not conclusive on this matter—hence my ponderings.

As much as I would like to get farther on with our review at this point, all of this does bring up an interesting question: How did anyone in Old Testament times get "saved" anyway, since the way of salvation had not come yet? Difficult question, but we love those, don't we? More tomorrow morning.

TUESDAY

"Jesus said to him, 'I am the way, the truth, and the life. No one comes to the Father except through Me'" (John 14:6).

"And how shall they believe in Him of whom they have not heard?" (Romans 10:14).

"In the day when God will judge the secrets of men, by Jesus Christ, according to my Gospel" (Romans 2:16).

"Then I saw a Great White Throne, and Him who sat on it. ... And I saw the dead, small and great, standing before God, and books were opened.

And another book was opened, which is the Book of Life. And the dead were judged according to their works, by the things which were written in the books. ... And anyone *not* found written in the Book of Life was cast into the lake of fire" (Revelation 20:11–15; emphasis added).

Throughout this whole work, we have confronted the deep questions of life, and without trepidation as the Word of God indeed has the answers. This beautiful Christian faith of ours is so intellectually challenging, and everything else (science, politics, business, even medicine) is so inferior when it comes to giving settled answers to our human condition. How was the universe formed? Why do we exist? What's the purpose of life? What happens after death? It all culminates in the Gospel of Jesus Christ. It is that Light, and that Light alone, that sets our minds and souls *free*—free to think deeply and clearly, and to love purely and unselfishly, and to live life abundantly and fully.

But what about the multitudes upon multitudes of humans who have never been presented the Gospel, both before and after the cross? How are they to be saved? How are they to know God? I've pondered this stuff a lot, and there's some basic concepts I've been shown that have helped me deal with this topic. I hope you find them helpful also.

1. First of all, be assured that every human's fate is in the hands of a *righteous, just*, and *loving* God. We've discussed these attributes of God thoroughly, along with the need to prove them to the universe through the great drama of humankind and the Fall and their redemption playing out on planet Earth. Paul goes on to say in Romans 2 that "we know that the judgement of God is according to truth." He calls His judgement "the righteous judgement of God" and states, "There is no partiality with God." Be assured that no human will be given a "raw deal" but will be dealt with justly, and will know it, for "they are without excuse" (Romans 1:20). I find that very comforting. More tomorrow.

WEDNESDAY

"It is appointed for men to die once, but after this the judgement" (Hebrews 9:27).

We're musing over the fate of humankind, and we were assured yesterday that the judgment of every human soul, which will be based on decisions made during their lifetime on this earth, is in the hands of a righteous, just, and loving God. Here's some other thoughts:

2. Faith in Jesus Christ is the *only* way to eternal life. Christianity is exclusive but is open to everybody. I gave the unambiguous statement of Jesus Himself yesterday in John 14:6, but further proof is found in the garden of Gethsemane, just before His betrayal, and it is chilling:

    "He knelt down and prayed, saying, 'Father, if it is Your will, take this cup away from Me; nevertheless not My will but Yours, be done.' Then an angel appeared to Him from heaven, strengthening Him. And being in agony, He prayed more earnestly. Then His sweat became like great drops of blood falling down to the ground" (Luke 22:41–44).

    Wow! This "cup" Jesus was agonizing over was God's righteous wrath, which would be expended solely on Him. He respectfully asked the Father for some *other* way of salvation, but there was none to be found. He is the only route—period.

3. Old Testament believers knew that, and they were looking *forward* to the cross and their ultimate redemption. After death, their souls were sent to a place of comfort and rest, known in Scripture as "Abraham's bosom" (Luke 16:22), where they were to await their Savior, who would come to them after the Crucifixion and defeat of Satan. They would accept Him and be escorted to heaven, to be with the Lord after His Ascension, in spiritual form until they received their immortal bodies at the time of the Rapture. I know this is a lot to digest, but it's all supported by Scripture. Look at this:

"'When He ascended on high, He led captivity captive and gave gifts to men.' Now this, 'He ascended'—what does it mean but that He also first descended into the lower parts of the Earth? He who descended is also the One who ascended far above all the heavens, that He might fill all things" (Ephesians 4:8–10).

"Do not be afraid; I am the First and the Last. I am He who lives, and was dead, and behold, I am alive forevermore. Amen. And I have the keys of Hades and of Death" (Revelation 1:17–18).

Interesting stuff. More tomorrow morning.

THURSDAY

Somehow in this yearlong discussion of this Christian doctor's views on the healing of humankind, we've managed to cover a bunch of the major doctrines of the Christian faith. We're currently looking at the judgment of humankind, pointing out the sovereignty and goodness of the Great Judge, God, and emphasizing the exclusivity of faith in Jesus Christ as the way to eternal life. We've come to the category of righteous believers who lived before the Atonement.

Please remember what I mean by righteous. The only righteousness recognized by God is that given to humans once they put their faith in Jesus Christ. It is a gift. It is not a work. The following two verses make this quite clear:

"But we are all like an unclean thing, and all our righteousnesses are like filthy rags" (Isaiah 64:6).

"For He [God] made Him [Jesus] who knew no sin to be sin for us, that we might become the righteousness of God in Him" (2 Corinthians 5:21).

But Old Testament believers lived and died *before* Jesus became sin for them. How can the Atonement apply to them? Well, it did; it was on credit. But the Gospel was known to them. Look at these verses:

"And the Scripture, *foreseeing* that God would justify the Gentiles by faith, *preached the Gospel* to Abraham *beforehand*" (Galatians 3:8; emphasis added).

"Your father Abraham rejoiced to see My day, and he saw it and was glad" (John 8:56).

"By faith, he [Moses] forsook Egypt, not fearing the wrath of the king; for he endured as seeing Him [Jesus] who is invisible" (Hebrews 11:27).

So *all salvation* of lost humans is by grace through faith in Jesus Christ. Believers before the cross were looking *forward* to it; believers since the cross look *back* to it. Amen! More on just how the Old Testament believers were united with their long-awaited Savior next time.

FRIDAY

Okay, so it's Friday, and we certainly haven't finished our review of the material we covered last year as we are off on a diversion, pondering over the final fate of various categories of humans. We're on my third point, dealing with Old Testament believers. We've seen that they were looking forward to the Messiah and that after death their souls went to a physical place of rest and peace known as Paradise, or Abraham's bosom, which may have been located deep in the earth (Ephesians 4:9). But they were *not* in heaven; they were *not* with the Father. Remember John 14:6 from earlier this week? Jesus proclaimed that the *only* way to the Father, and thus to heaven, was through Him and what He accomplished on the cross. So Jesus had to *go to them*, there in Paradise, to set them free and escort them up to heaven and the Father. We gave the Scriptural proof of that also earlier this week, Ephesians 4:8–10. After Jesus absorbed all of God's righteous judgment meant for humans into His own precious body, He "descended" to Paradise to "lead captivity captive" by "ascending" up to heaven. But then Scripture adds something else, something very interesting that follows all of this. Jesus "gave gifts to men" (v. 8). And that provides a great segue to my fourth point, the judgment of New Testament believers.

There is *no* judgment for sin in store for believers, whether Old Testament or New Testament saints. There can't be, because scripture makes it clear that once we put our faith in Jesus Christ, our sins are forever *forgiven*, and not only that, but also *forgotten*! Remember this? "For I will forgive their iniquity, and their sin I will remember no more" (Jeremiah 31:34).

But there is a "judgment" for believers. This was revealed to the apostle Paul. Look at this:

"For we [believers] must all appear before the judgement seat of Christ, that each one may receive the things done in the body, according to what he has done, whether good or bad" (2 Corinthians 5:10).

That sounds a little intimidating, doesn't it? Please rest assured that it is *all good*, this "judgment seat" of Christ for believers. I wish I had time to explain this today since it's a Friday, but it will have to wait. However, let me leave you with an analogy. When I started medical school at Vanderbilt University, the dean gave an early introductory speech trying to take the pressure off us by reminding us that even the lowest-ranked member of our graduating class four years in the future would still be an MD. Likewise, the worst-case scenario outcome for believers at the judgment for us is *an eternity of bliss in heaven with our Lord*! Amen!

37
WEEK

MONDAY

We start a new week. We're more than halfway through January, and we still haven't finished our review of material covered last year, but it's all good as we're discussing some really neat stuff, hopefully helping us to "give a defense to everyone who asks you for a reason for the hope that is in you" (1 Peter 3:15). We were reviewing our journey through God's plan of salvation, and we got stuck in the garden (we spend a lot of time there, don't we?), mulling over the fate of Adam and Eve. Now we've expanded to pondering the final disposition of all humans. I've put forth the following: (1) Our Judge is good, righteous, and just. (2) Jesus Christ is the *only* way to eternal life. (3) Old Testament saints were a special case; their souls were kept safe and secure in a place called Paradise after death, until the victorious Jesus Christ, now with the "keys of Hades and of Death" (Revelation 1:18), came to reveal Himself to them and escort their souls to heaven to be with the Father.

Now we're looking at the "judgment" of all believers. There is indeed a judging going on, and it's administered by our Lord Jesus Christ, but it's not for *sin*; it's for *rewards*! There are different levels of rewards for believers (there goes socialism!). This concept of rewards for believers is made super-duper clear in scripture. We'll look at those verses shortly, but I first want to make a distinction, subtle but important, between how the world rewards and how God rewards. One has a posture of *works*, and the other has a posture of *rest*.

"There remains, therefore a *rest* for the people of God" (Hebrews 4:9).

Counterintuitive, isn't it? But that's the kingdom of God. It's very different from the kingdom of the world, where one is rewarded for how hard they work and for what they accomplish on their own with their own sweat and blood. And you know what? That's the way it should be for the carnal things of our life. It is a Christian thing, this work ethic. It wasn't easy for me to become a doctor, nor is it easy being one, responsible for just under five thousand patients, so I'm all about hard work and being compensated for such. It's known as capitalism, and again, it's a good thing. But it only works when applied to things we as humans are capable of doing in the earthly realm. And here's the key point: we *cannot* please God or do anything *worthwhile* in His sight *on our own*! He only recognizes *faith* in His Son, and acceptance of what He (Jesus) accomplished at the Atonement, and the "righteous works" performed by us *because* and *through* our Savior via the Comforter (Holy Spirit) living in us!

Wow, that's a mouthful. Enough to ponder today. More tomorrow.

TUESDAY

There are rewards for believers in heaven, given out by Jesus Christ at His bema seat, or judgment seat (2 Corinthians 5:10). This is a separate, and very different, event from the Great White Throne judgment for unbelievers; there is no fear or intimidation in this judicial proceeding, but still it is a consequential event for believers.

So wouldn't this mean we should really make it a priority in our Christian lives to earn as many rewards as we can while on this earth? Read the Bible as much as possible, pray incessantly, fast for prolonged times, give abundantly to the Lord's work, go door-to-door witnessing? I mean, doesn't that stuff sound good? Shouldn't we be frenetically *working* to earn heavenly rewards?

You know what I'm going to say, don't you? But let's look at this very beautiful story, relayed by Dr. Luke, of the interplay between our Lord and two sisters, both of whom He loved very much, and see what He has to say about how best to serve Him and gain rewards in heaven:

> Now it happened as they went that He entered a certain village, and a certain woman named Martha welcomed Him into her house. And she had a sister called Mary, who

also sat at Jesus' feet and heard His word. But Martha was distracted with much serving, and she approached Him and said, "Lord, do You not care that my sister has left me to serve alone? Therefore tell her to help me." And Jesus answered and said to her, "Martha, Martha, you are worried and troubled about many things. But *one thing* is needed, and Mary has chosen that good part, which will not be taken from her." (Luke 10:38–42; emphasis added)

Wow! Do you see what's going on here? Mary is *resting* at Jesus's feet, soaking in His Word and meditating on Him, while Martha is frantically *working* to please Jesus! She wasn't doing anything bad; she was trying her best to serve Jesus. Yet our Lord gently corrected her and pointed out the one priority He wanted for her, and that was Him.

So how does anything get done then? Who *is working* if we are not to? I have just the answer—tomorrow morning.

WEDNESDAY

"For it is *God* who *works* in you, both to *will* and to *do* for *His good pleasure*" (Philippians 2:13; emphasis added).

Remember the question we ended with yesterday? *This* is the answer! It is God who is behind every good, righteous thing we believers do; He gives us the *desire* (will) to do the good work, then He gives us the *ability* to do the good work, and then you know what? This is what is most amazing to me: He *rewards* us for doing what He actually did! Our only role is to allow Him to work through us, to yield to His will. That is a very difficult thing for us as boastful, proud, self-serving humans.

I'm convinced that the primary way we effectively yield our will to His will is to become more like Jesus in our minds, to have our minds renewed, and to have the perfect spirit part of us (as believers) permeate our minds and bodies. I believe we accomplish that by *seeing* Jesus in all of Scripture and meditating on Him and His Word. That's what Jesus was trying to get

Martha to see in Luke 10. He is the "one thing" that unlocks everything else for us as Jesus stated so beautifully in the Sermon on the Mount:

"But seek first the kingdom of God, and *His righteousness*, and all these things shall be added to you" (Matthew 6:33; emphasis added).

That righteousness is what Jesus gives us, as believers, when we put our faith in Him, as seen in 2 Corinthians 5:21, which we have quoted frequently thus far (look it up). The point is that it is *His* righteousness, not ours, as we have none on our own. It's all about Him.

Just as we started this morning's discourse with one of the most revealing verses in the Bible, we'll end with another. Just think what this really means:

"For of Him and through Him and to Him are all things, to whom be glory forever. Amen" (Romans 11:36).

So the works we are rewarded for originate with our Lord, but Scripture seems to indicate that there are believers who do not get rewards. Can that be? Isn't faith without works *dead*? Great questions. We'll tackle those tomorrow.

THURSDAY

We are discussing the judgment of believers; it is an adjudication of rewards, given by Jesus Christ, based on the righteous works we performed on this earth through the empowerment of the Holy Spirit. We act as the vehicle for these works, the "hands and feet" of our Lord. Self-righteous works don't count. It all has to be for the glory of Jesus as seen in yesterday's verse, Romans 11:36.

But will all Christians be rewarded? In a sense, yes, because eternal life is every true Christian's guarantee. But look at this Scripture from Paul:

"For no other foundation can anyone lay than that which is laid, which is Jesus Christ. Now if anyone builds on this foundation with gold, silver, precious stones, wood, hay, straw—each one's work will become clear; for the Day will declare it, because it will be revealed by fire, and the fire will test each one's work, of what sort it is. If anyone's work which he has built on it endures, he will receive a reward. If anyone's work is burned, he will suffer loss; but he himself will be saved, yet so as through fire" (1 Corinthians 3:11–15).

Paul is addressing believers, people who are saved, who have faith in Jesus Christ as their foundation but who have built on that foundation in very different ways: the worthwhile works of righteousness (characterized by gold, silver, and precious stones) and the worthless works of self-righteousness (wood, hay, and straw). The "Day" referenced is the bema (the Greek word for the judgment seat mentioned in 2 Corinthians 5:10) seat ceremony, during which Jesus distributes our rewards. Look at the drastically different outcomes, but please notice the super important last verse. Although the believer's unworthy *works* are consumed, his or her *soul* is *saved*! That's because true salvation by grace through faith is *eternal*. Never forget that. Never question your salvation! Listen to these beautiful words of our Lord: "My sheep hear My voice, and I know them, and they follow Me. And I give them *eternal life*, and they shall *never perish*, neither shall anyone snatch them out of my hand" (John 10:27–28; emphasis added).

Amen! Could Jesus make that more clear? "But," you say, "what if I don't feel like I'm saved anymore? What if I've *lost* my faith?" No worries. "If we are *faithless*, He *remains faithful*; He *cannot* deny Himself" (2 Timothy 2:13; emphasis added).

Your eternal life is *sealed* by the Holy Spirit when you are saved (2 Corinthians 1:21–22). Rest in that. More on this tomorrow.

FRIDAY

"Thus also faith by itself, if it does not have works, is *dead*" (James 2:17; emphasis added).

We've just seen how there will be believers in heaven, having inherited eternal life, who were *not* fruitful during their lives on this earth. They receive no rewards at the bema seat of Christ. Yet James seems to indicate that a supposed believer who is *not* fruitful actually doesn't have true saving faith and never did. Isn't that the way we've been conditioned to interpret this verse and how we ourselves "judge" Christians, by their works?

Here's what I think: James states their faith is *dead*, but not *canceled*, or *voided*, or *annulled*. These Christians still have saving faith but have not sold out to Jesus or followed Him, that process we call sanctification. That's tragic, but it does not affect their *position* in Christ. God still views them as flawless. I know that's a difficult concept, but remember, this great God *forgives* us and *forgets* our sins when we put our faith in His Son. The real tragedy here is that the fruitless Christians have missed out on the abundant *life* here on this earth that Jesus wants to give every one of us. These souls will receive no rewards in heaven, but they'll be there!

Nowhere is this conception that our salvation is not dependent on *works* more misunderstood than in Jesus's beautiful Last Supper discourse about the vine and the branches, recorded in John 15. I've heard this preached errantly (again, based on my understanding of Scripture and the "whole counsel of God") many times with the unfruitful branches in the vine being "taken away." It's super scary and condemning. Most everyone leaves one of those sermons questioning their faith. But the problem all has to do with what I believe to be an errant translation of the Greek word *airo*; not a single translation could I find that translates that word the way I think it was intended to be translated. Of course that could very well be because I'm crazy, but you already know that and you're still reading, so hear me out on this one, because I think we'll see a beautiful, uplifting, encouraging, and *true* principle emerge.

This is important, so we'll not rush through it this morning. We'll pick up next week in John 15 and focus on verse 2, specifically, the phrase *takes away*, which was translated from the Greek word *airo*. Look it up in Strong's Concordance (it will be under Strong's G142), and see what you think. Have a great weekend.

WEEK 38

MONDAY

It's a new week, the last week of January, and we're exploring the final disposition of the human soul. We certainly don't shy away from the deep questions of life. It is all dependent on faith in Jesus Christ. Before looking at the judgment of the unrighteous, we'll finish up the judgment in store for the righteous (believers), which is not regarding sin but rewards. The rewards are determined by how "fruitful" we are as Christians, and that fruit must be born of the Holy Spirit working in and through us, not by our own efforts to please God. Unfortunately, not all believers will be fruitful; they do not "prove what is that good and acceptable and perfect will of God" (Romans 12:2). But they are still believers, and they are still in heaven, right? Look at this; look at it closely:

"I am the true vine, and my Father is the vinedresser. Every branch in Me that does not bear fruit He *takes away* (airo), and every branch that bears fruit He *prunes* (kathairo), that it may bear more fruit. You are *already clean* because of the Word which I have spoken to you. *Abide* (meno) in Me, and I in you. As the branch cannot bear fruit of itself, unless it abides in the vine, neither can you, unless you abide in Me" (John 15:1–4; emphasis added).

What a beautiful picture of our relationship with Jesus! It's not like a tree with branches coming off the rather sterile and boring, straight and rigid trunk; the grapevine itself is vibrant and curvy and winds all over the place, and the "branches" come off so smoothly and contiguously that it's hard to tell where the vine ends and the branch begins. That's how tight and intimate our relationship is to be with our Lord. *Every branch* of that grapevine is *in* the vine (v. 2). All of these branches are saved; they are already in Christ, whether they bear fruit or not. The branch is not productive, but it's still a branch! Are you with me?

So what gives with this "He takes away" statement? It's all in the Greek. Again the word is *airo*, and here's the *first* definition given in the highly respected Strong's Concordance (G142) for this Greek word:

airo. (1) to raise up; elevate; lift up; to raise from the ground.

Wow! Doesn't that dramatically change the meaning here? The *third* definition listed for *airo* is "to bear away, take away, remove." That's what every translation went with, but I should point out that the main reference Bible we've been using in this series, the NKJV, does point out in the center-column notes that "takes away" could also mean "lifts up."

I'm telling you, this translation preference makes all the difference in the world, and *so* much more fits with the entire context of this chapter, and, indeed, the true heart of God. We'll discuss it more tomorrow.

TUESDAY

"These things I have spoken to you, that My *joy* may remain in you, and that your *joy* may be full" (John 15:11; emphasis added).

In John 15, Jesus gives us a beautiful visual image of who we are in Him; He is the grapevine, we are the branches that produce fruit from the life He gives us, and the Father is the vinedresser. There are two actions the Father performs on the branches: "takes away" and "prunes." There is one and only one action for the branches: "abide." At the end of this passage, Jesus gives the reason why He spoke these words: for our (believers') *joy*! Yet Satan, true to form, has worked hard to twist and distort the Word of God (just like in the garden and with the sacrament of Holy Communion) such that we actually come under condemnation because of words and phrases like *take away* and *prune*, and we miss out on the true, joyful meaning of this Scripture. I hate that. Here's how I believe we are to understand John 15:1–4, the text of which we gave yesterday:

First of all, all the branches are saved; they are all *safely* in the Vine. We've already covered that awesome truth, that of eternal security. Jesus first discusses unfruitful Christians. To better understand this, picture a vineyard. I'm no expert by any means, but every vineyard I've ever seen has the vines growing on trellises, up and off the ground, as I would think those branches lying on the ground would not do well—would not be fruitful. I suspect that was the deal in Jesus's time also, and that's why it makes such sense to me that the proper meaning of the Greek word *airo* is not "takes away" but is "lifts up"! These are God's precious children, but they have not experienced the fullness of their salvation, so our Lord will do everything He can to encourage them and protect them and show His goodness to them, such that they yield more and more of their carnal natures to the Holy Spirit, become more like Jesus, and *abide* in the Vine, rather than settle for just being *in* the Vine (more on this distinction later). Doesn't this interpretation fit more with the heart of God?

Then Jesus discusses fruitful Christians and how the Father "prunes" them to bear more fruit. I think we all have an intuitive sense of what that means. I used to have a little "orchard" of about a dozen fruit trees of different varieties (and "used to" is the operative term here. Let me just say that if you have two sprayers, one with a liquid pesticide and the other with Round-Up, label them!), and I would trim the trees back in the fall so the remaining buds would have more fruit, but still it is a rather severe word. The Greek word is *kathairo*. Let's again turn to Strong's Concordance and look at the first definition given (#2508):

> **kathairo.** to *cleanse* of filth/impurity.

Wow! That is just awesome to me. The second definition has to do with clipping back, with removing part of the plant; I'm going with that first definition. The Father is attempting to clean up His faithful, fruitful children, dusting off the impurities and filth inherent with living in this fallen world.

And just how does He do that? I think it has to do with staying in His Word, and I think that makes the difference between *existing in* Jesus and *abiding in* Jesus. Our Father wants us to do more of the latter. Look at what Jesus says right after the "pruning" verse. It has to do with being clean: "You are already clean *because of the word* which I have spoken to you. Abide in Me, and I in you" (John 15:3–4; emphasis added).

Isn't this stuff great? More tomorrow.

WEDNESDAY

"Then Jesus said to those Jews who *believed* Him, 'If you *abide* in My *Word*, you are My *disciples* indeed. And you shall know the truth, and the truth shall set you free'" (John 8:31; emphasis added).

We're discussing the topic of eternal rewards for believers, namely, *fruitful* believers, in the context of our relationship with Jesus so beautifully illustrated in John 15. We've seen that only Christians who *abide* in the Vine (Jesus) will be fruitful and therefore have rewards. But what does it mean to abide? The Greek word used for "abide" is *meno*. Back to Strong's Concordance (#3306):

> **meno.** to remain in, sojourn, tarry.

So basically it means to "hang out" in Christ. He's our place of rest and joy that we can't wait to get to and where want to stay as long as possible. The opening verse, in addition to the vine analogy of John 15, indicates that not all believers who put their faith in Jesus go on to become followers, or disciples, and therefore they are not very fruitful. Their salvation is just for them; they aren't interested in impacting others for Christ. That "abiding" comes from staying in His Word (Scripture); that's what the "pruning" (cleansing) of the fruitful believers is all about. Daily meditation on His Word keeps us firmly connected to the Vine.

But there's another aspect of this deep relationship with our Lord that need be discussed, this empowered, fruitful Christian life that longs for others to know our Savior and live abundant lives, this evangelical bent to tell others that Jesus commanded us to have, something so important to Him that it was His last command to us, the Great Commission:

"And He said to them, 'Go into all the world and preach the Gospel to every creature'" (Mark 16:15).

The Holy Spirit has been prompting me to write about this aspect for some time now. I've resisted because it's not the purpose of this treatise. Or so I thought. But maybe it's actually the driving force behind this these writings. Can you wait until tomorrow? Do you have a choice?

THURSDAY

Did you know there are actually *three* baptisms available to believers? The first is essential to salvation, to eternal life; the second is not essential for salvation but is one of just two sacraments instituted by Jesus, and is expected of all believers; and the third is entirely optional but entirely beneficial, and was a big deal to first-century believers, but it is quite misunderstood and, sadly, often abused in the modern church. It is this third one that I believe facilitates the *abiding* in Christ we talked about yesterday, allowing Him to completely work through us and "prove what is that good and acceptable and perfect will of God" (Romans 12:2) in our lives.

First of all, what is baptism? Actually, it is a transliteration, not a translation, of the Greek word *baptizo*. The alphabet was simply changed from Greek to English; there was no prior English word to translate it to. Here's the Strong's Concordance definition (G907):

> **baptize.** to dip repeatedly, to immerse, to submerge.

You get the picture. The thing being baptized is completely surrounded, engulfed, and overwhelmed by whatever it is being baptized in. It is all in.

So at salvation the Holy Spirit baptizes the new believer *into* Jesus Christ. It is the Holy Spirit who draws the unbeliever in, but it is the unbeliever who has to, through his or her own faith, accept the free gift of salvation. At that point, the person is placed firmly in Jesus and sealed by the Holy Spirit, never to be snatched away. This is the *only* requirement for salvation. Want scripture?

- "No one can say that Jesus is Lord except by the Holy Spirit" (1 Corinthians 12:3).
- "And do not grieve the Holy Spirit of God, by whom you were sealed for the day of redemption" (Ephesians 4:30).
- "And I give them eternal life, and they shall never perish; neither shall anyone snatch them out of My hand" (John 10:28).

Isn't this amazingly wonderful? We really don't value our salvation as much as we should. At least I know I don't. Another benefit of frequent Communion!

Next is the baptism that probably first came to your mind when I mentioned this topic, and that is water baptism. We'll address that beautiful ceremony tomorrow.

FRIDAY

"Then Jesus came from Galilee to John at the Jordan to be baptized by him. ... When He had been baptized, Jesus came up immediately from the water; and behold, the heavens were opened to Him, and He saw the Spirit of God descending like a dove and alighting upon Him" (Matthew 3:13, 16).

"Go therefore and make disciples of all the nations, baptizing them in the name of the Father and of the Son and of the Holy Spirit" (Matthew 26:19).

Water baptism. Jesus modeled it for us and commanded us to keep it. It is for all believers. In this baptism, the believer is baptized *by* another believer *into* water. It is a public proclamation of belief in Jesus Christ, of the death of the old self and the birth of a "new creation" (2 Corinthians 5:17). It is the fulfillment of Romans 10:9: "If you confess with your mouth the Lord Jesus and believe in your heart that God has raised Him from the dead, you *will be saved*" (emphasis added). It is a beautiful, moving experience; I will never forget mine, although it was a good fifty years ago (I'd like to say I was baptized in utero, but that would be a lie).

So we have the Holy Spirit baptizing us into Jesus, and a fellow believer baptizing us into water. Does Jesus baptize us into anything? What does scripture have to say? Look at the words of John the Baptist right before he baptized Jesus in water:

"I indeed *baptize* you with *water* unto repentance, but He who is coming after with me is mightier than I, whose sandals I am not worthy to carry. He will *baptize* you with the *Holy Spirit* and *fire*" (Matthew 3:11; emphasis added).

Wow! That's indicating there is a third baptism; it's not referring to salvation or water baptism. We'll look at that next week. I want to end today with this important observation: there is no evidence in scripture that Jesus Christ did anything miraculous until the Holy Spirit came upon Him in Matthew 3:16. Remember, although 100 percent God, Jesus obediently gave up that power to live as a human man on this earth. This is an awesome truth, but *everything* He did after this point was through the power of the Holy Spirit. Look at the start of the very next chapter, after the baptism of Jesus:

"*Then* He was led of the Spirit" (Matthew 4:1; emphasis added).

Do you realize what that means? That same power is available to us through that same Holy Spirit who indwells us as believers. We absolutely *need* that power to fully *abide* in Christ, to be fruitful Christians. Think on this as we prepare to look at the great second chapter of Acts next week.

39
WEEK

MONDAY

So it's the second month of the new year, and we're (theoretically) reviewing the material we covered last year before embarking on the home stretch of this treatise, realizing that we are also covering most of the basic doctrines of the Christian faith along the way. Like the vine in the imagery of John 15, these writings have been of a winding, serpentine, nonlinear nature, basically unpredictable (even to me, and I'm writing them!), but I at least find that aspect of things refreshing and consistent with the beautifully wild and fresh nature of God.

We started recapping our journey through God's plan of salvation for humans, and we tarried over Adam and Eve and their attitude toward God and their possible fates. That led to a discussion of the fates of all classes of humans. We're now on the judgment of believers. We've seen it is a judgment of rewards, and we're examining how to be a *fruitful* Christian, which means *abiding* in Christ, which means staying in His Word and being cleansed by it on a daily basis.

But for me there is also something else very important involved, which is a key to living a vibrant, energized, powerful life of impact for the kingdom of God on this earth, being an effective witness for Jesus Christ and His cross. And that has to do with a baptism. So we've reviewed the baptism of new believers into Jesus Christ (permanently) at salvation and the baptism of believers into water at the time of water baptism, and we're about to explain, as I see and experience it, the baptism of believers *by* Jesus Christ *into* the Holy Spirit, which is available to all believers and leads to a more intimate and powerful relationship with our Lord.

But I first must lay the context, because this beautiful element of the Christian life has been so distorted and abused and maligned that it actually carries a negative connotation among many believers. That is clearly the purpose of the enemy, because if he can get our focus off of Jesus and the Atonement and on to *anything* else, even a good thing, then he has accomplished much harm to the body of Christ. Believe me, the *only* goal of the Holy Spirit is to *glorify* Jesus Christ and His sacrifice for us. That's the only goal. It is not to create a new category of "super-Christians." He will only operate within the confines of the cross of Jesus Christ.

I have asked for guidance on how best to word this important doctrine, and the Lord has been gracious. We start tomorrow.

TUESDAY

"Then the seventy returned with joy, saying, 'Lord, even the demons are subject to us in Your name.' And He said to them, 'I saw Satan fall like lightning from heaven. Behold, I give you the authority to trample on serpents and scorpions, and over all the power of the enemy, and nothing shall by any means hurt you. Nevertheless do not rejoice in this, that the spirits are subject to you, but rather rejoice because your names are written in heaven'" (Luke 10:17–20).

I will start with this beautiful portion of Scripture because it puts everything in the proper context and order. Just look at the power given these disciples of Jesus. They had *authority* over *all* the power of Satan and his minions, yet Jesus reminded them that this earthly manifestation of power could not compare to the importance and magnificence of *salvation*, of *eternal life*. Everything else good and acceptable and perfect in our Christian life is a consequence of that singular act—the Atonement, the cross. This includes an abundant, grace-filled life on this earth for believers, but that shouldn't be the main thing we're about as Christians, not our great desire. Our passion should be to "be witnesses to Me [Jesus] in Jerusalem, and in all Judea and Samaria, and to the end of the earth" (Acts 1:8).

That's the *reward* I'm after, to bring others into the kingdom of God, to a saving knowledge of Jesus Christ. And that involves "abiding" in Christ. The Holy Spirit is all about that. That's our topic now, and it's an important topic as the enemy works hard to keep us ignorant about the Holy Spirit's role in our Christian walk because he does not want us empowered to further the Gospel. So let's jump in to this discussion. I've spent more time in prayer and meditation on this part of these writings than on any other, and I'm excited to share what I've been given.

It all starts with salvation, when we become a new creation, all old things pass away, and everything is made new (2 Corinthians 5:17). When we are saved, our dormant spirit person, killed at the Fall, becomes alive and is 100 percent filled with the Holy Spirit. Every believer is *indwelt* by the Holy Spirit.

"But you are not in the flesh, but in the Spirit, if indeed the Spirit of God dwells in you. Now if anyone does not have the Spirit of Christ, he is not His" (Romans 8:9).

"Or do you not know that your body is the temple of the Holy Spirit who is in you, whom you have from God, and you are not your own?" (1 Corinthians 6:19).

Got it? The spirit aspect of believers is Spirit-filled and *perfect*. But here's the problem: that's just one-third of you! We'll pick it up here tomorrow.

WEDNESDAY

"And do not be conformed to this world, but be transformed by the renewing of your mind, that you may prove what is that good and acceptable and perfect will of God" (Romans 12:2).

How many times have we quoted this verse? A common thread of thought throughout this treatise has been that the goal of sanctification, of becoming more like Jesus, is to allow the perfect renewed spiritual aspect of our triune human lives [remember, we are made up of a spirit (dormant at birth), a soul (mind/intellect/emotions), and a physical body (including the five senses)] to infiltrate and permeate our minds and bodies, such that we can enjoy emotional stability, a sound mind, and a healthy body as that is God's perfect will for us.

"Beloved, I pray that you prosper and be in good health, just as your soul prospers" (3 John 2) "Because as He is, so are we in this world" (1 John 4:17).

Now just think of what that last verse is saying. Is that true? Are we believers, while stuck in these bodies on this earth, in this world, just like Jesus? Yes … and no. Our spirits are indeed. Remember, that aspect of us is perfect and flawless, just like Jesus. But the transformation of our minds, souls, and bodies is a work in progress; it's a journey. My point in all of this is that it is the Holy Spirit living inside of us who facilitates that process; He is our Helper. Jesus told His disciples at the Last Supper that it was to their advantage that He leave them so that the Holy Spirit could come! Look at this:

"It is to your advantage that I go away; for if I do not go away, the Helper will not come to you; but if I depart, I will send him to you. … When He, the Spirit of truth has come, He will guide you into all truth. … He will take of what is Mine and declare it to you" (John 16:7, 13, 14).

We discussed all of this in the very first installment of these writings. It might have been difficult to understand then, but it should make more sense now since we've already seen how vital it is to see Jesus in Scripture and cleanse ourselves every day by washing in the Word of God. This is how we remain fruitful Christians and abide in the Vine. It is the Holy Spirit who accomplishes this by taking what is Jesus's, namely, the Word, and declaring it to us as stated in the foregoing verse. As we pointed out on the road to Emmaus, it is better for us to see Jesus in our spirit, through His Word, than to see Him even with our physical eyes, because as Jesus said, "It is the Spirit who gives life; the flesh profits nothing. The words that I speak to you are *spirit*, and they are life" (John 6:63; emphasis added).

Man, this is really good stuff! More tomorrow.

THURSDAY

> And He said to them, "Go into all the world and preach the gospel to every creature. He who believes and is baptized will be saved; but he who does not believe will be condemned. And these signs will follow those who believe: in My name they will cast out demons; they will speak with new tongues; they will take up serpents; and if they drink anything deadly, it will by no means hurt them; they will lay hands on the sick, and they will recover." So then, after the Lord had spoken to them, He was received into heaven, and sat down on the right hand of God. (Mark 16:15–19)

> For with stammering lips and another tongue He will speak to this people, to whom He said, "This is the rest with which you may cause the weary to rest," and, "This is the refreshing." (Isaiah 28:11–12)

Hmm, what am I getting at here? We've seen that every believer, at the very moment of salvation, is *indwelled* by the Holy Spirit (which, by the way, is why no believer can be demon possessed. Just as Jesus completely expelled Satan from heaven *forever* after the Ascension, evil spirits are completely and forever cast out of our spirit realm when the Holy Spirit enters at salvation). He is *in* us.

But remember what the word *baptized* means? There is a deeper level of interaction with the Helper where we can become *engulfed, submerged, overwhelmed* with Him, where we are *in* Him, in addition to Him being *in* us. It's an *empowering* sort of thing, and I've been blessed to experience it. This is what John the Baptist was referring to in Matthew 3:11: "He will baptize you with the Holy Spirit and fire."

In this third baptism, Jesus Christ baptizes the believer into the Holy Spirit. I think of it like this: My vehicle is an FJ Cruiser with a 4.0 V-6 engine—adequate but not powerful. My wife has a vehicle with a supercharged V-6 engine made by Jaguar, and I *love* to drive it! The power is amazing and gives one a sense of confidence when behind the wheel. That's what I liken my Christian life to now, as opposed to before I had this experience. It's just better and certainly more fruitful.

And how does one receive this? What are those verses about "tongues" and "fire" about? Tomorrow.

FRIDAY

"He commanded them not to depart from Jerusalem, but to wait for the Promise of the Father. ... He said, '... but you shall be baptized with the Holy Spirit not many days from now. ... You shall receive power when the Holy Spirit has come upon you'" (Acts 1:4–8).

"When the Day of Pentecost had fully come, they were all with one accord in one place. And suddenly there came a sound from heaven, as of a rushing mighty wind, and it filled the whole house where they were sitting. Then there appeared to them divided *tongues*, as of *fire*, and one sat upon each of them. And they were filled with the Holy Spirit, and began to speak with other *tongues*, as the Spirit gave them utterance" (Acts 2:1–4; emphasis added).

Wow! There it is, the second chapter of Acts, as controversial a portion of Scripture as there is. But you can't ignore it, can you? The apostle Paul, the first human to understand fully the Gospel, wrote a lot about this baptism in the Holy Spirit and its proper role in glorifying Jesus. This is what he said about this "tongues" thing:

"I thank my God I speak with tongues more than you all" (1 Corinthians 14:18).

Now the general take on all of this by the modern church is that this manifestation of a deeper relationship with the Spirit was unique to the first believers and is not for us today. Commentators will go to extreme lengths to make that point. It's fine to believe that; it doesn't change your status in Christ. You're still perfect in God's eyes. But I know what I'd be missing out on if I weren't Spirit-filled, and I'll tell you this: I greatly doubt I would have been able to write this work. This has all been Spirit-driven; I've simply yielded to Him.

That is exactly how to receive this gift, if you so desire: to yield to His calling. You have complete control, and always will, of your actions and thoughts; God is not a dictator. He is a "perfect gentleman" and will not force Himself on anyone—not ever. Think about it. He didn't even force His will that His only Son become a human and suffer and die for us. Jesus had to *yield* His will to that of the Father (see Luke 22:42).

There's only one requirement: you must be saved. If that's the case, all you have to do is *ask* Jesus for this free gift and, as is always the case with this faith of ours, *believe* that you have received it. He wants you to have it more than you do. And then worship Jesus; praise Him (worship music such as "Holy Spirit (You Are Welcome Here)," by Katie and Bryan Torwalt, is helpful) with your voice and words. What happens next is the amazing thing; it's a beautiful thing, but it's also an unnatural thing since it's spiritual.

My, my. We're out of time this Friday. Ponder these things over the weekend, and we'll finish up this particular topic of the Holy Spirit on Monday, I promise. Then we'll move on to the "elephant in the room": What does God do with unbelievers?

40
WEEK

MONDAY

"The Spirit Himself bears witness with our spirit that we are children of God … likewise the Spirit also helps in our weaknesses. For we do not know what we should pray for as we ought, but the Spirit Himself makes intercession for us with groanings which cannot be uttered. Now He who searches the hearts know what the mind of the Spirit is, because He (the Holy Spirit) makes intercession for the saints according to the will of God" (Romans 8:14, 26–27).

"But the hour is coming, and now is, when the true worshipers will worship the Father in spirit and truth; for the Father is seeking such to worship Him. God is Spirit, and those who worship Him must worship in spirit and truth" (John 4:23–24).

Happy Monday. We've been talking a lot about "spirit" things, and that makes some uncomfortable because things that cannot be seen or touched or in some other way physically experienced are unnatural for us, because we are programmed at birth, as fallen humans, to be carnal. But God *is* Spirit—completely. As is the Holy Spirit. Only Jesus has a physical body, and He always will.

Maybe it's just me, but I quite honestly can't picture God. Isn't that terrible? I can't picture the Holy Spirit. But I can picture Jesus. I can very clearly imagine what He must look like, and through that I can "see" the Father, for "the light of the knowledge of the glory of God is in the face of Jesus Christ" (2 Corinthians 4:6).

But we can worship what we can't see; we can worship in spirit. The Holy Spirit wants to facilitate that, to help release us from the carnal constraints we all must deal with. That includes giving us a new language, a new "tongue," that "intercedes" for us according to the will of God in a way far superior to what we can accomplish with our innate intellect and emotions. It's a truly beautiful and edifying thing. As you're praising the Lord, you'll feel a warm sensation emanating from your core (not your head). It's like a fire. As you yield to that unnatural sensation, sounds that are foreign to you effortlessly come out. It is awkward at first (stammering lips) as new things are, but it becomes more natural and awesome over time. You're communicating with God on a purely spiritual level. And you can stop it at any time; you don't lose control of your will or intellect. It's something above, not instead of or against.

That's all I'm going to say about this third baptism. I know it's real and beneficial, but I don't want to belabor the point because I don't want to lose any reader over this, and we have much more to cover. We're done with the judgment of believers. The unrighteous still need to be dealt with—tomorrow.

TUESDAY

> Then I saw a great white throne and Him who sat on it, from whose face the earth and the heaven fled away. And there was found no place for them. And I saw the dead, small and great, standing before God, and books were opened. And another book was opened, which is the Book of Life. And the dead were judged according to their works, by the things which were written in the books. The sea gave up the dead who were in it, and Death and Hades delivered up the dead who were in them. And they were judged, each one according to his works. Then Death and Hades were cast into the lake of fire. This is the second death. And anyone not found written in the Book of Life was cast into the lake of fire. (Revelation 20:11–15)

> But the heavens and the earth which are now preserved by the same Word, are reserved for fire until the day

of judgement and perdition of ungodly men. … The Lord is not slack concerning His promise, as some count slackness, but is longsuffering toward us, not willing that any should perish, but that all come to repentance. (2 Peter 3:7–9)

Chilling, isn't it, this final judgment of unredeemed humans? Let me say this right off the bat: if you are in this category, what in the H-E–double hockey sticks is wrong with you?! Seriously! Please don't reject this great salvation we've been discussing for nine months, because the alternative is really not good. Every human's way out from the curse of sin was provided for at the cross; everyone's name was written in the book of life as all the sins of every man and woman were dealt with. But you have to *accept* this free gift of grace by putting your faith in Jesus (Ephesians 2:8), or else your name will be *removed* from that book of life. Look at these words of our Lord:

"He who overcomes [is saved] shall be clothed in white garments, and I will *not* blot out his name from the Book of Life" (Revelation 3:5; emphasis added).

You see the heart of God in that verse from 2 Peter; He is not willing for anyone to perish in hell. Actually, hell was not made for humans; it was never God's intention for them to be there. Hell is described as "the everlasting fire prepared for the devil and his angels" by Jesus in Matthew 25:41. You see, it was never even *created* originally, but specially *prepared* for Satan and his minions after his rebellion. Humans were not meant for eternal punishment. But they'll be there. If nothing else, knowing this should serve as an impetus and provide an urgency to spreading the Gospel, that good news of salvation from hell. Why? Ponder this scripture for tomorrow:

"How then shall they call on Him in whom they have not believed? And how shall they believe in Him of whom they have not heard? And how shall they hear without a preacher?" (Romans 10:14).

WEDNESDAY

So we're wrapping up this diversion on the eternal disposition of humans, tackling the age-old question "What happens after I die?" We've pointed out that every human's fate is ultimately in the hands of a just and righteous and good God and that the *only* way to the Father, heaven, and eternal life is through Jesus Christ. We've seen how Old Testament believers were handled prior to the cross and how all believers will be judged—a judgment of rewards. We've seen the absolute importance of *abiding* in Christ. Now we're pondering over the unsaved, those who have *died* a physical death without putting their faith in Jesus Christ. It seems straightforward enough: If a person presented with the Gospel, given the opportunity to accept Jesus, rejects Him, then the individual dies separated from God, never to be reunited, and he or she will spend eternity that way, separated from our Lord. Such was the severity of the Fall.

But what about all of those millions and millions of humans who have lived and died without ever hearing the Gospel message? That seems to be a whole different scenario. Certainly they have an excuse, don't they?

Paul obviously thought this question through a lot, and the Holy Spirit inspired him to write the book of Romans (an awesome book; I've always thought that if I had to get by with just two books of the Bible, I would pick the Gospel of Luke—it's that doctor thing—and the book of Romans), the first four chapters of which deal with this very thing in detail. They are certainly worth reading in their entirety, so please do read them. But here's the bottom line: no, there is no excuse for any human; their judgment will be *righteous* and *true*. Here are some verses:

"For the wrath of God is revealed from heaven against all ungodliness and unrighteousness of men, who *suppress the truth* in unrighteousness, for what may be known of God is *manifest in them*, for *God has shown it to them.* For since the creation of the world, *His invisible attributes are clearly seen*, being understood *by the things that are made*, even His eternal power and Godhead, *so that they are without excuse*" (Romans 1:18–20; emphasis added).

Wow! No excuses! Even if they've never heard the Gospel! Does this seem a bit unfair? Severe? Remember, God loves for us to question these things because He has nothing to hide. He is good all the time. I'll explain further tomorrow.

THURSDAY

"Then one of the criminals who were hanged blasphemed Him, saying, 'If you are the Christ, save Yourself and us.' But the other, answering, rebuked him, saying, 'Do you not even fear God, seeing you are under the same condemnation? And we indeed justly, for we receive the due reward of our deeds; but this Man has done nothing wrong.' Then he said to Jesus, 'Lord, remember me when You come into Your kingdom.' And Jesus said to him, 'Assuredly, I say to you, today you will be with Me in Paradise'" (Luke 23:42–43).

"But in accordance with your hardness and your impenitent heart you are treasuring up for yourself wrath in the day of wrath and revelation of the *righteous* judgement of God, who will *'render to each one according to his deeds'* ... to those who are self-seeking and do not obey the truth, but obey unrighteousness—indignation and wrath, tribulation and anguish ... but glory, honor, and peace to everyone who works what is good ... for there is *no partiality* with God" (Romans 2:5–11; emphasis added).

My two favorite books, Luke and Romans, and what they're revealing here go a long way toward helping us understand the way our righteous Lord deals with unbelievers who have never had a chance to reject the Gospel. Here's what I think: They will be judged based on the *light* of the truth of the Gospel that they have been exposed to and what they did with that light, that truth, as Paul goes on to say further in Romans 2, "In the day when God will judge the secrets of men by Jesus Christ, *according to My Gospel*" (v. 16; emphasis added).

And "Paul's Gospel" is the Gospel of Grace. Look at the thief on the cross. We have no reason to think he had any knowledge of Jesus Christ before that last-minute encounter at the Crucifixion, yet he realized just *who* Jesus

Christ was at that moment and put his faith in Him, and he was definitely *saved*! We'll meet him in heaven! I think *that* happens a lot. *Before* the last breath, Jesus appears to the unbeliever who has responded to the light he or she was given in life, and reveals Himself to the person, and gives him or her a choice, Yes, I think "deathbed conversions" happen a lot. Just my musings on all of this, but this thinking is not contrary to Scripture. And it rests well with me and what I know of the heart and "whole counsel" of God.

One more point on this topic I want to make tomorrow: *There are no second chances after death. None.*

FRIDAY

"People are destined to die once and then the judgement" (Hebrews 9:27 CEB).

So we end this week completing our discussion of the afterlife. We've covered a lot of stuff, and some have been my ponderings, but one thing is for certain from Scripture, and it is stated above. Physical death is a onetime occurrence, and then it's *game over*! There are no mulligans—no second chances. I know this flies in the face of the biggest Christian church on the planet, but it's really important to understand that everyone's eternal destiny is set *before* they take their last breath.

But isn't that the way it has to be for us to be truly free-willed creations who have the unique ability to determine our own destinies? Would it make any sense for other factors to have a say in the final result of our choices? I think this all has to do with our being created in the image of God, and it's a tremendous responsibility.

I want to explain one little obscure portion of scripture that can bring this doctrine into question. Look at this:

"By whom He also went and *preached* to the spirits in prison, who formerly were disobedient, when once the Divine longsuffering waited in the days of Noah, while the ark was being prepared" (1 Peter 1:19–20; emphasis added).

Wow! Does this mean Jesus, after the Crucifixion and defeat of Satan on the cross, went down to hell and preached salvation to unbelievers? Some people interpret it this way. But look at this:

"And the angels who did not keep their proper domain, but left their own abode, he has reserved in everlasting *chains* under darkness for the judgement of the great day" (Jude 6; emphasis added).

Considering that one of the meanings of *preach* is to "publicly proclaim, or teach, a belief," it seems to me that this scripture is referencing how Jesus went before the imprisoned fallen angels who had messed with the human women back in Noah's time to *proclaim His victory* over them, after the cross, when He descended to Hades to set the Old Testament believers free as we've discussed previously. Isn't that just awesome?! We start afresh next week; have a great weekend.

41
WEEK

MONDAY

Happy Monday! So now we'll pick up where we left off in our review of the topics we covered last year (I know it's already late February, but these little diversions into the doctrines of the Christian faith keep getting in the way (although I must say that the last one about the judgment of humankind was good…we're all going to face this judgment, yet we never talk or even think about it) and then set the stage for the last three months of this one-year treatise. Yes, there is an end in sight!

We pick up after the Fall of Man. We've been expelled from the garden, and Adam and Eve have a great many kids, and they all have a great many kids, and there's an intriguing and, I think, very sad verse in Genesis 4:26: "Then men began to call on the name of the Lord."

Think of that; what does that mean? To me this shows the inherent *hunger* in every human soul for something other and greater than what is within it, what is carnal. These early humans had a conscience, a sense of right and wrong, but that only went so far; they yearned for something deeper, something eternal, as they realized that they were mortal, that they would eventually die.

But they couldn't commune with God because He is Spirit and they were entirely carnal, and the bridge between the two was out because their spiritual aspect was dead. All the universe was watching uneasily because this experiment, this creation of free-willed humans made in the image of God, was not going well. It would just get worse, and worse until "the wickedness of man was great in the earth, and *every* intent of the *thoughts* of his heart was only *evil continually*" (Genesis 6:5; emphasis added).

That, my readers, is the ultimate outcome of a world devoid of the Spirit of God, and it would prove an important point: humankind in their unredeemed form, relying just on their carnal abilities and desires and strength, will become only more and more evil over time. They could not redeem themselves; they needed a Savior. Things became so "corrupt and violent" (Genesis 6:11) that God had to righteously judge both the earth and everything living on it, washing the earth clean with a worldwide flood and starting over with a representative couple of every species of animal life, along with a family of just eight humans who still had perfect human DNA. The plan of salvation would play out through them, but a very important lesson was learned by humankind, right? Things could never get that evil again, right? Well, look up Matthew 24:37 for tomorrow and see what Jesus had to say about this.

TUESDAY

"But as the days of Noah *were,* so will the coming of the Son of Man *be*" (Matthew 24:37; emphasis added).

Wow! Those days of Noah were not cool; they were really, really bad, and Jesus is comparing them to the period of time on this earth right before His Second Coming, which occurs a matter of years (the number of years is controversial, but the maximum would be seven) after the Rapture of the church, of believers. I've explained previously that the reason for this oppressive, overwhelming evil is not that Satan was freshly thrown out of heaven, as he's been here fully engaged since Jesus ascended back to heaven and kicked him out two thousand years ago, but that the restraining power of the Holy Spirit will be pretty much gone once all the Christians, in whom the Holy Spirit resides, are pulled out.

Just as the sinful earth had to be judged the first time, it will be judged again. But God had promised "Never again shall there be a flood to destroy the earth" (Genesis 9:11) after the Great Flood, and He is faithful. He will keep His word. There will be no flood, but there will be something much quicker and more effective, because this time the earth (and heavens) will be annihilated—obliterated! Look at these verses:

"But the heavens and the earth ... are reserved for *fire* until the day of judgement and perdition of ungodly men" (2 Peter 3:7; emphasis added).

"But the day of the Lord will come ... in which the heavens will pass away with a great noise, and the elements will *melt* with fervent *heat*; both the earth and the works that are in it will be *burned up*" (2 Peter 3:10; emphasis added).

"All things will be *dissolved* ... the heavens will be *dissolved*, being on *fire*, and the elements will *melt* with fervent *heat*" (2 Peter 3:11, 12; emphasis added).

Hmm, that seems pretty persuasive. Peter was not one to mince his words. But no worries. When this happens, all humans will have already been judged, and there will a *new* heaven and a *new* earth formed "in which righteousness dwells" (2 Peter 3:13; emphasis added). Praise God!

So when you hear a Christian say when they (and by they, I mean me) are jealous of something nice that someone else has, "It's all gonna *burn* someday!" they're actually right, and there's the Scriptural proof. However, it's still not a nice thing to say. More tomorrow.

WEDNESDAY

Our review continues. We saw how after the Flood, humankind, unredeemed but created in the image of God, reproduced quickly and stayed cohesive in one location and with one language (this idea of a "one world" government is obviously pretty old, and God has never been a fan). They were up to no good again, building a ridiculously tall tower, presumably to avoid their ancestors' fate. The Lord therefore scattered humans over all the earth and gave them different looks and abilities and propensities. That's why we have different ethnic groups, all of one species, one DNA. This was a good thing. It seems to me God really likes diversity. All creation screams that out. Just go to any zoo or aquarium.

But the humans were still lost, and God was aching to break the stalemate.

"The Lord searches all the earth for people who have given themselves completely to Him. He wants to make them strong" (2 Chronicles 16:9 NCV).

He found one: Abram (later named Abraham). This guy was really different in that he *believed* what God said without any proof in the carnal realm. He definitely went all in with God. It was this kind of belief that God had to see in humans to crack open the door of salvation as it was *this* that God counted as *righteousness.*

"And he [Abraham] believed in the Lord, and He [God] accounted it to him for righteousness" (Genesis 15:6).

Super important verse there. So we saw how Abraham and Sarah had the miracle baby, Isaac (so very much a type of Christ), and Isaac married Rebekah (the twenty-fourth chapter of Genesis is devoted solely to the romance between Isaac and Rebekah; it is simply spellbinding, especially when you consider it is a type of the romance between Jesus and the Church), and they had Jacob, and he had twelve sons, the twelve tribes of Israel.

Because of Father Abraham's unwavering belief in God, these "children of Israel" were chosen to shine the light of the Gospel, of salvation, to the world. But that wasn't going to take place right away; they weren't ready. They were going to enter a dark period, a period of four hundred years of unprecedented hardship, and the wondering, ever-observing universe was trying to figure it out. Had God forgotten them? Was humankind always going to stay lost? Where was that "seed of the woman" who was supposed to crush Satan? I'm sure Satan was feeling pretty good about things around this time. Everything seemed to be going his way. He truly had outfoxed God in the garden; God's precious little humans were all his, and their only hope was a nation of slaves who had seemingly forgotten their God.

Isn't this exciting? More tomorrow.

THURSDAY

"Then He [God] said to Abram: 'Know certainly that your descendants will be strangers in a land that is not theirs, and will serve them, and they will afflict them *four hundred years*'" (Genesis 15:13; emphasis added).

"Behold, I will send you Elijah the prophet, before the coming of the great and dreadful day of the Lord. And he will turn the hearts of the fathers to the children, and the hearts of the children to their fathers, lest I come and strike the earth with a curse" (Malachi 4:5–6).

"The book of the genealogy of Jesus Christ, the Son of David, the Son of Abraham" (Matthew 1:1).

Hmm, interesting assortment of verses, eh? Well, today we're going to contemplate another one of those relatively obscure, yet very revealing, nuggets of truth tucked away in this Bible of ours. It has to do with a period of time—four hundred years.

Between the Old and New Testaments in your Bible, there should be a page that says the following: "Four Hundred Years of Silence," as that is the period of time between the last verse of the book of the last Old Testament prophet Malachi and the first verse of the New Testament. Note the Malachi passage is talking about John the Baptist. Four hundred years of no recorded interaction between God and His chosen people—none. That struck me as weird and as something worth pondering over. So I looked for another four-hundred-year period and found this was the period of time the children of Israel were captive in Egypt, another period of apparent silence from God.

Wow! So are there similarities here? Why these hundreds of years of God lying dormant, and Satan seemingly winning in this awesome drama being played out on planet Earth? Specifically, where was the Gospel in all this, because as you know *all* of Scripture is ultimately about Jesus and His cross. I asked the Lord for insight as to how to see Jesus in this stuff.

Here's what I was given. You know what, I don't want to break this next part up, so we'll save it for tomorrow, okay? But one quick word of explanation for you Bible scholars out there: I'm well aware the actual time of the Israeli captivity in Egypt was 430 years, not 400 (Exodus 12:40–41), but that wasn't God's plan. The period of captivity was extended thirty years by a man's mistake (Moses's). But that's a whole other story, one we will not cover in this series of writings. We can't cover everything! We'll talk more tomorrow morning.

FRIDAY

"For His anger is but for a moment, His favor is for life; weeping may endure for a night, but *joy* comes in the morning" (Psalm 30:5; emphasis added).

Happy Friday! We're looking at these two *long* (four-hundred-year!) periods of time when God seems to be "missing in action" as far as His plan of salvation is concerned, the time of captivity as slaves in Egypt for the children of Israel and the of absence of communication from God to His people between the prophet Malachi and John the Baptist. Nothing is insignificant in the Word of God, and everything ultimately points to the Gospel (Jesus), so what could it all mean?

Here's the analogy I was given. I know it seems weird, but bear with me. I like to watch women's figure skating; there's something otherworldly and perfect about it. A particular jump called a triple lutz came to my mind when thinking of these long silent periods of time before something absolutely *spectacular* happens. Google it. The skater is gracefully and seemingly effortlessly gliding backward toward the end of the rink, when *suddenly* she leaps high (and I mean high!) into the air and twirls around three times before landing beautifully with her arms spread wide in jubilation. It is a period of nothing happening leading up to an awesome climax. That's exactly what we see in the Bible with these two events.

We'll expound on this further, but first I need, in this culture I live in, to state that I am not being sexist using *women's* figure skating as an example.

There is something absolutely awesome about men on skates also; it's called *hockey*, and I like that too. Second, I must also admit that, as beautiful as ice-skating is, the *primary* reason I watch it is to see the skater fall (and don't act like that's not the reason you watch it also). Enough said.

Here's the deal: remember, the universe is watching, and these two prolonged periods will prove to them that the ultimate salvation of humankind would have nothing to do with humankind! The children of Israel, heirs of believing Abraham, would turn their backs on their God (except for Joseph, who is a type of Christ) and not *believe* Him for His provision and protection. They will end up slaves in a foreign land. Centuries later, their descendants, even after having been given the Law, and the prophets, and the priests, and temporary atonement for their sins, would completely reject His love and mercy, holding on instead to the letter of the Law, which was death. It was as if in both instances *God was completely forgotten*!

But look at the opening verse for this morning. Hmm, what would that *joy* be after these periods of abject darkness? You know, I could be rude and wait until Monday, but ... yeah, I will be that and do that. But it's *really good*, so have a great weekend!

42
WEEK

MONDAY

So we're discussing two four-hundred-year periods of time, separated by one thousand four hundred fifty years, during which God is strangely distant from His chosen people, the children of Israel. My proposition is that in both cases the purpose was to show to the observing universe (remember, the cross had not occurred yet, and the universe was unsettled) that humankind, left to their own devices, would stray horribly from the love of God and basically forget Him. We will see at the end of both periods of time the absolute *goodness* and *mercy* of God would become manifest, in the first case as a beautiful shadow of the ultimate salvation to come, and in the second, that perfect salvation Himself. I think this is just an awesome thing with huge implications, and it's ultimately about Jesus. So we'll dwell on it a bit.

First of all, did the children of Israel lose their identity as God's chosen people while captive in Egypt? Yep. Look at this:

"Then the children of Israel *groaned* because of the bondage, and they *cried out*; and their cry came up to God because of the bondage. So God *heard* their groaning, and God *remembered* His covenant with Abraham, with Isaac, and with Jacob. And God *looked* upon the children of Israel, and God *acknowledged* them" (Exodus 2:23–25; emphasis added).

Wow, what a one-way relationship this is! Look closely at the one thing the children of Israel did: they groaned and cried, *but not to God*! They were just crying out in complete distress and brokenness, but they had forgotten whom even to pray to. They were completely lost. It was God who heard, and remembered, and looked upon, and acknowledged. As I pointed out many moons ago in this treatise, that Hebrew word for "acknowledged," *yada*, means to have intimate (like sexual) relations. It's the same word used in Genesis 4: "Now Adam *knew* his wife, and she conceived" (emphasis added). It was God and God alone who purposed and planned for and enabled His people to leave Egypt, but only after the ceremony of Passover was initiated, heralding the sacrificial Lamb of God, which we spent many weeks on previously. There was all that darkness and eerie quietness, but then an explosion of grace, mercy, goodness, *joy*. Just like a divine triple lutz!

But what about that second four-hundred-year period of time? Had God's people, the Jews, forgotten Him again? We'll see tomorrow.

TUESDAY

Remember the last words of the Old Testament, from the prophet Malachi? "Behold, I will send you Elijah the prophet before the coming of the great and dreadful day of the Lord" (Malachi 4:5).

Four hundred years later, during which time there was no fresh Word from the Lord to His people, that prophecy was fulfilled, at least partially. John the Baptist arrived on the scene, and "he will turn many of the children of Israel to the Lord their God. He will also go before Him in the spirit and power of Elijah" (Luke 1:16–17).

Now I say the prophecy was only partially fulfilled because Elijah, you may recall, never died; he was caught up to heaven by a whirlwind (2 Kings 2:11) and will return himself to earth during the Great Tribulation to be a witness for the Lord (probably along with Moses, who also probably never died a physical death; see Deuteronomy 34:5–6). Further evidence for this interpretation lies in the transfiguration on Mount Hermon, where both of these guys, Moses and Elijah, show up in their regular physical bodies; only Jesus was "transfigured" to His glorified body (see Luke 17:1–8). Interesting stuff, eh?

But let's get back to John the Baptist and see what he thought of the spiritual status of the Jews of that time and how far they had distanced themselves from the faith of Abraham:

"Brood of vipers! Who warned you to flee from the wrath to come? Therefore, bear fruits worthy of repentance, and do not think to say to yourselves, 'We have Abraham as our father.' For I say to you that God is able to raise up children to Abraham from these stones. And even now, *the ax is laid to the root of the trees*" (Matthew 3:7–10; emphasis added).

Wow! These Jews, even though they had the temple and priests and animal sacrifices and experts in the Law (Pharisees), were *so lost* that they didn't even know they were lost, because they were trusting in the *letter*, not the *spirit*, of the Law. The whole purpose of John the Baptist was to point this out to them, to get their hearts somewhat ready to hear the Gospel, because they first had to realize they needed it. I think that is so much still the case today, thinking that performing the usual "rituals" of Christianity, like going to church once in a while, putting something in the offering plate on occasion, and giving to the local food bank (which is a really good thing, by the way) gets us to heaven. Dangerous territory, and so plentiful in this "Christian" land of ours. But we know it's only through *faith* in Jesus Christ and the Gospel of Grace that we are saved. I'm convinced it's only by that grace that we can even know we are lost and need Him. We'll end today with my favorite verse from the greatest hymn ever, which sums this all up so concisely and beautifully:

"'Twas grace that taught my heart to fear, and grace my fears relieved"— from "Amazing Grace" written by John Newton in the eighteenth century.

WEDNESDAY

"But He answered and said, 'I was not sent except to the lost sheep of the house of Israel'" (Matthew 15:24).

So we've seen that Israel was spiritually dead at the time of Jesus Christ's incarnation, and they didn't even know it. That would be obvious because Jesus fulfilled every prophecy about the coming Messiah in the Old Testament, which was complete, and even available in Greek, yet they missed it. They did not accept Him. They rejected Him, and that was absolutely crucial to God's plan of salvation, which was for all humans, not just the Jews. But as can be seen above, He came for the Jews and them alone. What if the Jews *had* accepted Jesus as their Messiah? Where would that leave you? Where would that leave me? Where would it leave anyone who is not a Jew? Jesus would have set up His kingdom on this earth then, and ushered in His reign on this earth, with no apparent provision for forgiveness of sin, or the Atonement, or the salvation of any Gentile! No, they *had* to reject Jesus. That is why I believe the four hundred years of silence before He came. Paul spoke a lot about all of this in Romans, chapters 9–11. Look at these verses:

"You will say then, 'Branches were broken off that I might be grafted in'" (Romans 11:19).

"For I do not desire, brethren, that you should be ignorant of this mystery … that blindness in part has happened to Israel until the fullness of the Gentiles has come in" (Romans 11:25).

Here's how I put all this together: God would purposely distance Himself from His chosen people for four hundred years in Egypt to demonstrate to the universe His unmerited and complete *love* for them by setting them free from bondage and giving them a preview of their future Messiah (in the Passover). Then, almost fifteen hundred years later, that same God would again fall silent toward His people for four hundred years and basically sacrifice them (temporarily) to allow for the opportunity for the salvation of *all humans* through their rejection of that Messiah.

Wow! Double wow! This is just so amazing to me. I don't want to end this morning's discussion without pointing out the very next verse in Romans 11:

"And so, *all Israel will be saved*" (vv. 26; emphasis added).

God didn't "throw them under the bus"; they will be grafted back in.

This makes a lot of sense to me, but why the length of four hundred years? What's so special about that? We have more to ponder tomorrow.

THURSDAY

"Know certainly that your descendants will be strangers in a land that is not theirs, and will serve them, and they will afflict them four hundred years … but in the *fourth generation* they shall return here" (Genesis 15:13, 16; emphasis added).

This is God speaking to Abraham about the Egyptian captivity. He equates the four-hundred-year sojourn with four generations. Does that seem odd? Not for back in the time of the patriarchs. We've discussed the longevity of humankind previously, but remember, guys lived routinely over a hundred years then (Abraham was one hundred years old when he had Isaac), so a generation was one hundred years. But this phrase "fourth generation" seemed familiar to me, and this is why. Look at these verses:

"For I, the Lord your God, am a jealous God, visiting the *iniquity of the fathers* upon the *children* to the third and *fourth generations* of those who hate me, but showing mercy to thousands, to those who love me and keep my commandments" (Exodus 20:5–6; emphasis added).

This was spoken just before the giving of the Ten Commandments. It reflects the nature of the Law and Old Testament times. This Scripture is *repeated* word for word in Exodus 34:7, Numbers 14:18, and Deuteronomy 5:9. God is trying to make a point. His righteousness is so perfect and awesome that any sin against Him, unless it is *remitted, atoned for*, will continue to impact the subsequent children of the offender out to four generations! Four hundred years! Wow!

But *then* what happens? What takes place *after* that period of time? Redemption. Salvation. That's what happens! This was previewed in the Passover and Exodus of the children of Israel from Egypt, after four hundred years of suffering, and fulfilled in the incarnation, life, death, and resurrection of Jesus Christ, the Lamb of God, after the four hundred years of judgment between the Old and New Testaments.

That's awesome, isn't it? But I got to thinking further about this four-hundred-year period thing and the generations of humans. And I saw something just as awesome, but this time we'll use the more conventional period of time for a generation, which is forty years, not one hundred. The children of Israel had to wander in the wilderness for a "generation" after refusing to believe God the first time they came to the Promised Land, and that wandering was for forty years. So we'll use that. That means there were ten generations fulfilling this four hundred years of struggle before salvation, before a new start, a new life. Got it?

Rats. We'll have to wait until tomorrow, Friday, to finish this. That's okay. I love ending the week with something really new and neat, and that will be the case tomorrow.

FRIDAY

The number forty is significant in the Bible. It delineates a period of time associated with judgment, or testing, or proving. Think of forty days and nights, the period of continuous rain causing the Great Flood; the amount of time Moses spent on Mount Sinai receiving the Law (from angels, not God Himself); and the length of the temptation of Jesus Christ by Satan. Think of forty years, the amount of time Moses spent in the wilderness after killing the Egyptian (which, as I alluded to cryptically previously, was the reason the length of time of the Jews' captivity in Egypt was extended); the period of time the children of Israel wandered in the wilderness before entering the Promised Land; and the length of the time of the reigns of both King David and King Solomon.

But four hundred? What gives with that, if anything, besides the extension of judgment for sin going out four very long generations as discussed yesterday? I think there is something more, and it has to do with the more common forty-year definition of a generation. That would involve ten generations of humans. Where in the Bible would ten generations delineate a period of time until severe judgment, and then redemption, with a fresh, new start following?

As we've done so many times in this series, we will go back to the beginning, Genesis, and what transpired after the Fall. We'll turn to chapter 5, which looks really boring because it's a genealogy. But it's not boring, trust me. Let's go through the generations from Adam to the Flood: Adam had Seth, who had Enosh, who had Cainan, who had Mahalalel, who had Jared, who had Enoch, who had Methuselah, who had Lamech, who had *Noah*. Count them. Go ahead, count them! *Ten* generations. Ten generations of lost humankind struggling and deteriorating, so distant from their Creator God. The Great Flood was not the end, but the beginning of a new covenant, the Noahic covenant. God would establish the rainbow as a sign to all humankind that He cares for them and would never destroy the earth by flood again. To me this equates with the ten forty-year generations that make up the four hundred years of the Egyptian captivity and the divine silence between the old and new covenants as both periods of time ushered in (the former as a type; the latter as the reality) the ultimate redemption and salvation for humankind, Jesus Christ and the atonement.

So we end up seeing Jesus in even these obscure, seemingly meaningless portions of scripture. I just love the Word of God. You can call me overly obsessed, but you know what I could be spending my time on? I could be pondering over sudoku, or putting jigsaw puzzles together, or watching *Jeopardy!* incessantly. There is nothing wrong with those things, but they really are lame as all that stuff is temporal and passing, but the Word of God is eternal and edifying, renewing my mind and soul. So don't judge me! Have a great weekend.

43
WEEK

MONDAY

"Most assuredly, I say to you that you will weep and lament … and you will be sorrowful, but your sorrow will be turned into joy. A woman, when she is in labor, has sorrow because her hour has come; but as soon as she has given birth to the child, she no longer remembers the anguish, for joy that a human being has been born into the world. Therefore, you now have sorrow; but I will see you again, and your heart will rejoice, and your joy no one will take away from you" (John 16:20–22).

The foregoing are the beautiful words of our Lord to His disciples at the Last Supper.

It's March, a transition month, as the hardships and trials of winter give way to the rebirth of spring, a beautiful reminder of this constant Christian theme of *sorrow* turning to *joy*. That's been our theme also as we have looked at two four-hundred-year periods of hardship giving way to redemption, restoration, and blessing. That's what Jesus was reassuring His followers about, that "joy comes in the morning" (Psalm 30:5), that the darkest time of the night is right before the dawn. That is *so* reassuring to us as Christians and why we are not to give in to Satan's fearmongering and anxiety-provoking lies. Remember, "God has not given us a spirit of fear" (2 Timothy 1:7).

I'm sure the Evil One was thrilled to see God's children of promise enslaved and powerless in Egypt and to see that God had apparently given up on saving His lost people during the years of silence before Jesus's time. He thought he was actually winning the war, and I would think the observing universe thought the same. But that was *before* he was absolutely crushed at the cross, utterly defeated (Colossians 2:15). Here's what really gets me *mad* about Satan in this time of ours: although already defeated, and clearly exposed to the universe as the horribly evil and inferior creature he is, he is so delusional that he thinks he can still win, that he still has a chance to overthrow God. He is going to do all he can to destroy the precious human race now that he has been (as we have recently shown) expelled fully from heaven and unleashed on this earth. He refuses to acknowledge the certain end for him and his followers: the "lake of fire burning with brimstone" (Revelation 19:20). What a fake; what an impostor!

Do you think I'm overly hard on Satan? Well, it's because I absolutely hate him, and that's a good thing. There is such a thing as righteous anger, and it's biblical. Ponder this verse for tomorrow morning:

"Be angry and do not sin; do not let the sun go down on your wrath, nor give place to the devil" (Ephesians 4:26–27).

TUESDAY

"The Lord *rebuke* you, Satan! The Lord who has chosen Jerusalem *rebuke* you!" (Zechariah 3:2; emphasis added).

"Then Jesus went into the temple and began to *drive out* those who bought and sold in the temple, and *overturned the tables* of the money changers *and the seats* of those who sold doves. And He would *not allow* anyone to carry wares through the temple" (Mark 11:15–16; emphasis added).

Wow! Do you think Jesus might have been a bit angry in that scenario in the temple? There's no way to spiritualize this; He was getting *physical* with those blasphemers of His Father. So much for any thought of Jesus Christ being a milquetoast. He was, as the poet Carl Sandburg would say, made of velvet and steel, in perfect possession of a heart of tenderness and a will of iron. We are to be like Him. It's okay to get angry, even very angry, at Satan and evil. Remember the last verse from yesterday, where Paul actually admonishes believers to be angry and not to let the "sun go down" on that anger (Ephesians 4:26)?

Now, indeed, the conventional interpretation of that is that one must not *stay* angry very long since it's not a good thing, but I think Paul actually meant exactly what he said. It is far too easy for us as Christians to become complacent with evil, to look the other way, to choose to be non-confrontational. But Paul is asking us not to "give place to the devil," to stay vigilant in our opposition to sin (but not toward the sinner, as Jesus so beautifully exemplified, since he was actually called the "friend of sinners" [Matthew 11:19]). Paul is saying we should be passionate about our opposition to evil 24/7. We are to be strong men and women of faith, trusting not in our strength but in the Lord, as David said:

"In God I have put my trust; I will not be afraid. What can man do to me?" (Psalm 56:11).

My point is that there is a place for righteous anger, and an important place at that. As a pediatrician, I see things that make it so very easy to fan the embers of this righteous anger into a fiery flame. I'll share a personal story about all of this tomorrow morning.

WEDNESDAY

I'll call her Emmy. She was my patient from birth through eighteen years of age. She was born with a rare genetic condition known as Treacher–Collins syndrome. These children have perfectly normal intelligence but disfiguring facial anomalies, including severely sunken-in, small cheekbones, defects of the lower eyelids, and very malformed ears. Google it. The findings are not subtle and are immediately noticeable. I note again, Emmy was perfectly normal intellectually. She knew what she looked like. I've often wondered how I would have handled that, to see the look of shock in strangers' eyes when they looked at me, followed by the look of pity. And that would be from the caring people she would encounter in life; she would have had experiences much worse in interacting with expectedly unsophisticated kids her age and cruel adults.

God didn't make her that way; He doesn't do that. No, her nightmare was caused by *sin*, not hers, but a direct consequence of the Fall and the inherited sinful condition of all humankind—all part of Satan's plan to get back at God and make His most treasured creations in all the universe suffer and suffer terribly. This little girl was innocent in God's eyes—yes, born "already ruined" and lost, but not able to determine her own destiny yet. We know clearly from Scripture that all children, until they reach whatever the age of accountability is for them, go to heaven after death and have eternal life (see 2 Samuel 12:15–23). By the way, that includes fetuses who die before birth, either naturally or by murder, meaning that there will be an extra sixty-million-plus American citizens in heaven, as it stands now, who were never given the chance to live in our country because of the legalization of abortion in 1973. Really, just think of that.

Every time I would see Emmy, I would be reminded of just how evil, debased, and ugly Satan is. What kind of absolute monster could do such a horrible thing to an innocent little girl?

But there is a balance to that anger—a *big* balance. Because I noticed something else stir within me every time I looked at Emmy, a supernatural, amazingly real, unconditional love. I found myself seeing in front of me the most beautiful girl in the universe. I could just gaze at her forever; she looked amazing to me.

Then I got it. That is exactly how our Lord saw her and how He sees every one of us. The imperfections just melt away when He gazes upon us. We are treasured, and priceless, and flawless. That's what Emmy became to me.

You know what? I believe she sensed that, that perfect acceptance and worth. She was one of the several children, over the years, with whom I was impressed by the Holy Spirit to do something that some may think unusual and maybe wrong, but I knew it was right. It was this: As I was examining her ears with my otoscope, which was hard because her ear canals were so small, I would have my mouth right close to that terribly malformed, flawed ear and would whisper, so only she could hear, five words, just five words: "*I wish you were mine!*"

We have to stop for today. I wish we didn't have to. More tomorrow.

THURSDAY

We ended yesterday with a human example of one man's unconditional
love for a physically imperfect and flawed little girl. It is a moving thing,
but there is a much greater truth here, and that is the ageless true story
of the perfect, flawless, all-powerful, lovely King of the Universe and His
unconditional love for fallen, sinful, carnal, lost humans. I want us to look
at John chapter 11, which illustrates one of the most moving and dramatic
stories of all time. We'll take our time as Jesus did His in this story.

"Jesus wept" (John 11:35).

Known for being the shortest verse in the Bible, its significance is huge.
Let's look at the context: Lazarus was dead and had been dead for four
days. He was beloved by Jesus, the brother of Mary and Martha, and
they had sent word to Jesus before Lazarus died that he was very sick. No
doubt, they assumed, He would come right away and heal their brother,
but He did not. He purposely delayed. "So, when He heard that Lazarus
was sick, He stayed two more days in the place that He was" (vv. 6). He
wasn't physically close; He was staying by the river Jordan, and Lazarus
was in Bethany, just outside Jerusalem, days away.

Just think about that next time your prayers don't seem to be answered
immediately. Jesus knew what He was doing, and His purpose was greater
and more beneficial. His ways are not our ways, and we must learn to
patiently trust in His timing. At just the right divinely appointed time,
Jesus said to His disciples, "Let us go to Judea again" (v. 7).

He arrived seemingly embarrassingly late; Lazarus was in the tomb, obviously
dead as a doornail, for four days. On His casual way there, Jesus spoke to
the disciples about the state of Lazarus: "Our friend Lazarus sleeps" (v. 11).
The disciples thought that was indeed the case, that Lazarus hadn't actually
died yet. But Jesus was telling us something profoundly true and reassuring,
for Lazarus was a believer, and Jesus was looking forward to the cross, where
He would *defeat death*. You need to know this: When we as believers "die,"
it really is going to sleep and waking up with Jesus! Look at this:

"Death is swallowed up in victory. O, Death where is your sting? O Hades, where is your victory?" (1 Corinthians 15:54–55).

Wow! Profound, but lost on the disciples. Let me paraphrase their response: "That's great, Jesus, 'cause if he's just sleeping, he'll be well when he wakes up! So why even go there?" (vv. 12–13). You see, they didn't want to go anywhere near Jerusalem because they knew they were wanted men there. I love our patient Lord's dealing with these guys. Look at the next verse:

"Then Jesus said to them *plainly*, 'Lazarus is dead'" (v. 14; emphasis added).

What a wonderful and kind Lord we have. We'll pick up here tomorrow.

FRIDAY

We pick up the story of the raising of Lazarus from the dead, found in John chapter 11. Interestingly, no other Gospel records this amazing account of the miraculous power of Jesus Christ, but John spends a lot of time on it. To me, the most compelling part of this story is Jesus's compassion and love for us.

So Jesus and the disciples are on their way to Bethany, which is basically a suburb of Jerusalem, and the disciples are worried. The last time they were in Jerusalem, the Jews tried to stone Jesus for blasphemy (John chapter 10), but He wasn't deterred. He knew His time was not yet. Such was not the case with the disciples. But look who settles the matter:

"Then Thomas … said to his fellow disciples, 'Let us also go, that we may die with Him'" (John 11:16).

Wow! Good old doubting Thomas, the Eeyore (from *Winnie the Pooh* fame) of the disciples, who sees everything in a negative vein, including this situation. Don't you just love his reasoning? So pessimistic and gloomy, just like Eeyore. But there are a ton of Christians just like that, saved, washed in the blood of the Lamb, and inheriting eternal life yet living a downer life, thinking it's such a sacrifice to serve the Lord. Have you ever met anyone like that? What comes to my mind is a very popular old classic hymn of the church "Farther Along" by W. B. Stevens, which perfectly embodies this thinking. Look at these lyrics!

> Tempted and tried, we're oft made to wonder.
> Why it should be thus all the day long
> While there are others living about us
> Never molested, though in the wrong?
> Sometimes I wonder why I must suffer,
> Go in the rain, in the cold, and the snow,
> When there are many living in comfort
> Giving no heed to all I can do.

Wow! And it goes on and on like that. It's a super popular all-time hymn! I don't want to live like that, and I'm telling you, Jesus doesn't want me to live like that. What did He have to say about the quality of our lives?...

"I have come that they may have *life*, and that they may have it *more abundantly*" (John 10:10; emphasis added).

I'm going with that. Have a wonderful, abundant, joyful weekend.

WEEK

MONDAY

It's Monday, and we press on with the raising of Lazarus:

"Now Jesus loved Martha and her sister, and Lazarus. So, when He heard that he was sick, He stayed two more days in the place that He was" (John 11:5–6).

Hmm, isn't this weird? It seems as though John is saying that *because* Jesus loved this family, He delayed coming to rescue them, doesn't it? Strange way to show love. But I think there's something very deep and beautiful here, and it has helped me to understand, to some degree, why prayers of devout Christians are not seemingly answered sometimes: so that we may see a deeper truth in disappointment.

The key person in this whole story, to my way of thinking, is Mary (Martha's sister). This is the Mary who sat at Jesus's feet in Luke 10, listening to His every word, soaking Him in. This is the Mary who anointed those same feet with costly oil and wiped His feet with her hair six days before the Crucifixion, in John 12. She was totally sold out to Him. She was special, and I think she fully expected her Messiah to drop everything when He heard of her brother's life-threatening illness.

So when Jesus finally arrived outside of Bethany, at least four days after Mary asked for Him, He was greeted by—no, it was not Mary. Look at this:

"Now, *Martha*, as soon as she heard that Jesus was coming, went and met Him, but *Mary was sitting in the house*" (v. 20; emphasis added).

Wow! Don't think Jesus didn't notice this. Mary, I believe, was nearer to Jesus than Martha, and she was hurt terribly and didn't have the strength to go out to see Him. That's a very real thing. The more we are invested in a person, the more we are exposing ourselves to disappointment and pain if let down. Mary was experiencing this, and Jesus knew He had caused that pain, but Jesus also knew why He had to and that Mary could be counted on not to turn from Him. His waiting for Lazarus to die, to die beyond question, was to serve a very important purpose for the kingdom of God, but it would be at Mary's expense; in a sense, He was depending on her and her deep love for Him.

Is any of this making sense? I think it will as we have much more to see in this story, but when I finally saw the deep truths wrapped up in all of this, it really helped answer that nagging question of why God seems unresponsive to our earnest prayers at times. Here's what we can be reassured of: He is *never* unresponsive or uncaring. He's always on His throne, and He always has our best interests in mind. This week will be great!

TUESDAY

"Therefore, when Jesus saw her [Mary] weeping, and the Jews who came with her weeping, He groaned in the spirit and was troubled" (John 11:33).

When we ended yesterday, Jesus was greeted outside of Bethany by Martha, but Mary was mourning at home. She was devastated. But look what happened after Jesus was done talking with Martha:

"Then she [Martha] left and hurried off to her sister, Mary, and called her aside from all the mourners and whispered to her, 'The Master is here, and *He's asking for you*" (v. 28 TPT; emphasis added).

Wow! Do you see what Jesus was doing here? Mary had doubts that she didn't want to have; she needed reassurance, and that whisper in the ear was just like my whisper to Emmy. It was affirming and encouraging, and it assigned a special worth to her because her love for Jesus was so deep. How did she respond?

"As soon as she heard that, she arose quickly and came to Him. … Then, when Mary came to where Jesus was, and *saw Him*, she fell down at His feet" (vv. 29, 32; emphasis added).

The very next verse is what I opened with this morning, and it is very beautiful. Seeing Mary visibly distraught, weeping loudly, and suffering moved our Lord greatly and deeply such that even He, the greatest orator of all time, could only "groan in the spirit." And then comes the shortest, but possibly most significant, verse in all of scripture:

"Jesus wept" (v. 35).

Wow! Just picture this scene. Meditate on it today. Imagine the face of Jesus weeping. Tomorrow we'll look closely at the Greek and see that the weeping described in verse 33 is different from the weeping described in verse 35. It will be awesome.

WEDNESDAY

"I am the resurrection and the life. He who believes in Me, though he may die, he shall live. And whoever lives and believes in Me shall never die. Do you believe this?" (John 11:25–26).

Lazarus was dead, really dead: four days dead! Mary was broken and "weeping" in front of Jesus. The Greek word used is *klaio*. Remember our Strong's Greek Concordance? We'll look at entry G2799:

> **klaio.** to weep, mourn, lament, bewail.

You get the picture. Mary was visibly shaken and loudly weeping, as were those around her. Now look at this: "When Jesus saw her weeping [klaio] … Jesus wept [dakryo]" (vv. 33, 35). A different Greek word is used for Jesus's weeping! What does that mean?

Strong's G1145 shows the following:

> **dakryo.** to silently, quietly shed tears.

I know exactly what that is like: a welling up from the soul of emotion that is overwhelming, and the tears, often embarrassing for me, just keep coming. But it's not demonstrative or flashy; it's silent and deep. The Jews saw the tears, and they thought they knew why. "Then the Jews said, 'See how He loves him!'" (v. 36).

But I don't think that's why Jesus was weeping. Sure, He loved Lazarus, but He already knew Lazarus would be raised from the dead and currently was not suffering. But Mary was suffering; she was suffering mightily because Jesus had let her down! Those divine tears were for her and all of suffering humanity. O how He hated to see us suffer under the bondage of sin. How He wanted to protect us and soothe us, to "gather us together as a hen gathers her chicks under her wings" (Matthew 23:37). His tears were for you and for me!

But He wasn't falling apart, not wailing, or thrashing about, or raising His voice, for He knew that salvation was coming and coming soon. He knew the end of the story. He Himself would provide a way out, a way to safety and eternal life, a way to defeat death itself. He knew His beloved Mary would see—and soon—that He hadn't let her down at all, that only He knew the perfect plan for all of us. It's described in the opening verse.

So, dear believer who has struggled with inexplicable loss, please hold on to this: you are His, and He is yours. That is good enough for now. Amen.

THURSDAY

So I've really enjoyed this latest diversion about waiting on God's timing and trusting that it is better than ours as "all things work together for good to those who love God, to those who are the called according to His purpose" (Romans 8:28). And by the way, what's "His purpose"? It's spreading the Gospel, furthering the kingdom of God on this earth. Our emotional and physical healing as believers is part and parcel of that, so I think it's high time we push on with our review of last year's journey through God's plan of salvation and get on with the rest of this treatise.

Both times we progressed to the liberation of the enslaved children of Israel from Egypt and got bogged down with two periods of time—fifty days and four hundred years. The latter we just dealt with, but last year we spent a good amount of time comparing the fifty days from Passover to Mount Sinai with the fifty days from the Crucifixion to Pentecost. And we saw that Jesus stayed with His followers after the resurrection for forty days, not fifty, leaving that unusual period of time, after Satan was defeated on the cross, when neither Jesus nor the Comforter was present with the believers. I believe that left them vulnerable. They were to stay sequestered in Jerusalem, awaiting the Holy Spirit.

Why this unusual timing? My conclusion is that Jesus Christ ascended to heaven when He did to lead the battle against Satan and his fallen angels, resulting in the expulsion of all evil from heaven, and this had *huge* implications for planet Earth and its inhabitants, both saved and unsaved, because all that evil was now unleashed on this little orb. Such had not been the case previously.

Here's the main point I was trying to make: We need not be afraid of Satan or give him any more power or credit than he deserves, because he is obviously *limited* and *finite*. He has been trying to destroy this earth and all of humanity for almost two thousand years, and he has failed. He won't have any more power in the future than he has now. He's been trying as hard as he can. He is a failure who makes horrible decisions all the time, and he's *not* in heaven any more! Look at this for tomorrow, these awesome words of Jesus:

"I saw Satan fall like lightning from heaven" (Luke 10:18).

Hmm, when did He say that? More tomorrow.

FRIDAY

"And Jesus spoke to them, saying, 'All authority has been given to Me in heaven and on earth'" (Matthew 28:18).

These words were some of the last our Lord proclaimed before He ascended to heaven, right before He gave the Great Commission. I've pondered over them because they seem to indicate that Jesus didn't always have that authority, that this acquisition was possibly a recent thing. Now I didn't question the authority on earth part. As we had discussed previously, Adam and Eve had voluntarily relinquished the authority over earth that God had given them to Satan, and only a perfect, sinless man (the seed of the woman) could win it back. That I knew. But what about the authority in heaven? Wouldn't Jesus have always had that? Hmm, let's look deeper into Luke 10 as I think the good doctor Luke records the answers to these questions there.

"After these things, the Lord *appointed* seventy others also, and sent them two by two *before His face* into every city and place where He Himself was about to go" (Luke 10:1; emphasis added).

The Greek word for "appointed" is *anadeiknymi*. Here's the definition, from Strong's Concordance G322:

> **anadeiknymi.** to proclaim; to announce, as a king, etc.;
> to lift up and exhibit for all to behold.

Now, remember, as I love to point out, up until the cross the universe was still unsettled as to this God vs. Satan thing, and they were intently observing this absolutely beautiful blue planet. I think this "appointing" was for their benefit because these seventy close followers of Jesus were endued with His power—a temporary anointing as the cross had not occurred yet—and they would demonstrate the power of the Lord over the earthly authority of Satan and his demons. Look how they fared:

"Then the seventy returned with joy, saying, 'Lord, even the demons are subject to *us* in *Your name*'" (Luke 10:17; emphasis added).

Wow! This really is important; for the first time *ever*, human believers in the very human, yet 100 percent God, Jesus Christ would have dominion over the enemy, a preview of what would be available to all believers after the cross! Amen!

Right after this is that exclamation of Jesus that I gave yesterday morning about Satan falling like lightning from heaven. What I've been shown about that is absolutely empowering and awesome. But it will have to wait until Monday. (Don't you just love me?!) Have a great weekend.

45

WEEK

MONDAY

Happy Monday! Spring is right around the corner, the beautiful yearly reminder of renewal and refreshing, of that which is dormant becoming alive and vibrant. My prayer is that what we'll discuss today will have that effect on our souls because it is a transformative truth.

Jesus Christ once and for all defeated Satan on the cross. That's when all authority was given to Him as He stated in Matthew 28:18. But here's the fascinating thing I began to see: Jesus stayed here on this earth for weeks after the resurrection, and Satan was *still in heaven*! He was still the representative of the human race before God. There was still something very unholy in the celestial sanctuary, contaminating it, making it impure. We addressed all this late last year when we closely examined Hebrews 9, and we tied this portion of scripture with Revelation 12. We saw that Jesus ascended to heaven, after forty days of lingering with His beloved followers, to accomplish the expulsion of the *already defeated* Satan from heaven *forever*! Jesus *purified* the heavenly sanctuary!

Why is this so important for us as believers? This is why:

"Do you not know that you are the temple of God and that the Spirit of God dwells in you? ... For the temple of God is holy, which temple you are" (1 Corinthians 3:16, 17).

Wow! This is huge. We need to see this. Satan is like a corrupt ruler who has been legitimately overthrown and rejected yet refuses to leave the palace, continuing to pretend he's in power. Jesus took care of that situation in heaven, kicking him out. But where did he go? This is where Luke 10 comes back into play, where Jesus "saw Satan fall like lightning *from* heaven" (v. 17; emphasis added), but He doesn't mention what he fell *to*. It was earth, as we already saw in Revelation 12:9. Now get this: Satan is *still* trying to get back into the purified earthly sanctuary, which is the soul of believers, even though he has been completely and forever expelled from our spirits and can never get us back. The thing is, he doesn't want us to realize that. He loves to condemn us and depress us and accuse us and to tell us that we're not to be healthy or joyful or prosperous. All *lies* as he is the "father of lies" (John 8:44).

So when he starts playing his little games with you, *remind* him that he's been forever kicked out of your world by the blood of Jesus Christ and that you will *not* listen to him. Praise God! We'll end this morning with this now more easily understood verse from James:

"Resist the devil and he will flee from you" (James 4:7).

TUESDAY

"Woe to the inhabitants of the earth and the sea! For the devil has come down to you, having great wrath, because he knows that he has a short time" (Revelation 12:12).

This is pretty much where we left off last year, seeing how Jesus purified heaven, cleansing it of all evil by expelling Satan and all his demons, who came bursting onto earth, intent on destroying the Jews, the Christians, and basically everything good about humanity (see verses 13–17 of Revelation 12). This already happened, after the Ascension and before Pentecost. We started looking at evidence for that, starting with the continuing persecution of the Jews. We then looked briefly at the persecution of the early church, but there is much more to say about that as we just saw how our earthly sanctuaries, inside every believer, were also purified and made holy, perfect in God's eyes. Why then do we believers still struggle with evil? We get depressed, discouraged, ill, anxious, scared, poor, etc., yet we are still believers. What gives?

Two things. First, although Satan is not in heaven, he is here. Although defeated, he is still functional because God has not closed the curtain on the opportunity for eternal salvation for humans—and for humankind to be saved, they have to have something to be saved from. To be given the chance to put your faith in the Savior, there has to be a choice, an alternative, and that is Satan. He should know his ultimate end, but he is so delusional that I honestly think he thinks he has a chance yet to overthrow God!

Second, remember, we are *human*, composed of three entities—spirit, soul, and body—and only one of those is redeemed, holy, and completely resilient to the enemy, and that's the spirit. So Satan still can attack our emotions, our reason, and of course our bodies. As I've said before, the enemy directs most of his efforts on believers, not to try to win them over to him, because he can't (and he does know that), but to keep us down and out, thus stunting our ability to further the kingdom of God on this earth. I'm telling you, we can't have lives of impact if we are resourceless and sick all the time.

But—really good and important news here—because our "sanctuary" is perfect and holy, we are in right standing before God. We are *His righteousness* (2 Corinthians 5:21), we have received *His grace* (Romans 5:15), and we don't have to give in to *anything* Satan throws at us! Amen! We end this morning with this awesome verse, which will make your day:

"If death ruled because of one person's [Adam's] failure, those who receive the multiplied *grace* and the *gift of righteousness* will even *more certainly rule in life* through the one person Jesus Christ" (Romans 5:17 CEB; emphasis added).

WEDNESDAY

In case you're wondering, yes, I do know where we are on our journey through God's plan of salvation, and it's right where we've been for about six months now! We're still just about to accompany the children of Israel on their way out of Egypt and to Mount Sinai. This treatise is obviously not progressing in a linear fashion; that's not the way my mind works, nor is it the way the Holy Spirit operates. I've used this verse before:

"The wind blows where it wishes, and you hear the sound of it, but cannot tell where it comes from and where it goes. So is everyone who is born of the Spirit" (John 3:8).

When I try, as impossible as it is, to picture God's mind, I don't see things that are linear or straight, but things that are roundish and curvy and soft. Look at Creation: the earth is round (if anyone in the past actually thought the earth was flat, they didn't know Scripture—"It is He who sits above the *circle* of the earth" [Isaiah 44:22; emphasis added]—and they didn't know God's mind, as He would never create such a thing), the sun is round, the moon is round, and New Yorker donuts are round (okay, maybe not part of original creation, but they should have been). What about curvy? Waves are curvy, clouds are curvy, women are curvy (okay, I probably shouldn't even go there, but it's true and it's good), and even our DNA is curvy—*very* curvy. It is a helix, a tightly wound spiral, which it has to be, because if all the DNA in your body were unwound and stretched out in a linear fashion, it would be *fifteen billion miles* long! That's twice the diameter of our solar system. Wouldn't that scientific fact alone make one wonder if, *just maybe*, something more than natural selection of random processes is going on here?

So we've weaved and circled all over the place in these writings, but we've covered a lot of neat stuff, I think. We're currently dealing with Satan and his minions, expelled from heaven two thousand years ago, and how he's trying to take down humans and torch the earth. He's especially enraged with the Jews and the Christians.

"Now when the dragon saw that he had been cast to the earth, he persecuted the woman whom gave birth to the Child … and the dragon was enraged with the woman, and he went to make war with the rest of her offspring, who keep the commandments of God and have the testimony of Jesus Christ" (Revelation 12:13, 17).

We'll pick up tomorrow with our discussion of Satan's persecution of Christians by looking at the early church's first martyr, a wonderful Christian Jew by the name of Stephen.

THURSDAY

I'm looking forward to talking about Stephen because, even though he was "killed" for his faith, there are some very uplifting and reassuring truths we'll uncover that should help us not be afraid to proclaim this "blessed hope" (Titus 2:13) within us.

But first, one more afterthought regarding this straight vs. curvy analogy I was pondering over yesterday. I'm fairly passionate about this one. I have a flip phone. I will always have a flip phone. It is *so* much cooler than a smartphone, which is not a phone at all but a personal computer with a phone function. The advantages of flip phones are too numerous to list here in full, but the durability, super long battery life, and superior sound quality are among them. However, there is one overarching reason that I will *never* have a smartphone: they are *straight*, and my face is *curved*! Sure, you can envision a straight line between your ear and mouth, but there's something in the way: it's called your *face*! Unless you're a *giraffe* (and they probably have smartphones too—every third grader I see does), there is no way the straight rectangle of the smartphone connects your ear to your mouth; you're talking into space. How lame is that? My flip phone is beautifully curved to accommodate my face. I just love that. Face it (pun intended), smartphones aren't cool anymore; join me in the flip phone revolution. Back to Stephen:

"But he [Stephen], being full of the Holy Spirit, gazed into heaven and saw the glory of God, and Jesus standing at the right hand of God, and said, 'Look! I see the heavens opened and the Son of Man standing at the right hand of God!' ... And they stoned Stephen as he was calling on God and saying, 'Lord Jesus, receive my spirit.' Then he knelt down and cried out with a loud voice, 'Lord, do not charge them with this sin.' And when he had said this, he fell asleep" (Acts 7:55–56, 59–60).

Wow! Who was this Stephen character, and where and why did this stoning to death occur? Well, he was what the Bible calls a "Hellenist," meaning that he was a Jew by birth, indeed, but he had lived in, and was influenced by, Greek culture. He was saved, a believer, and he moved to

Jerusalem, where the above-mentioned event took place. He was a leader of the early church (comprised mostly of Jews) in Jerusalem and was described as "full of faith and the Holy Spirit" (Acts 6:5). He was on fire for the Lord, preaching the Gospel without fear, doing "great wonders and signs among the people" (Acts 6:8), and the religious leaders had had enough. He was arrested for blasphemy and taken before the Sanhedrin, a kind of Jewish supreme court of religious leaders headed by the high priest. He was about to give these learned men an amazing lecture on the history of their Jewish faith, culminating in the Messiah and *their* murder of Him. That's where the foregoing verses kick in. More tomorrow.

FRIDAY

So it's Friday. Stephen is being stoned to death; he'll be Christianity's first martyr. Many, many more will follow, and it's fair to ask why. Why, if Christians are "more than conquerors" (Romans 8:37) and have the power of the Holy Spirit in them ("But you shall receive power when the Holy Spirit has come upon you" [Acts 1:8]), is Satan allowed to kill them? I've asked that, and I believe this awesome story of Stephen gives us some insight into this question. We'll deal with just one aspect today. I trust it will prove to be a great way to end the week. Here's what I'm going to propose: we don't have to feel sorry for Stephen or any other believer who gives up his or her life for the kingdom of God. Do you find that hard to believe? Here we go …

First of all, it doesn't appear that Stephen had any consternation about his predicament. Look how Dr. Luke, who was probably there, describes him at the onset of his trial before the Sanhedrin:

"And all who sat in the council, looking steadfastly at him, saw his face as the *face of an angel*" (Acts 6:15; emphasis added).

Wow! Stephen was glowing with the power of the Holy Spirit; it was physically noticeable! I don't think there was any room for anxiety or fear.

Then at the end of his powerful oration to the Sanhedrin, when it became obvious things were not going to go well for him, Stephen actually experienced heaven on earth as we noted in the Scripture from Acts 7 we gave yesterday. He *saw* the glory of God and *saw* Jesus Christ. As the stones started flying, he *asked* Jesus to "receive my spirit." Just look at this:

"And when he had said this, he *fell asleep*" (Acts 7:60; emphasis added).

Does that make it sound like Stephen was in anguish and suffering terribly? No, of course not. This is what I want to end with, which will blow your socks off: the words of Jesus in Matthew 10:29:

"Are not two sparrows sold for a copper coin? And not one of them falls to the ground *apart from your Father's will*" (NKJV; emphasis added).

That's from my favorite translation of the Bible, but it's not right on with this awesome verse. The American Standard Version is, though. Look at this:

"Are not two sparrows sold for a penny? And not one of them shall fall to the ground *without your Father*" (ASV; emphasis added).

Our loving God is right there, comforting, holding, and protecting every seemingly worthless little sparrow as it dies and falls. Wow! How much more do you think He was protecting Stephen, and every one of us who have put our trust in Him? Just think of that this weekend. I love it.

46
WEEK

MONDAY

"Hereafter the Son of Man will *sit* on the right hand of the power of God" (Luke 22:69; emphasis added).

"But this Man, after He had offered one sacrifice for sins forever, *sat* down on the right hand of God" (Hebrews 10:12; emphasis added).

"Look! I saw the heavens opened and the Son of Man *standing* at the right hand of God" (Acts 7:56; emphasis added).

Happy Monday! It's another week in the Lord, and we're looking at the martyrdom of Stephen, trying to make sense of seemingly "bad" outcomes for believers wholly sold out to Jesus Christ. We saw last week that the Godhead is fully engaged with these situations, and this morning we'll see further proof of that.

There are actually many more scriptures, in addition to the two above, stating that the risen and ascended Jesus Christ is *sitting* at the right hand of Father God in heaven. Now, do you remember when we discussed Zechariah chapter 3 in regard to Satan's presence and dealings in heaven before he was cast out by Jesus? The preincarnate Jesus is referred to as the "Angel of the Lord" there as Zechariah depicts a courtroom scene where Joshua the high priest is accused by Satan, who was standing at Joshua's right hand. Both were before the Angel of the Lord—and He was *standing*. How do I know? Look at verse 5 of Zechariah 3: "And the Angel of the Lord *stood* by" (emphasis added).

Isn't that awesome! You see, Jesus had additional work to do in Old Testament times. Satan was not only not defeated but also free to contaminate heaven. Things (actually the whole universe) were unsettled as I like to say. There was no rest.

But after the cross, Jesus's work was already done. When he yelled out, "It is finished" (John 19:30), He meant it. His position now is one of *rest*; He is *seated*.

So what gives with Stephen's vision of Jesus *standing* at the right hand of God? He must have really believed what he saw because he mentions it twice, in consecutive verses (Acts 7:55–56). Is there a contradiction here? Or did Jesus actually stand up to witness this dramatic scene? I think it's the latter, and here's why: this sacrificial giving up of one's life for others moves Jesus as nothing else because it was His laying down of His sinless life that changed everything. Just look at these verses:

"This is My commandment, that you love one another as I have loved you. Greater love has no one than this, than to lay down one's life for his friends" (John 15:12–13).

"By this we know love, because He laid down His life for us. And we also ought to lay down our lives for the brethren" (1 John 3:16).

Wow! Enough to ponder today. More tomorrow.

TUESDAY

"And they cast him [Stephen] out of the city and stoned him. And the witnesses laid down their clothes at the feet of a young man named Saul" (Acts 7:58).

We've looked at the martyrdom of Stephen from the perspective of Stephen and have seen how our loving God was taking care of him during this ordeal, but now we'll look at the effect Stephen's sacrifice had on *others*. The first person to be affected is none other than the apostle Paul, whose name was Saul but who would later be known as Paul. We'll just refer to him as Paul. He was a devout Jew and Pharisee, an expert in the Law, and a Christian-killer who was "breathing threats and murder against the disciples of the Lord" (Acts 9:1). But he would have an encounter with Jesus and become the greatest of the apostles; he would be the first human to have the full Gospel of Grace revealed, and he would write more of the New Testament than anyone else.

He was at the stoning of Stephen, and it affected him deeply, I believe. I say this because of what Jesus said to Saul at his conversion on the road to Damascus. Look at this:

"As he journeyed he came near Damascus, and suddenly a light shone around him from heaven. Then he fell to the ground, and heard a voice saying to him, 'Saul, Saul, why are you persecuting Me?' And he said, 'Who are you, Lord?' Then the Lord said, 'I am Jesus, whom you are persecuting. It is hard for you to *kick against the goads*'" (Acts 9:3–5; emphasis added).

The King James Version translates that last part as "kick against the pricks." What does that mean? It means that Paul, although an avowed persecutor of the church, was struggling internally. The Holy Spirit was working on him. *Goad* and *prick* are older words for a cattle prod, a long stick with a pointed end used to "urge" or "spur" the animal in the desired direction. I believe the martyrdom of Stephen was one of those goads, one of those promptings, that was drawing Paul to accept the Way, the Gospel of Jesus Christ. But he was fighting against those urges of the Spirit. I think Paul fully knew he was going to end up serving the Lord because he saw what Stephen had, that power and peace and joy, and he wanted it. Jesus knew that and didn't waste any time knocking the self-righteous Paul to the ground (for some reason I've never understood, Paul is often pictured as being on a horse at the time, but that's not in Scripture) and pointing out to him that He was real and Paul was wasting time fighting his destiny. Here's his response:

"So he [Paul], trembling and astonished, said, 'Lord, what do You want me to do?'" (Acts 9:6).

Wow! Paul immediately called Jesus "Lord," no questions asked, and submitted himself to Him. That's because of the work the Holy Spirit had already begun in his heart. I think a big contributor to Paul's salvation was the testimony of Stephen and his death, his giving of the ultimate sacrifice. Where would the early church have been without Paul? Remember what we've proposed before, that the plan of salvation is being orchestrated to ensure the maximum number of saved souls. The martyrdom of Stephen leading to the conversion of Paul is an example of that. Tomorrow we'll look at another Pharisee impacted by Stephen.

WEDNESDAY

"Then one in the council stood up, a Pharisee named Gamaliel, a teacher of the law held in respect by all the people … and he said to them, 'Men of Israel, take heed to yourselves what you intend to do regarding these men … keep away from these men and let them alone; for if this plan or this work is of men, it will come to nothing; but if it is of God, you cannot overthrow it—lest you even be found to fight against God.' … And they agreed with him" (Acts 5:34, 38–40).

The council in question here is the Sanhedrin again, but this time Peter and John are before them, having just been miraculously delivered from prison. They are defying the council's command that they not preach the Gospel. "We ought to obey God rather than men" (v. 29). The council wants to kill them. This event occurred before Stephen's appearance in front of the council that we already covered; Gamaliel would have been at both events. Though we don't know whether this Pharisee ended up believing in Jesus Christ like Paul and Nicodemus did, we do know God used his sense of reason to help the disciples, at least in this case. And I think there's a good chance Gamaliel continued to facilitate the spread of Christianity through his position as a trusted religious leader because he would have seen the majesty of Stephen's martyrdom. Paul stated in Acts 22 that he himself was a pupil of Gamaliel (v. 3) when he was trying to establish legitimacy before a violent Jewish mob, so I think Gamaliel's restraint in purging the early church in Jerusalem greatly helped to get it established—another consequence of the testimony of Stephen, accomplished through his death.

Now not many of us will be asked to pay the ultimate price for our faith, but what I'm trying to show here is that if we are so asked, the same grace that initially saved us will be with us all the way, and that grace is sufficient (2 Corinthians 12:9). Our suffering and possible death for the cause of Christ is not a reflection of failure or a win for the enemy. Look at this amazing scripture:

"Stand fast in one spirit, with one mind striving together for the faith of the Gospel, and *not in any way terrified by your adversaries* ... for to you it has been *granted on behalf of Christ*, not only to believe in Him, but also to suffer for His sake" (Philippians 1:27–29; emphasis added).

Wow! *Granted*, like a making a wish possible, like giving a gift. Could we as believers be so into Jesus that we actually view suffering as something to request, to look forward to? Difficult stuff we're covering, eh? Enough for this morning, but I'll try to make this all easier by going back to a portion of scripture we covered previously, the beautiful last chapter of the Gospel of John—tomorrow.

THURSDAY

"My brothers and sisters, when you have many kinds of troubles, you should be full of joy" (James 1:2 NCV).

Hmm, that statement is counterintuitive, isn't it? Is James, the half-brother of Jesus, serious? He is. I will share with you today a portion of Scripture that helped me to understand this liberating truth. We looked at it before. During the forty days when Jesus walked this earth after His resurrection, He had many encounters with His disciples, but none was more moving and poignant than the one recorded in John 21, on the shores of Jesus's beloved Sea of Galilee. Remember, most of Jesus's disciples were fishermen, and although all the remaining disciples were solid believers (Judas was dead, and Thomas was no longer doubting), they had not been empowered by the Holy Spirit, so they were without purpose. Peter was still struggling with how he had failed Jesus after His arrest, denying Him three times, so he went back to what he was comfortable doing, what he knew he could do well. "I am going fishing," he said to the others (v. 3). There were seven of them, and they fished all night but caught nothing.

Dawn arrives, and Jesus is on the shore. He's making a fire of coals and cooking breakfast for His friends, even though they don't know it's Him. Please try to picture this. This is the *perfect, victorious, all-powerful* God of the universe, and He's excited about being with His human *friends*, and eating with them, and fellowshipping with them! This brings me to this powerful obscure verse in Zechariah, which has always stayed with me:

"And one shall say to Him, 'What are these wounds in your hands?' Then He shall answer, 'Those with which I was wounded in the house of my friends'" (Zechariah 13:6).

Wow! Doesn't that just send chills down your spine? How He loves us!

He calls out to His friends, "Children, have you any food?" (v. 5). Now please note that Jesus didn't need their fish; we see in verse 9 that He already had fish on the fire. And bread. No, He was after something bigger. Remember, the disciples still didn't recognize Him, and He was now going to do something to again show them who He was, something that would stay with them forever.

They yell out to this stranger that they hadn't caught a thing, not all night, which was the prime fishing time. Jesus yells back, "Cast the net on the *right* side of the boat, and you will find some" (v. 6; emphasis added). Interestingly, they obeyed. What happened next is worth waiting until tomorrow for. I love ending the week with something truly uplifting and inspiring!

FRIDAY

"So they cast, and now they were not able to draw it in because of the multitude of fish" (John 21:6).

We pick up the story in John 21 that will shed some light on the suffering of devout, Jesus-loving, grace-filled Christians. The unrecognized Jesus is illustrating for His disciples the *power* and *perfection* and *victory* found only in Him. The imagery is phenomenal. These skilled fishermen had been fishing all night in fishless waters, catching nothing, but then Jesus arrived and took over. He instructed the disciples to try the *right* side of the boat, which is significant because that will be the position of Jesus after He ascends to heaven, on the right hand of the Father. That is the position of authority and *power*. There are *seven* disciples there (not eleven), which is significant as that is the number associated with *perfection* in the Bible. And there's something even more subtle to see here. Look at this:

"The other disciples came in the little boat … dragging the net with fish. … Simon Peter went up and dragged the net to land, full of large fish, *one hundred and fifty three*" (vv. 8, 11; emphasis added).

Now there is another Bible number that is associated with perfection, but even more so with *victory*, and that's the number 17. So hauling in 17 fish would have been consistent with our theme, albeit a little underwhelming; 153 fish is much more impressive. Here's what will blow your socks off: try adding the 17 integers (separate whole numbers) of the number 17, that is, $1 + 2 + 3 + 4 + 5$ and on and on to $16 + 17$. Go ahead, do it! What did you get? Awesome! Nothing is insignificant in scripture. This little scene is all about the *power* and *perfection* and *victory* of Jesus Christ. This is so important to get right because it has everything to do with understanding the difficult portion of scripture that is to follow, where our Lord will gently but firmly let His beloved disciples know, in no uncertain terms, the fate that awaits them. We'll look at all of that next week, but know this: no matter what we are asked to do for the Lord during our earthly walk with Him, we will always be surrounded by His *love*. His *perfect power* will ensure our *victory*, no matter what the circumstance, because He will cradle us, and protect us, and *fall with us* just like He does with every little sparrow. We have nothing to fear! Rejoice in this truth this weekend.

47

WEEK

MONDAY

Happy Monday! This week we transition from March to April; the Easter season is here, the last major holiday we'll see before the end of these writings, unless we count Cinco de Mayo, which we're not counting. We're deep into John 21, gleaning truths regarding our life in Christ and how we can understand, and actually rejoice, when seemingly bad things happen to us. The bigger picture is the war that Satan and his demons have waged on Jews and Christians since his expulsion from heaven about two thousand years ago. We've already discussed the Jews, we're now discussing the Christians, and after that we'll look at the obvious, at least to me, deleterious effect this unleashed evil has had on planet Earth in general.

Our focus now is on Peter and his prophesied end, but first this troubled but deeply loved disciple who is struggling with his faith and his worth to the kingdom of God has to be restored. How our Lord accomplishes this is priceless, absolutely priceless. But if you don't have a Strong's Greek Concordance, you'll miss it. This brings up something I should have made a point of at the start of this treatise: the only resource I have used in a lifetime of studying God's Word, as a layperson with a very busy professional career, is a good study Bible (the New King James Version) with a Greek and Hebrew dictionary. That's it. Now there are a great many helpful commentaries out there, and that's a good thing, but I don't want you overwhelmed, thinking you have to invest in a whole library of Christian books and study guides, because you really don't. You *need* to read only *one* book, the Bible, and you need to read it with understanding. That's the job of the Holy Spirit as seen in John 16:12–14. Ask Him to reveal the truth in the Word, and He will. But you need to know what the actual original words mean. That's where the dictionaries of the original languages, Hebrew and Greek, come in. Nowhere is this more demonstrable than here in John 21:

"So, when they had eaten breakfast, Jesus said to Simon Peter, 'Simon, son of Jonah, do you *love* Me more than these?' He [Peter] said to Him, 'Yes Lord; You know that I *love* You'" (John 21:15; emphasis added).

This timeless question from Jesus, and the answer from Peter, will be repeated two more times: three affirmations to match the three denials of Christ by Peter before His crucifixion. But the transforming truth in these exchanges is brought out in the word *love*, because although translated as the same English word, there are two distinctly different Greek words used here. We'll unravel that tomorrow!

TUESDAY

"So, when they had eaten breakfast, Jesus said to Simon Peter, 'Simon, do you love [agapao] Me more than these?' He [Peter] said to Him, 'Yes, Lord, You know that I love [phileo] You'" (John 21:15).

First of all, what does Jesus mean by asking Peter if he loves Him "more than *these*"? More than what? Remember, six other disciples were sitting right there at breakfast. Now I suppose, knowing just how gentle and sophisticated Jesus was, that He had taken Peter aside for this discussion, but the others were still there. Was Jesus gesturing toward them when He asked Peter this question? Many would say so, because Peter, before his miserable fail the night before the Crucifixion, was boastful about his unfailing love for the Lord and had exalted himself above the other disciples.

"Peter answered and said to Him, 'Even if all are made to stumble because of You, I will *never* be made to stumble'" (Matthew 26:33; emphasis added).

Do you see the self-righteousness there? Never works. So Jesus would have been justified in bashing Peter in this way, confronting him about his selfish pride, but that is *not* our Lord; He is never that way. Not only is our Savior great, but also He is good, and He is way above taking hurtful shots at others. He is "altogether lovely" (Song of Solomon 5:16) all the time. O if I could be more that way!

So if not the disciples, who are the "these"? Well, if I can paraphrase James Carville's famous political statement: "It's the *fish*, stupid!" Remember, they had actually counted all 153 of them, so the fish would have been lying all over the place on that shore. And Peter was a fisherman by trade. Do you see the absolute beauty of our Lord in this? He knew Peter loved Him but was bruised, and He gently started a difficult conversation about Peter's commitment to Him with something obvious and easy for Peter to answer. Indeed, Peter had left his trade at Jesus's first calling years before and *followed* Him. Jesus was about to restore that excitement and joy, but in an even better way, such that this "bruised reed" would become a mighty tree and lead the early church. We'll see how He accomplished this soon, and get into the Greek, but I need to emphasize again the loving and gentle nature of our precious Lord and how He deals with those of us believers who are bruised and broken, because He is misrepresented all the time in this area, and it grieves me. Read this for tomorrow, and ponder it. This is our Jesus:

"Behold! My Servant whom I uphold, My Elect One, in whom My soul delights! I have put My Spirit upon Him; He will bring forth justice to the Gentiles. He will not cry out, nor raise His voice, nor cause His voice to be heard in the street. A bruised reed He will not break, and a smoking flax He will not quench" (Isaiah 42:1–3).

Wow! March goes out like a lion!

WEDNESDAY

First thing this morning, let's look at why Peter needed to be "restored" to a proper relationship with Jesus Christ, although I would point out that *restore* may not be the best term since Peter's prior revelation of the Lordship of Jesus Christ was "Peter-centric," not "Christ-centric." I would call it the "transformation" of Peter, resulting in something much more powerful and liberating than what he had before.

> Having arrested Him, they led Him and brought Him into the high priest's office. But Peter followed at a distance ... and a certain servant girl, seeing him as he sat by the fire, looked intently [atenizo] at him, and said, "This man was also with Him." But he denied Him, saying, "Woman, I do not know Him." And ... another saw him and said, "You are also one of them." But Peter said, "Man, I am not!" Then ... another confidently affirmed, saying, "Surely this fellow also was with Him, for he is a Galilean." But Peter said, "Man, I do not know what you are saying!" Immediately, while he was speaking, the rooster crowed. And the Lord turned and looked [emblepo] at Peter ... so Peter went out and wept bitterly. (Luke 22:54–62)

Man, the visual imagery in this is moving. Note that Peter comes under the scrutiny of two entities: the accusers and the Lord. There are two different verbs used. You know how much I like using that Strong's Concordance to get a fuller picture of the intended meaning, so here we go:

Strong's Concordance #816:

> **atenizo.** to look steadfastly and earnestly.

This is the verb used to describe how the servant girl was scrutinizing Peter, because as a Galilean, he would have appeared a bit different and would have had an accent (they were in Jerusalem, not Galilee). She was looking, very closely and intently, at his *physical* characteristics and figuring that if he was a Galilean, he must be associated with Jesus, who was also one.

Strong's #1689:

> **emblepo.** to stare; look at with a "locked-in" gaze; a *penetrating look*.

This is how Jesus looked at Peter. Do you see how much using the actual Greek verb adds to the meaning? This was no casual glance; this was a *soul-penetrating*, piercing stare, and it shook Peter to his core.

And it had to. Peter had to be transformed from the inside out. We'll examine that tomorrow.

THURSDAY

So we've seen how Peter failed our Lord when his faith was put to the test, and now we'll see how our Lord lifts up and strengthens this fruitless, fallen branch (I'm using terminology we already discussed about the branches [believers] and the Vine [Jesus] in John 15) to transform him into a fruitful, strong, confident branch as recorded in John 21. I think our Lord had started this process even before this breakfast encounter on the shores of the Sea of Galilee. Actually I think it was a priority of the risen Savior as the last interaction we see recorded in Scripture between Peter and Jesus before the Crucifixion was that piercing gaze from the beautiful eyes of our Lord. Peter was not at the cross. As far as we know, there was only one disciple there: John. As the scripture says, "Strike the Shepherd, and the sheep will be scattered" (Zechariah 13:7).

Jesus wasted no time meeting with Peter after His resurrection. Indeed, Peter had *run* to the tomb on resurrection morning, after the women (including Mary Magdalene) had told him and John they had found it empty, but Jesus wasn't there. However, look at Luke 24, where the two followers who were on the road to Emmaus arrive back in Jerusalem that same night and find the eleven disciples all together, saying, "The Lord is risen indeed, and has appeared to Simon!" (v. 34). This would have been a private meeting, and it's not recorded for us in Scripture, but my hunch is that Jesus let Peter know he was forgiven and loved and needed, preparing him for this encounter. This brings us back to John 21, that unusual back-and-forth with Jesus asking Peter if he loved Him and Peter responding that he did. But there's an important play on words going on here in the Greek, which is absolutely missed in the English, and it has to do with the word translated "love." The first two times Jesus asks Peter if he loves Him, He uses the word *agapao*.

Strong's G25:

> **agapao.** to love dearly and deeply.

It is the kind of love God has for us, completely devoted and committed. Just a few weeks prior, Peter would have answered that question in the affirmative without hesitation—but not now. He's a "bruised reed," a "smoking flax," and he knows he can't make that commitment. He responds with the word *phileo*.

Strong's G5368:

> **phileo.** to be fond of; have affection for.

Much less involved, isn't it? Good for Peter! He is being brutally honest. He knows his weakness and frailty, and he is broken before our Lord. How does Jesus respond to this lower level of commitment on Peter's part? Does He tell him he's not ready for service yet, that he needs to pray and fast and go to Bible school and thereby prove himself worthy to serve? Does He? Here's what He says: "Feed My lambs" (v. 15).

Wow! Maybe our Lord misspoke. Surely He didn't mean that. Maybe He ought to ask Peter again, which is exactly what He does in verse 16. We'll get to that tomorrow.

FRIDAY

"He said to him again a second time, 'Simon, son of Jonah, do you love [agapao] Me?' He said to Him, 'Yes, Lord; You know that I love [phileo] You.' He said to him, 'Tend My sheep'" (John 21:16).

Amazing! Do you see what Jesus is doing here? He is acknowledging Peter's humbleness and self-doubt and telling him that He can use him anyway because He's trying to get Peter to see something of crucial importance: It's not really about Peter; it's *all* about Jesus. Peter simply has to be willing to be used of the Lord, to yield to Him. As awesome as this is, what Jesus does next is simply incomprehensible. Look at this:

"He said to him the third time, 'Simon, son of Jonah, do you love [phileo] Me?' ... And he [Peter] said to Him, 'Lord, you know all things; You know that I love [phileo] You.' Jesus said to him, 'Feed My sheep'" (John 21:17).

Wow! Jesus comes right down to Peter's level, meets him right where he's at, like a *friend* relationship, rather than a Master–servant relationship. If that seems odd to you, look at Jesus's words to His disciples at the Last Supper:

"You are My *friends* if you do whatever I command you. No longer do I call you *servants*, for a servant does not know what his master is doing; but I have called you *friends*, for all things that I heard from My Father I have made known to you. *You did not choose Me, but I chose you*" (John 15:14–16; emphasis added).

Incomprehensible! The King of Kings and Lord of Lords, the apple of the universe's eye, the Beloved Son, left the glory of heaven to come to this earth as a man, to become one of us, to become our *friend*, to love us just as we are. "While we were still sinners, Christ died for us" (Romans 5:8). Better yet, He came not to leave us the way we were but to save us from the curse of sin and give us abundant lives and the ability to commune with His Spirit. And *that* is what not only restored but actually transformed Peter. What a great way to end the week and start the weekend!

48
WEEK

MONDAY

Another Monday. We've been considering the deleterious effects of the unleashing of the full evil powers of Satan and his kingdom of darkness on the earth after he was completely and forever expelled from heaven two thousand years ago. We're currently focused on Christians, specifically, the early Church, and puzzling over the martyrdom of all the disciples except one. We've just seen the beautiful restoration of Peter and improvement of the relationship between Jesus Christ and Peter. Right after that, immediately after that, Jesus delivers this bombshell to Peter:

"I tell you the truth ... when you were younger, you tied your own belt and went where you wanted. But when you are old, you will put out your hands and someone else will tie you and take you where you don't want to go" (John 21:18 NCV).

Wow! There's nothing cryptic about this. Jesus is foretelling Peter's death, showing that he would reach out for help but be bound as a condemned criminal and led to his execution. Peter absolutely *knew* what He meant. Look at the very words of Peter written right before his death, in AD 68:

"Yes, I think it is right, as long as I am in this tent, to stir you up by reminding you, knowing that shortly I must put off my tent, *just as our Lord Jesus Christ showed me*" (2 Peter 1:13–14; emphasis added).

Back to John 21...then our absolutely splendid, lovely, and beautiful Lord Jesus Christ looked squarely at Peter and said, "Follow Me" (v. 19).

Now freeze-frame; stop right there! If we were writing a Hollywood script about all of this, wouldn't we have this encounter end with Peter bowing to our Lord and saying something like, "As You will, my Lord. I am Yours"? The sun would be setting over the sea, reflecting over the water, as the scene fades. Wouldn't that be awesome! Wouldn't it?

But this is *Peter*, remember? Impulsive, impetuous Peter. And he does the most unusual thing. Seemingly disregarding those last words from Jesus, he looks over to John (who's writing this) and says, "But Lord, what about *this* man?" (v. 21; emphasis added).

Weird, right? Did it really happen, as the guy writing this is the subject here? But everything in the Bible is true; John wasn't making it up. I've pondered over this a lot. I'll tell you what I think tomorrow.

TUESDAY

"Then Peter, turning around, saw the disciple whom Jesus loved following, who had also leaned on Jesus's breast at the supper, and said, 'Lord, who is the one that betrays you?' Peter, seeing him, said to Jesus, 'But Lord, what about this man?'" (John 21:20–21).

Peter has just been told he will die a violent, criminal's death for following Jesus, and surprisingly his interest immediately turns to John. Why? Did he love John so much that he was concerned he would suffer the same fate? Possibly, but I don't think so. Look how John is described in the foregoing Scripture. He is the disciple who leaned on Jesus "at the supper." What supper? The Last Supper. Looking closely at that story, also recorded by John, may give us a clue as to what was going on here. It's in John 13:21–30. This is what happened: They were all eating, lying around Jesus, when the Lord, "troubled in spirit … said, 'Most assuredly I say to you, one of you will betray Me.'" This apparently caught the disciples off guard, which in and of itself is surprising to me since it's easy (and perhaps convenient) to think Judas was obviously a very troubled and messed-up person. That apparently was not the case; the other eleven must have thought of him as just like them. That's a commentary on how we simply can't judge a person's sincerity of faith; only the Lord knows.

So the disciples are "perplexed" and impulsive, hyperkinetic Peter wants to know, but he's afraid to ask the Lord, so what does he do? He motions to John, who is lying right up *on* Jesus's chest, and motions to him to ask Jesus. This is what John does:

"Then the dearly loved disciple leaned into Jesus' chest and whispered, 'Master, who is it?'" (John 13:25 TPT).

I used this particular translation rather than the NKJV because I think it fits most closely with what subsequently happened. There was this intimacy, this closeness, between John and Jesus that no other disciple had with Him. Remember, although Jesus loves each of us equally, there are different levels of closeness of His followers to Him, then as now. There were the "seventy," then the "twelve," and then the three closest disciples— Peter, James, and John. It appears John was the closest, and Peter knew it. I think that troubled him because he was the one disciple who boasted the most of his love for the Lord as we've already seen. Yet John seemed to have the inside track as we see in this amazing encounter. The Passion Translation captures that intimacy. The NKJV indicates that John spoke out loud (said) the question to Jesus, for all to hear, but that makes no sense, nor would the next verse:

"Jesus answered [apokrinomai], 'It is he to whom I shall give a piece of bread when I have dipped it.' And having dipped the bread, he gave it to Judas Iscariot" (John 13:26).

Yep, again it's all in the Greek. Tomorrow.

WEDNESDAY

You know, it just dawned on me—really—that this is Passion Week. Good Friday is just two days away, and look where we're at in this treatise: the Last Supper! Wow! This Lord of ours is so amazing as I didn't plan any of this. Remember Thanksgiving? We were talking about manna and unthankfulness. Remember Christmas? We were discussing the Roman Empire and how it provided the perfect, stable environment for our Savior to be born. Now it's Easter, and we're about to see who would betray Jesus. We're at the Last Supper. I am overwhelmed by His goodness and guidance!

We left off with John quietly asking our Lord who the betrayer was as he was comfortable enough with Jesus to know He would answer him. The word translated "answered" in John 13:26 is the Greek word *apokrinomai*.

Strong's #611:

> **apokrinomai.** to reply in like manner.

So I believe that Jesus very quietly, in a whisper, answered back to John, and John alone, indicating that He was about to give a piece of bread, dipped in wine, to the betrayer. Why was this so important? Well, this is just conjecture on my part, but I know it fits with the heart of this Jesus I know as I believe that our Lord *loved* Judas just as much as He loved the others and was not willing to lose him (I think this is primarily why He was "troubled in spirit" in verse 21). He would give him one more chance to accept Him as his Messiah because, you see, Judas also had to be lying very close to Jesus for Jesus to hand him the dunked bread. He was probably on the other side of where John was. I think Jesus had him there on purpose. It was a place of honor, and having the host of the meal offer bread to him was also an honor. Jesus was offering Judas His love and acceptance. That's why it would have made no sense at all for Jesus to acknowledge out loud who the betrayer was before this opportunity was given. The back-and-forth between John and Jesus was private and intimate, and Peter saw that. He wanted that kind of closeness to His Lord. Does this make sense? Here's further confirmation:

"Now after the piece of bread, Satan entered him [Judas]. Then Jesus said to him, 'What you do, do quickly.' *But no one at the table knew for what reason He said this to him*" (John 13:27–28; emphasis added).

So it's pretty obvious the other disciples had no clue that Judas was the betrayer, even after he abruptly left the supper (v. 29). That lovely, sophisticated nature of Jesus is so awesome!

But that's not even the point I'm trying to drive home here. It has to do with this unique relationship between Jesus and John. Why was John special, special enough that Peter would question Jesus's plans for him in John 21? I think we'll find the answer in the very words of John himself tomorrow.

THURSDAY

"Now there was leaning on Jesus' bosom one of His disciples, *whom Jesus loved*" (John 13:23; emphasis added).

"Then Peter, turning around, saw the disciple *whom Jesus loved* following" (John 21:20; emphasis added).

Those are the words of the disciple John, describing the disciple John. Wow! What nerve, right? No, what *insight*! He simply had a deeper understanding of Jesus's love than any of the others. John was focused in on *Jesus's love for him*; Peter was focused in on *his love for Jesus*. Do you see which expression of love Jesus honors more? Remember Mary and her sister Martha entertaining Jesus in their house as told in Luke 10:38–42? Martha was all about showing Jesus love by cooking and serving and bustling about, to the point of frustration, while Mary was simply sitting quietly at the feet of Jesus, absorbing His love for her through His words. And what did Jesus say? "One thing is needed, and Mary has chosen that good part, which will not be taken away from her" (Luke 10:42).

So that was John's secret! And may I point out that this disciple, although often portrayed as soft and mild-mannered, was not that way at all. He was unrefined and rough and tough—a fisherman from a family of fishermen who was such a strong force that Jesus Himself referred to him and his brother James as the "Sons of Thunder"! It was these same brothers, two of Jesus's closest companions, who wanted Jesus to "command fire to come down from heaven" to obliterate a Samaritan village that had rejected Him (Luke 9:54)!

Yet even John was forever changed by the grace and love of our Lord and immersed himself in that. It was only this disciple who was with Jesus at His crucifixion, and to whom Jesus entrusted the care of His own mother (John 19:26–27). John was empowered by his realization of the love of Jesus Christ for him. That should be an example to us all.

Do you know whom else John reminds me of? King David. David was a mighty warrior, responsible for many deaths of the enemy, tough as they come (as Goliath could attest to), yet he became totally dependent on God's love.

"Do not withhold Your tender mercies from me, O Lord; let Your lovingkindness and Your truth continually preserve me" (Psalm 40:11).

This is how God describes this aspect of David: "I have found David ... a man after my own heart, who will do all My will" (Acts 13:22).

Tomorrow, Good Friday, the most revered and treasured day in the calendar of the universe (trust me), we'll see why we today have every right to claim that love, that incomprehensible love, for ourselves. I can't wait. This stuff is amazing.

FRIDAY

"And Jesus said to him, 'Foxes have holes and birds of the air have nests, but the son of Man has nowhere to lay [klino] His head'" (Matthew 8:20).

It is Good Friday morning. Jesus Christ, the Lamb of God, would be led to Mount Calvary at 9:00 a.m. and nailed to that rugged wooden cross, which would then be lifted up and thrust into the ground. He would hang there, suspended between heaven and earth, until 12:00 noon, at which time everything would go black. For the next three hours, this sinless Son of God, who voluntarily left all the glory and splendors of heaven to become one of us, to live among us as a vagabond, without anywhere to call His home and rest His precious head, took all of the sin and shame and curse of the human race—*all of it*—upon Himself.

This suffering would not be like that we as believers face, because we are actually deserving of such, whereas He was not. We have the love, protection, and encouragement of our heavenly Father constantly with us in our comparatively inconsequential trials, and He did not, as the Father had to turn from His Son, had to forsake His Son, because He could not save Him from this judgment.

At 3:00 p.m., after Jesus had absorbed all the Father's righteous judgment meant for us, as the darkness cleared, we see am amazing thing…Jesus was *still there*! He was not consumed by the judgment; He conquered it! And look at this, recorded by the eyewitness John:

"Jesus … said, '*It is finished!*' And bowing [klino] His head, He gave up His spirit" (John 19:30).

Do you see this, the use of that Greek word *klino* being used in both the opening verse in Matthew for "lay" and in this verse in John for "bowed"? What's the Greek meaning?

Strong's Concordance #2827:

> **klino.** to cause to bend.

Wow! This was an active act of Jesus. He had no ability to rest during His time on this earth; He had to save the entire human race. He had nowhere to *klino* His head. *But* after defeating sin and death, His work was finally *over*, and He voluntarily gave up His life, which caused His head to bend down. He had found His rest.

That incomprehensible act of *love* was for each and every one of us. John knew that. May we all. God bless.

49
WEEK

MONDAY

It's Monday, the day after Easter. I hope you had a blessed one. Beautiful time of year, isn't it? We have just one month of these morning devotionals left before we complete the year, and we have a great deal of ground to cover, but no worries. Jesus is able to compress time. That was actually His very first miracle as recorded in John 2:1–10. This is one of my favorite stories in the Bible as I just love the playful mother–son interaction between Mary and Jesus. Wait a minute, do we have time for this? It would be yet another diversion.

Hmm. Yep! We do. Jesus hadn't performed any miracles yet on this earth since His incarnation, but He was filled with the Holy Spirit now, and He and His disciples were invited to a wedding, where His mother was also. "And when they ran out of wine, the mother of Jesus said to Him, 'They have no wine'" (v. 3). Now remember, Jesus had *never* done anything miraculous during His childhood or young adulthood, but Mary knew full well who He was and what He was capable of. The exchange that follows is priceless:

"Jesus said to her, 'Woman, what does that concern have to do with Me? My hour has not yet come.' His mother said to the servants, 'Whatever He says to you, do it'" (John 2:4–5).

Wow! That's adorable. Jesus is lovingly toying with His mom. I can see her just demurely smile and roll her eyes because she knew He couldn't deny His mom. I love it! Jesus immediately turns six large waterpots into six large wine containers. He turned water into wine, His first miracle. The point here is that it was a miracle of compression of time, as water does become wine, but it's a lengthy process, one that Jesus accomplished instantaneously. That's what He's going to have to do to help us cover the ground we have left. I'm trusting Him fully.

Just one more observation this morning regarding Jesus's demeanor and bearing, which I find very attractive. Remember Isaiah 42, the prophecy about the Messiah not crying out or raising His voice? Think of that when you hear these very *loud* preachers who somehow think that yelling makes what they're saying more important. It doesn't, and it's not Christlike. Jesus was a quiet man.

We'll quickly finish up the persecution of believers tomorrow and then start looking at how poorly the whole earth fared after Satan and his friends invaded this little planet fully two thousand years ago.

TUESDAY

"Jesus said to him, 'If I will that he remain till I come, what is that to you? *You follow Me*'" (John 21:22; emphasis added).

That's the crux of the matter, this question as to why some Christians face horrible persecution, even to the point of death, and some do not. The foregoing verse is Jesus talking to Peter about John. Peter had just been shown that he will suffer and die for Jesus, but he sensed that such would not be the fate for John. I think that's because he saw that super-close, intimate bond between John and Jesus, which was a result of John's embracing the love Jesus had for all of them. Did that make John a "better" Christian, deserving of divine protection? No, of course not. John was John, and Peter was Peter, and that's the point of Jesus's admonition, which is for *all* of us: "*You follow Me!*" As believers, we are all *in* Christ, but we are still all *individuals* and always will be. There is a *uniqueness* to each of our relationships with Jesus Christ, and only He knows that perfect will for our lives; our responsibility is simply to *follow* His lead and trust fully that He will be there every step of the way, no matter what the challenges. Paul, who suffered much for the kingdom of God, said this about what Jesus had told him regarding this topic, "And He said to me, 'My grace is sufficient for you, for My strength is made *perfect* in weakness'" (2 Corinthians 12:9; emphasis added). So we can *rest* in His love and be reassured that He's got this! It's as simple, yet profound, as that little rhyme we learned as toddlers that we never forgot because it is deep in our souls: "Jesus loves me, this I know, for the Bible tells me so."

Amen! So that ends what I wanted to say about the qualitatively different persecution Jews and believers (the "woman" and "her offspring" of Revelation 12) experienced after Satan, full of great wrath, came down to earth just after Jesus's time. Now we'll look at how he almost destroyed humanity and why he was able to accomplish all that evil. After that, we'll get right back on that trip through God's plan of salvation, finally accompanying the children of Israel as they leave Egypt (where we left them many months ago), and *speed* through the rest of the journey to the cross, hitting some highlights along the way. *Then*, having completed our task of showing that healing is in the atonement for believers and just how God's plan to save humans got to that place (for we are to know these things, to "be ready to give a defense to everyone who asks you a *reason* for the *hope* that is within you" [1 Peter 3:15; emphasis added]), we will address the role of modern medical science in healing (and there *is* a role). Then we'll briefly address the nonbeliever, the unsaved. Is supernatural healing available to them? Then we'll be done! Got it?

WEDNESDAY

As Martin Luther wrote in his 1521 work *Diet of Worms*, "I am bound by the Scriptures I have quoted and my conscience is captive to the Word of God. I cannot and will not recant anything ... here I stand. I can do no other. May God help me. Amen."

Fifteen hundred years after Jesus Christ, the Son of God, came to earth to save humankind from the ravages of sin, and the light of the Gospel burst forth with the power to transform all of humankind, this man Martin Luther was forced to defend his faith in the Word of God upon penalty of death. What happened? How did we get to this point, where proclaiming the truths *written* in the Word of God is considered heresy, considered something foreign to Christianity? Well, remember this?

"Woe to the inhabitants of the earth and the sea! For the devil has come down to you, having great wrath" (Revelation 12:12).

That's why. Let's briefly look at some of the woes Satan and his minions inflicted on this earth and discover how he tried to completely snuff out the light of the Gospel. When we finished out last year, we had looked at the relatively stable great empires that brought order to the earth, namely, Assyria, then Babylon, then Medo-Persia, then Greece, then the Roman Empire, during the height of which Jesus was born and lived and died. We also discussed how that stability was important to the early and rapid spread of the Gospel.

But shortly thereafter, everything would change as the great and glorious Roman Empire would start to crumble and eventually fall, and there would be no further governmental stability in the world for many centuries. The world would enter the Dark Ages, or Middle Ages, which would span the time from the fall of the Roman Empire in the fifth century to the renewal of Western Europe in the fifteenth century, a time known as the Renaissance. From my unashamedly Christian world viewpoint, that would coincide with the Reformation, with the rekindling of the light of the Gospel in the world.

It's truly amazing to me that the human race made it that far, under the onslaught of evil unleashed against it. Not since the Flood had the survival of humankind been so tenuous. We'll look at some evidence for that claim tomorrow, because it's important to see that Satan, given a golden opportunity to wipe us out, couldn't pull it off. He is *finite*, he is *limited*, and he is *ignorant*, for "the fear of the Lord is the beginning of knowledge" (Proverbs 1:7). In other words, he is a fool, and we need not fear him. Amen.

THURSDAY

"The thief does not come except to steal, and to kill, and to destroy. I have come that they may have life, and that they may have it more abundantly" (John 10:10).

Did you know there were just about 175 million humans on earth during Jesus's time, about half the current population of the United States? Over the next 1,400 years, that number would only double, to 350 million, by the 1400s. Now just think of that; it's really an impressive statistic. In the intervening

600+ years since 1400, the world's population would soar to over 7 *billion*, an increase of twenty-fold! And that's not the result of increasing fertility rates; women had way more kids in the past than now. And considering that a fertility rate of just four would double a country's population in just 32 years...no, there was just a lot of *death*. I mean a lot of death. The population of the earth actually *declined* during the 1300s, primarily because of the bubonic plague (the Black Death), which is estimated to have knocked out around half of Europe's population. These were really dark times.

So where were the Christians? Weren't they supposed to "go into all the world, and preach the Gospel to every creature" (Mark 16:15)? Weren't they supposed to "receive power from the Holy Spirit" to accomplish this (Acts 1:8)? Satan was reigning supreme, it seems. The universe knew better as they had witnessed Satan's defeat and expulsion from heaven, but the world was suffering, and the reason for this was that the light of the Gospel, revealed in the Word of God, was just a little flickering ember; it was suppressed and all but snuffed out as people did not have access to it.

Remember, the early church was birthed during the rule of the Roman Empire, and it was contrary to the dominant heathen culture and terribly persecuted. But even with (and maybe because of) that persecution, the church flourished and grew. Christianity is meant to be countercultural in this fallen world of ours. Look at these words of Jesus:

"Do not think that I came to bring peace on earth. I did not come to bring peace, but a sword" (Matthew 10:34).

Wow! What's that all about? We'll see tomorrow.

FRIDAY

"Glory to God in the highest, and on earth peace, goodwill toward men!" (Luke 2:14 NKJV).

So we left off yesterday with Jesus telling His disciples that He didn't come to bring peace on earth, but a sword (Matthew 10:34). Did the foregoing, well-known verse immediately come to mind? These were the words of the heavenly host to the shepherds upon Jesus's birth, and although we love the NKJV translation, this time it's inaccurate. That would make sense, wouldn't it, for the time after the birth of Christ was anything but peaceful. Here's a better translation:

"Glory to God in the highest, and on earth peace among men with whom He is pleased!" (NASB).

We as believers are pleasing to God. *We* have peace. Doesn't that make more sense? My point is that Christianity is diametrically opposed to the values and desires of this sinful world, which is ruled by Satan. The things the world treasures and worships hold no sway over us believers, and that's unnerving to nonbelievers. I haven't quoted Bob Dylan in a while; the following is a reflection, I think, of how he felt after his conversion:

> When the whip that's keeping you in line doesn't make
> him jump,
> Say he's hard of hearing, say that he's a chump.
> Say he's out of step with reality as you try to test his nerve
> Because he doesn't pay tribute to the king that you serve.
> He's the property of Jesus.
> Resent him to the bone.
> You got something better;
> You got a heart of stone!
> —from "Property of Jesus"

Hmm, that's pretty accurate, isn't it? Ever been treated like that? Well, the early Christians faced extreme persecution; they were outsiders, radicals. But then something *really* unexpected and dramatic happened, and the course of Christianity would be altered, seemingly for the good but actually very much for the bad, almost resulting in its death! It was the fourth century, the Roman Empire was fading, and to paraphrase Dr. Seuss, the emperor had an idea. An awful idea. The emperor had a wonderful, awful idea. Mull over that this weekend.

50

WEEK

MONDAY

"If the world hates [miseo] you, you know that it hated Me before it hated you. If you were of the world, the world would love its own. Yet because you are not of the world, but I chose you out of the world, therefore the world hates you" (John 15:18–19).

Wow! What a way to start the week, eh? Could Jesus be any clearer? There's no misunderstanding the Greek here.

Strong's Concordance #3404:

> **miseo.** to hate, detest.

But the emperor of mighty Rome, Constantine, is going to show these "hated" little Christians some major love. He will "convert" to Christianity in AD 312 and make it the official, acceptable religion of the Roman Empire! They won't be persecuted anymore! Great, right? No, it wasn't great, because Christianity would be paganized, institutionalized, and ritualized, such that the "good news" of the Gospel would be basically lost. It would become a religion of humankind and their efforts, not a relationship with the One who reached down to His sinful humans and, by His efforts and His efforts alone, saved them. Liturgy ruled the day; there was no room for the spontaneity of the Spirit, and most importantly, the Word of God would be taken out of the hands of the masses and kept sequestered among the religious folk. Salvation by grace through faith was unknown; condemnation and fear was the norm. It seemed that all was lost.

But remember Jesus's words on the cross? "It is finished" (John 19:30) was yelled out strongly for the whole universe to hear. The "smoking flax" of the Gospel would not be quenched. Starting in the fourteenth century, great men and women of God would once again turn to the power of the Holy Spirit, proclaim the Gospel, and start prying off the lid that was keeping Scripture captive. John Wycliffe would, for the first time, translate the Bible into English, which is when the light of the Gospel started to shine. This was greatly augmented by the invention of the printing press in the fifteenth century. By the time of the sixteenth-century stand of Martin Luther and his translation of the Bible into German, the Protestant Reformation was in full swing, and conditions in the world began to improve dramatically. People were becoming free again; they were allowed to think again. And remember, Christianity is all about *freedom*:

"Therefore if the Son makes you free, you shall be free indeed" (John 8:36).

That freedom of the Gospel is very much evident today. Sure, there's a lot of evil and repression around, but "where sin abounded, grace abounded much more" (Romans 5:20). So Satan failed miserably in his two-thousand-year effort to destroy humankind. Here is where we will end this topic. We start the long-awaited journey out of Egypt tomorrow.

TUESDAY

We press on through God's plan of salvation. And why? What does this have to do with healing? Well, we've already shown that healing for believers is part and parcel of the Atonement of Jesus Christ on the cross—that is the focal point of the universe—but I think it's beneficial to see just how humankind got to that point because this helps us to believe in the providence and goodness and righteousness of God, who laid out this beautiful plan before the foundations of the world (Revelation 13:8). We're joining God's chosen instrument to reveal that plan, the children of Israel, as they are set free from four hundred thirty years (yes, it was originally supposed to be four hundred years) of sojourning in Egypt, as slaves for most of that time. They leave healthy and prosperous with the actual blessing of the Egyptians. Look at this:

"Now the children of Israel had … asked from the Egyptians articles of silver, articles of gold, and clothing [may I just inject here that this sounds just like my stepdaughter] … and the Lord had given the people favor in the sight of the Egyptians, so that they granted them what they requested. Thus they *plundered* the Egyptians [yeah…my stepdaughter]" (Exodus 12:35–36; emphasis added).

Wow! What a God. His children went from being poor slaves to rich freemen overnight. And they headed out enveloped by the grace of God, who went before them in a pillar of cloud by day and a pillar of fire by night. Now get this: They were *not* redeemed; they were *not* forgiven. Their sin debt hadn't been paid yet. But it didn't have to be—not then. Remember what we pointed out before, that at this time in human history, humankind's sin was not being counted (imputed) against them? Paul explains this in Romans chapter 5. This would all change at Mount Sinai, which we are dangerously close to on our journey, but for now God is going to extend pure, unmerited grace on His people. Just like now, right? Oh no, it's not the same, as the grace extended to us, which we approximate by faith, *is merited, is just,* as Jesus Christ paid our sin debt for us. So we can fully approximate and live in that grace, but that was not the case with the unredeemed children of Israel thirty-four hundred years ago. They would not know how to handle that grace as we shall see tomorrow. This would be an important lesson for the universe to see; God couldn't just "look the other way" and ignore the sin problem. Let me end this morning with that little phrase of mine that I find helpful in understanding all this:

If the sin debt has not been paid, grace is ineffective.

WEDNESDAY

"For the Lord your God is a consuming fire, a jealous God" (Deuteronomy 4:24).

The children of Israel are headed toward the land promised to their forefather Abraham centuries before—Canaan. It's not a long journey at all if they go the direct route because they are located in Goshen, up in the northeast corner of Egypt, bordering the Mediterranean Sea, and they could have traveled along the coast (by way of the land of the Philistines [Exodus 13:17]) and gotten there in no time. But God had other plans. "So God led the people around by way of the wilderness of the Red Sea" (v. 18). There's a neat lesson to be learned here: God knew His people had basically forgotten Him during their long stay in an idolatrous country; they were not ready to possess the Land of Promise (the destination). The more important thing would be the *journey* toward that destination, where He could mature His people and have them experience Him more.

Isn't that a beautiful analogy of *sanctification*, our journey through this life as Christians, ever growing in the knowledge and grace of our Lord? I've always liked this quote of C. S. Lewis: "And what have you been saved *for*? For service and ministry, but also your *own transformation*. ... You are to become something *other* and *greater*" (emphasis added). Our journey with the Lord on this earth is important because it determines our role for eternity. Amen! And God's plan for these freshly liberated and ecstatic children of His is "just like God" as it is totally incomprehensible yet, in retrospect, absolutely perfect.

"Now the Lord spoke to Moses, saying, 'Speak to the children of Israel, that they *turn* and camp before ... the sea, opposite Baal Zephon; you shall camp before it by the sea'" (Exodus 14:1, 2; emphasis added).

Wow! Picture this. They could have crossed fairly easily from Egypt to the Sinai Peninsula if they had stayed up north, where they already were, but God *purposely* turned them southward toward a huge body of water, the Red Sea, which they had to cross to get to Canaan. What sense is there in that? Now I don't want to hear how this body of water was not actually the Red Sea (the Hebrew calls it the "Sea of Reeds") but a shallow marshy area that could be crossed without a miraculous parting of waters, because it had to be a large enough body of water to drown an entire huge Egyptian army, along with their horses and chariots! Why underestimate God? This is the God whose creation of all the stars, all one hundred billion of them, is mentioned as an afterthought in Genesis 1! No, this was a *sea* that the children of Israel knew could not possibly be crossed. And that's the point, right? How many times have we seen this? Our God is indeed a jealous God, for only He is all-powerful and only He is deserving of all glory and honor. We'll see what happened tomorrow.

THURSDAY

"And Moses said to the people, 'Do not be afraid. Stand still and see the salvation of the Lord, which He will accomplish for you today. For the Egyptians you see today, you shall see again no more forever. The Lord will fight for you, and you shall hold your peace'" (Exodus 14:13–14).

I just *love* those verses, so full of foundational truth. Let's set the scene again: God *intentionally* leads His children to the shore of an impassable body of water and then "hardens Pharaoh's heart, so that he will pursue them" (v. 4). God has big lessons in mind for His unbelieving children and the haughty, irreverent Pharaoh, who would quickly assemble a huge army, including six hundred chariots, and take off in pursuit of the former slaves. The army finds the former slaves, pinned against the sea with no way of escape: game, set, match! "So they were very afraid, and the children of Israel cried out to the Lord" (v. 10). That's when Moses gives the admonition above. Notice what the children of Israel were to do to escape this dire situation: they were to "stand still" and "see their salvation" and "hold their peace." Wow! That's all. Just *rest* in what the Lord "will accomplish for you today." God was to *perform*; they were to *stand still*. Please hold that thought, because just five chapters from now, this beautiful relationship will be *reversed* with disastrous consequences.

But we're getting ahead of ourselves. The parting of the Red Sea is one of the most dramatic scenes in human history. For one thing, it occurs at night, but the pillar of fire is *before* the Israelites, to light their way, while the pillar of cloud moves *behind* them, to enshroud the Egyptians in darkness. Then the waters are parted, and the children of Israel pass on dry land. "The waters were a wall to them on their right hand and on their left" (v. 29). That's pretty cool, right? But remember that verse from yesterday, about God being a jealous God?

"Then the Lord said to Moses, 'Stretch out your hand over the sea, that the waters may come back upon the Egyptians, on their chariots, and on their horsemen.' ... Then the waters returned and covered the chariots, the horsemen, and all the army of Pharaoh that came into the sea after them. *Not as much as one of them remained*" (Exodus 14:26, 28; emphasis added).

Wow! What a God! I want to briefly look at one other, little-known example of the power and superiority of our Lord; it's found in 1 Samuel 5. Remember the ark of the covenant that was in the holy of holies in the tabernacle? We now skip ahead a few hundred years. The children of Israel are in the process of possessing the Promised Land, and they are continually fighting with the Philistines. In one of these battles, the Philistines actually capture the ark! They take it back to one of their cities, Ashdod, and place it in the temple of their chief god, Dagan, right next to a statue of the false god. Then they go to bed, and the next morning ... Oh my, we're out of time! You'll just love what happened ... tomorrow.

FRIDAY

> When the Philistines took the ark of God, they brought it into the house of Dagon and set it by Dagon. And when the people of Ashdod arose early in the morning, there was Dagon, fallen on its face to the earth before the ark of the Lord. So they took Dagon and set it in its place again. And when they arose early the next morning, there was Dagon, fallen on its face to the ground before the ark of the Lord. The head of Dagon and both the palms of its hands were broken off on the threshold; only Dagon's torso was left of it. (1 Samuel 5:2–4)

Poor Dagon! And this ark was, as you'll recall, just a temporary shadow of the real thing in heaven. Yet even this symbol of the one true God's power is very impressive. I would point out how the fallen idol was positioned: *on its face!* It was prone as if bowing before our Lord! Just now, that brings something else really neat to my mind (this is why we didn't finish this series up months ago). Remember when Jesus was betrayed in the garden by Judas? John's version records that Judas came with armed troops and officers to capture Him, and they asked for Jesus of Nazareth. Jesus replied, "'I am He.' ... Now when He said to them, 'I am He,' they drew back and fell [pipto] to the ground" (John 18:5, 6).

Now, honestly, there's just too much really neat stuff in this to bypass, so we won't bypass it. First of all, you'll notice that the word *He* in those verses is italicized in your Bible. That means it wasn't there in the original manuscripts but was added by the translators for clarity. What Jesus said was, "I AM." And where did we hear that before? Yep, at the burning bush of Exodus 3, where Moses asks what name he should use for God when the children of Israel ask who sent him. "And God said to Moses, 'I AM WHO I AM.' and He said, 'Thus you shall say to the children of Israel, 'I AM has sent me to you'" (Exodus 3:14). Wow! Jesus is pointing out He is God, and look what happens to everyone around Him. One could picture this drawing back and falling as if a power blast had come out of Jesus and blew them all backward onto their backs, but that's not what happened. Look at the Greek word used here for "fell":

Strong's Concordance G4098:

pipto. to *bow down*; to *fall prostrate*.

Wow! Picture that now. They would have stepped back so as to fall down prone, as if in worship of the man they were arresting to kill. What an awesome way to end the week. Amen!

I know we have only two weeks left in this yearlong series. Don't panic (let me do that). Next week we'll follow the children of Israel a bit farther toward Mount Sinai and see water come from a rock. We'll discuss the role of modern medicine in the healing of believers from the perspective of that watery rock, then we'll see what happened at Mount Sinai. After that we'll take a brief look at the healing of nonbelievers, and then we'll be done. It's all good.

51

WEEK

MONDAY

"And Moses said to them, 'Why do you quarrel with me? Why do you test the Lord?'" (Exodus 17:2 ESV).

"You shall not put the Lord your God to the test" (Deuteronomy 6:16 ESV).

"And Jesus answered him, 'It is said, "You shall not put the Lord your God to the test"'" (Luke 4:12 ESV).

It's Monday. We look now at an amazing Old Testament event that foreshadows our salvation, sanctification, and healing and provides the perfect context to discuss the role of modern medicine in the healing of believers. Awesome, right?

The children of Israel have miraculously escaped the Egyptians and are now headed to Mount Sinai, passing through a desert (wilderness) but enjoying the blessings of their gracious God, who provides manna from heaven for them to eat and water for them to drink (Exodus 15:27). Yet surprisingly (or not; remember what we said about God's grace being ineffective if there's no forgiveness of sin?) they won't rest in this provision. In Exodus 17, they get thirsty again, and instead of *resting* and *trusting* and *waiting* on the Lord, they *demand from* and *question* and *test* the Lord. "Give us water, that we may drink" (v. 2). They wanted a *miracle* on demand, in essence saying, "If you're *really* God, then make water appear out of nothing. Make it come out of these rocks around us if You can!" They were putting God to the test, and that's a *big* deal to God as we'll see. But first, this great, loving, long-suffering God of ours does exactly what His children had asked:

"And the Lord said to Moses, 'Go out before the people … take in your hand your rod … and behold, I will stand before you there on the rock … and you shall strike the rock, and water will come out of it, that the people may drink.' And Moses did so" (vv. 5, 6).

Seems like no big deal, eh? But trust me, it's a *big deal*, this "putting God to the test." Note the opening verses from Deuteronomy and Luke; this concept would come up time and again, once with Moses and once with Jesus, and it comes up with us believers on a daily basis, this testing of the Lord. It was such a significant event that Moses renamed the place where it occurred: "And he called the name of the place Massah (to test) and Meribah (to quarrel) because … they *tested* the Lord by saying, 'Is the Lord among us or not?'" (v. 7; emphasis added). I think that's the key thing as the Lord *was* among them, very much among them, for that rock was a startling symbol of a person, of the greatest person who ever lived, of *the Rock* … tomorrow.

TUESDAY

"Ascribe greatness to our God. He is the Rock, His work is perfect. … Where are their gods, the rock in which they sought refuge? For their rock is not like our Rock" (Deuteronomy 32:3–4, 31).

There are two "Songs of Moses" in the Old Testament, the first right after the parting of the Red Sea and before the Massah incident, and the second forty years later, right at the end of Moses's tenure as leader of Israel. In the first, Exodus 15, there is no mention of a rock of any sort; the second song, Deuteronomy 32, is just full of rock references, including "the Rock" mentioned five times! Why? Why was Moses so fascinated with rocks?

What we must see is that the rock at Massah was a type of Jesus. Striking the rock was His crucifixion; the water gushing forth, His salvation. Remember Jesus's words to the woman at the well about the "living water"?

"Jesus answered and said to her, 'Whoever drinks of this water will thirst again, but whoever drinks of the water that I shall give him will never thirst. But the water I shall give him will become in him a fountain of water springing up into everlasting life'" (John 4:13–14).

But there's more—so much more. It involves another rock, this one forty years later, at the end of the wandering time, but the people haven't learned, as they are thirsty, and again they "contend" with Moses and demand water. He goes to the tabernacle to seek direction from the Lord:

"Then the Lord spoke to Moses, saying, 'Take *the rod* … gather the congregation together. *Speak* to the rock before their eyes, and it will yield its water.' … So Moses took *the rod* from before the Lord as He commanded him. And Moses and Aaron gathered the assembly together before the rock; and he said to them, 'Hear now, you rebels! Must we bring water for you out of this rock?' Then Moses lifted his hand and *struck* the rock twice with *his rod*, and water came out abundantly" (Numbers 20:6–11; emphasis added).

Wow, this is full of meaningful stuff; this Scripture is all about *not trusting* in what God has already done for us through His Son on the cross but putting Him to the test again *after* He accomplished *all* for us. First of all, there are two rods involved. Did you catch that? "The rod" was actually Aaron's budding rod, discussed in Numbers 17, as that was the one "before the Lord" in the tabernacle, and it represented rebirth and renewal. But at the last moment Moses substituted "his rod," which was the rod of judgment, the rod associated with the plagues on Egypt, the rod used to strike the Jesus-type rock at Massah. Moses was to simply speak to the rock, but he became very angry with the insolence of the people and *struck* the rock, essentially crucifying Jesus again! And, man, would He resent that. More about this tomorrow.

WEDNESDAY

"Then the Lord said to Moses and Aaron, 'Because you did not believe Me, to hallow Me in the eyes of the children of Israel, therefore you shall not bring this assembly into the land which I have given them'" (Numbers 20:12).

Wow! God loved Moses a great deal, but this unbelief in the finished work of Jesus Christ on the cross, this not accepting the gift already given, this asking/demanding something *more*, was *intolerable* in the eyes of God, and Moses was justly punished for it; he would not be allowed to lead Israel into the Promised Land. Satan would try this same ploy on our Lord Jesus Christ Himself with the last of his three temptations as recorded in Luke 4:

"Then he [Satan] brought Him to Jerusalem, set Him on the pinnacle of the temple, and said to Him, 'If You are the Son of God, throw yourself down from here. For it is written: "He shall give His angels charge over You, to keep You" and "In their hands they shall bear You up, lest You dash Your foot against a stone." And Jesus answered him, 'It has been said, "You shall not put the Lord your God to the test""" (Luke 4:9–11 NKJV; Luke 4:12 ESV).

Do you see what Jesus is saying here? God is not to be *tested*; He's to be *trusted*! Sure, God could easily have sent angels to keep Jesus from falling to the ground, but there was *no need* for Jesus to fall to the ground! There was *no need* for Moses to *strike* the rock; he was making God into something He isn't, a kind of talisman.

And *that*, my fellow believers, is how I believe God wants us to approach using the benefits and blessings of modern medicine as part of our healing, for *all healing* comes from God (as I like to say, it's not in Satan's skill set), and He means for believers and nonbelievers to benefit from His goodness. He is a *good* God, "for He makes His sun rise on the evil and on the good, and sends rain on the just and on the unjust" (Matthew 5:45). We are to utilize what He *has already provided* to stay healthy and get well when sick—preventative care (the classic example of which are vaccines) and acute care (such as diagnostic tests, medicines, and surgeries). It is certainly *not* a sign of *unbelief* to utilize modern medicine. *Believe* that these good things are from our loving Lord, and He will work through these interventions to accomplish our healing, which can only come from Him.

But here's the crucial distinction between our use of medical interventions and that of the nonbeliever: we are not *dependent on* or *limited by* the obviously flawed and imperfect efforts of modern medicine. We are to have that "unwavering conviction" that our healing has already been accomplished in the Atonement, even when the evidence in this carnal world says otherwise. Remember that quote from Pascal: "Faith tells us what our senses do not, but not the contrary of what they see. Faith is *above*, not *against*." I think that's exactly right. Isn't it just *great* being a Christian? More tomorrow.

THURSDAY

So April draws to a close, and those April showers aren't bringing just May flowers but also the end of this yearlong journey through one doctor's musings on the physical and spiritual healing of humankind. We finish next week! I've really been blessed putting these thoughts into writing, but we have a bit more to go. Today we will finally reach Mount Sinai and see the next big phase of God's plan of salvation for the human race, at that time being played out through the children of Israel. A quick recap: after the Fall, humankind was not given any more rules from God to keep, as He knew they wouldn't possibly be able to keep them now that their spiritual connection to Him was dead, as humans had failed while it was intact. The human race became so contaminated by mating with fallen angels that even the human conscience (the knowledge of good and evil) was ineffective. And the world became exceedingly evil and chaotic, beyond repair, so God mercifully wiped everything out, except Noah and his family, in the Great Flood. Afterward, humankind was more settled and orderly, but just as fallen, and they become arrogant and haughty. God separated them into different ethnic groups with different languages in different locations on earth (the Tower of Babel narrative). World governments came into play, to provide some semblance of normalcy, but there was still no hope of redemption from the sin curse. Then Abraham came along, and the first flicker of the Light of the Gospel, of salvation, was seen, because Abraham *believed* God, rather than carnal circumstances, and God accounted that to him as *righteousness* (Genesis 15:6).

God works miraculously in Abraham and his descendants, but they don't continue in that same faith of their forebears, and they end up in captivity in Egypt for centuries. But now, through no good work of their own, God will deliver them from bondage and show pure, unmerited grace to them by setting them free and making them healthy and prosperous. He will do this by parting the Red Sea, by providing constant guidance via the pillars of fire and cloud, and by providing (in a desert!) food to eat and water to drink. They get to Mount Sinai after several weeks' journey. And God, through Moses, reminds His people of all He has done for them. He says this in Exodus 19:5: "Now therefore, if you will indeed obey My voice and keep My covenant, then you shall be a special treasure to Me above all people; for all the earth is Mine."

Now this is important because it is so subtle, yet so crucial to *everything* I've been trying to proclaim this whole year. Look closely at just what the Lord is *asking* His people to *do*. It's straightforward, right? *Obey My voice* and *keep My covenant*. How would you answer that? Well, we'll close today with how they answered. Really mull this over for tomorrow, because, as has usually been the case, we'll have a great end to the week!

"Then all the people answered together and said, 'All that the Lord has spoken *we will do*'" (v. 8).

"And all the people answered with one voice and said, 'All the words that the Lord has said, *we will do*'" (Exodus 24:3; emphasis added).

"And they said, 'All that the Lord has said *we will do, and be obedient*'" (Exodus 24:7; emphasis added).

FRIDAY

We have reached a pivotal point in the history of humanity and the universe. Humankind is horribly lost, separated from their Creator Father, spiritually dead. God has not given them rules to keep; they've been on their own, standardless, except for their slippery consciences, which are fickle. They don't know how to respond to unmerited favor (grace) because they have not been forgiven. The time has come for a paradigm shift in how God will deal with them. He's going to reinstitute *rules* and *commandments* and *laws* for His chosen people to follow. But He first asks them if they are up to it. Can they obey His voice and keep His covenant?

And they answered as a whole, "*Yes we will!*"

You know what? That was sincere; they really wanted to be right with God, and they would subsequently, at times, seem to be able to pull it off. One example that comes to mind is found in Exodus chapter 38. God had given detailed instructions for the construction of His temporary earthly dwelling place, the tabernacle, and it would require *lots* of gold, silver, and bronze. The people brought their offerings and easily met the demand. According to the numbers given, they offered up two thousand pounds of gold, seven thousand pounds of silver, and five thousand pounds of bronze (Exodus 38:24 29). They had a heart for giving!

But there's a problem, a very *big* problem: those righteous acts wouldn't last, and they wouldn't have solved the sin problem anyway. Look at this:

"But we are *all* like an unclean thing, and all our *righteousnesses* are like *filthy rags*; we *all* fade as a leaf, and our iniquities, like the wind, have taken us away" (Isaiah 64:6; emphasis added).

Wow! Even our best intentions to please God are horribly inadequate in His eyes. He is that holy and His standards that high. So with the Law came a temporary fix as we've discussed previously, the sacrifice of animal blood for our human sins. Certainly less than perfect, but a very valuable lesson had to be learned by humankind for the universe to see. Humankind was horribly lost and could not save themselves, no matter how hard they tried, and now, even worse, they were sinning directly against God. The only way out would be a "divine exchange." Jesus, who was righteous, had to become sin, and humans, who were sinful, had to be made righteous.

"For He [God] made Him [Jesus] who knew no sin to be sin for us, that we might become the righteousness of God in Him" (2 Corinthians 5:21).

So, how should the Israelites have answered the Lord? I think they answered in the only way they could at that time, for Jesus hadn't come. Now, we believers would say, "Yes, we will obey You, completely trusting and relying on Your righteousness freely and justly given to us through our faith in Your Son." Amen! Enjoy our last weekend together during this series; we finish next week.

52
WEEK

MONDAY

> When we walk with the Lord
> In the light of His Word,
> What a glory He sheds on our way!
> While we do His good will
> He abides with us still
> And with all who will *trust* and *obey*.
> *Trust* and *obey*, for there's no other way
> To be happy in Jesus, but to *trust* and *obey*.
> —"Trust and Obey," John H. Sammis, 1887 (emphasis added)

I remember that little hymn from Sunday school (it was actually an old hymn even then; I'm not that old!) Come to think of it, *this* is how we live a victorious life in the Lord. We "renew our minds" by seeing Jesus in His Word, and we *trust* that we are the righteousness of God in Christ. We do His good will *because* He abides in us and enables us. Praise God!

So the children of Israel now have the rules they requested, and they head off again on their journey to the Promised Land, but now under the judgment of the Law. There would be many failures and setbacks, including their incredible lack of faith in God's promise that they could take the land the first time they got to it. So they are ordered to wander around in that "wilderness" (we've all been there, haven't we?) for forty years! But God still absolutely loves His people. What we'll cover next this Monday morning is an amazing example of that.

Even during their pre–Promised Land wanderings, the children of Israel had to fight battles with the peoples they met along the way. One of those encounters was with the Moabites. The Moabites' king Balak was appropriately scared of them and hired a well-known false prophet Balaam to pronounce a curse on Israel. This story takes up a full three chapters in Numbers. Three chapters! But here's the gist of it:

> So it was ... that Balak took Balaam and brought him up to the high places of Baal, that from there he might observe the extent of the people [of Israel]. ... Then the Lord put a word in Balaam's mouth, and said ..., "Balak the king of Moab has brought me from Aram, from the mountains of the east. Come, curse Jacob for me, and come, denounce Israel! How shall I curse whom God has not cursed? And how shall I denounce whom the Lord has not denounced? For from the top of the rocks I see him, and from the hills I behold him." (Numbers 22:41, 23:5–9; emphasis added)

Wow! This false prophet was being *paid* to curse Israel, but he *couldn't* curse them! Why not? What was he seeing from that high place? More tomorrow.

TUESDAY

"God is not a man, that He should lie, nor a son of man, that He should repent. Has He said, and He will not do? Or has He spoken, and will He not make it good? Behold, I have received a command to *bless*; He has blessed, and I cannot reverse it. *He has not observed iniquity in Jacob, nor has he seen wickedness in Israel*" (Numbers 23:19–21; emphasis added).

Wow! More proclamations from the false prophet Balaam, who is looking down at the encampment of the children of Israel. He's being paid to *curse* Israel, but what he sees changes everything! Do you remember way back when we demonstrated how the Israelites camped in the wilderness with the four columns of three tribes each emanating from the central tabernacle, forming a perfect Roman cross? This is found in Numbers chapter 2. *That* is what Balaam saw, the cross of Christ, and that's the only reason he could honestly say that God saw no wickedness or iniquity in His people. They *were* wicked and sinful, but God saw the cross and was looking ahead to the Atonement! Remember the hymn "Before the Throne of God"? "Because a sinless Savior died, my sinful soul is counted free. For God the just is *satisfied* to *look at Him … and pardon me.*" Amen! Amen!

Thus it would be for these children of Israel as they finally conquer the Promised Land, and go through a period of judges leading them and then clamor for a king like the other nations. So a king they would have, but he (Saul) would fail miserably. The royal line that would lead (via both parents) to the Messiah would begin with David, and then Solomon, who ruled during the height of Israel's power. But then the kingdom would be split in two (Israel and Judah), and be conquered by enemies and taken to strange lands as captives, and Israel would be dispersed, but Judah would be allowed to return to the Holy Land and rebuild the temple and resume the temple sacrifices.

But all along the way, the Israelites were terribly lost. God gave them prophet after prophet, but His people would give them no heed and often killed them. God would pull back for four hundred years, like the quiet, calm backward skate before a triple lutz, and then "a Child is born … a Son is given" (Isaiah 9:6), and *salvation* would finally arrive on planet Earth, accomplished in the Atonement of Jesus Christ on the cross!

Whew! We did it. We got through God's plan of salvation, which culminated in the Atonement, which is the source of our *salvation* and *healing* as believers. We've also covered, along the way, the role of modern medicine in all of this, pointing out that *all* healing comes from God ultimately and that He works through the beautiful innovations of modern medicine but is not *limited* by them. *Faith* is *above*, not *contrary*. One more topic yet, and we have just enough time for it: What about healing for the nonbeliever? Tomorrow.

WEDNESDAY

"What grace is given to me, let it pass to him" (Arwen to Frodo, *Fellowship of the Ring*).

As you've probably noticed, I've referenced two non-Bible sources in this series quite a bit—Bob Dylan and the J. R. R. Tolkien classic *Lord of the Rings*—but what I'm referencing above is found not in the book *Fellowship of the Ring* but in the movie. It really got my attention because something very deep is involved here. Frodo, who embodies goodness and innocence, has sustained a potentially fatal wound from the Morgul-blade of the evil witch-king, and Arwen, who is played by Liv Tyler and is half elf (elves are very good and have supernatural powers) and half human, is trying to save him. She whisks the badly wounded Frodo away by horse to safety, escaping the Nazgul (evil spirit men), but he is fading fast. Arwen then lays Frodo down and kneels down over him. In a barely audible whisper, just millimeters from his ear, she says the above line (translated from Elvish). Frodo does recover. I felt chills the first time I saw that scene (you can google it: "Arwen Rides to Save Frodo"), and it got me thinking about what role we, as grace-filled, Spirit-filled believers, have in the healing of the lost. Now I would point out that if I were Frodo, having Liv Tyler whisper anything in my ear would probably make me feel a lot better (I know I really shouldn't make ridiculous comments like that, but may I quote another Christian artist, Bono? "Time won't leave me as I am, but time won't take the boy out of this man"—from "City of Blinding Lights"). I like that. But this concept of being able to pass supernatural healing to nonbelievers is one I'm intrigued by, and I think it is Scriptural and serves an important role, for this one thing I know: the ultimate purpose behind such a miraculous thing is the *salvation* of the nonbeliever who is healed and others who have witnessed it. It is, in a very real sense, a "calling card" testifying to the power and love and goodness of our Lord, whose Spirit lives in us.

So are there Scriptural examples of such? What we're discussing is essentially supernatural healings that occur outside the Atonement, and for that we should certainly turn to the Old Testament, because as I've already endeavored to show, there was no atonement for healing in the old covenant. Yet there are recorded a few episodes of healing—as rare as hen's teeth, as I stated previously, but nonetheless there. Look at this, the first reference to healing in the Bible:

"So Abraham prayed to God; and God *healed* Abimelech, his wife, and his female servants" (Genesis 20:17).

Now the background story here is convoluted, but in short, Abraham had acted completely childishly toward this heathen king Abimelech, almost getting himself killed. But the story ends up with Abraham demonstrating the true nature of his God to this king and his family, revealing His grace and mercy and possibly turning their hearts toward Him. Physical healing, which included reversing barrenness in this case, was part of that revelation, but this incident was such a rarity in pre-Jesus times. We'll endeavor to explain why tomorrow.

THURSDAY

> Now it happened after these things that the son of the woman who owned the house became sick. And his sickness was so serious that there was no breath left in him (he died). So she said to Elijah, "What have I to do with you, O man of God? Have you come to me … to kill my son?" And he said to her, "Give me your son." He carried him to the upper room … and laid him on his [Elijah's] own bed … and he stretched himself out on the child three times, and cried out to the Lord, and said, "O Lord my God, I pray, let this child's soul come back to him." Then the Lord heard Elijah; and the soul of the child came back to him, and he revived. … Then the woman said to Elijah, "Now by this I know you are a man of God, and that the word of the Lord in your mouth is the truth." (1 Kings 17:17–24)

> When Elisha came into the house, there was the child, lying dead on his bed. He went in therefore, shut the door behind the two of them, and prayed to the Lord. And he went up and lay on the child, and put his mouth on his mouth, his eyes on his eyes, and his hands on his hands; and he stretched himself out on the child, and the flesh

of the child became warm. He ... again went up and
stretched himself out on him; then the child sneezed seven
times, and the child opened his eyes. And he called the
Shunammite woman [the child's Mom]; she went in, fell
at his feet, and bowed to the ground. Then she picked up
her son and went out. (2 Kings 4:32–37)

A couple of points here. These two moms were Gentiles; they weren't
even Jews! These two prophets, Elijah and his successor, Elisha, were two
of the greatest prophets of all time, yet look how awkward and difficult
these healings were to accomplish. They were able to perform absolutely
spectacular miracles involving the physical world, but the healing of a
human was pretty much off-limits to them and occurred only in these
two families who were not under the Law of Moses. Interesting, isn't it?

And here's why: These Old Testament believers weren't covered by the
Atonement of Jesus Christ, and they weren't indwelt by the Holy Spirit.
The Spirit would come upon them just temporarily and then leave. Their
sins were covered by an inferior and temporary sacrificial system involving
the blood of animals, but there was *no* sacrificial system in place for
healing. That's why healing was virtually unheard of in Old Testament
times.

But do you see in the foregoing scriptures the reverence for and interest
in God these healings accomplished from heathens, that is, nonbelievers?
And now we post Atonement believers have *within* us the power to heal
others; we have *way* more available to us than Elijah and Elisha did! We'll
neatly tie all this up tomorrow and bring this series to a close. I'm kind of
sad about that.

FRIDAY

"And when He had called His twelve disciples to Him, He gave them
power over unclean spirits, to cast them out, and to *heal* all kinds of
sickness and all kinds of disease" (Matthew 10:1).

"After these things the Lord appointed seventy others also. ... Then the seventy returned with joy, saying, 'Lord, even the demons are subject to us *in Your name*.' And He said to them ..., 'Nevertheless do not rejoice in this, that the spirits are subject to you, but rather rejoice because *your names are written in heaven*'" (Luke 19:1, 17–20; emphasis added).

That same power to heal that was manifested by Jesus Christ, after He was filled with the Holy Spirit, and was given by Him to the twelve and the seventy, and was given to us on the Day of Pentecost, and resides in us...that same power gives us authority to heal others *in His name*. And for what ultimate purpose? Their *salvation*, their *eternal life*. And what is eternal life? "And *this* is eternal life, that they may know You, the one true God, and Jesus Christ, whom You have sent" (John 17:3; emphasis added).

That is what this yearlong journey about healing has endeavored to show: the beauty and majesty and loveliness of the Healer, of Jesus, and what His finished work on the cross provides for us. I pray that reading these daily ponderings has been a blessing to you. I have certainly been blessed writing them. I end this with the last stanza of my favorite Bob Dylan song, "Every Grain of Sand." Remember how we saw how God loves even the little sparrows and "falls" with them? Look at this one last verse, from David: "How precious are Your thoughts to me, O God! How great is the sum of them! If I should count them, they would be more in number than the sand" (Psalm 139:17–18). Hmm...

> I hear the aged footsteps, like the motion of the sea.
> Sometimes I turn, there's Someone there; other times it's only me.
> I am hanging in the balance of a *perfect finished plan*
> *Like every sparrow falling ... like every grain of sand.*

Goodbye, and God bless.

Dr. DeMay, a 1985 graduate of Vanderbilt University School of Medicine, has been a general pediatician for over 30 years, starting as a Navy medical officer and practicing subsequently in the various settings of academic medicine, group practice, and now in solo private practice in Williamsport, PA since 1999.